# EARTH MEMORY

Other titles by Paul Devereux:
*Places Of Power*
*Earth Lights*
*Earth Lights Revelation*
*Lines On The Landscape* (with Nigel Pennick)
*The Ley Hunter's Companion* (with Ian Thomson)
*Earthmind – Is The Earth Alive?* (with contributing authors)
*Who Owns Stonehenge?* (contributor. Editor, C. Chippendale)

Paul Devereux is editor of the *Ley Hunter* magazine, and Director of The Dragon Project Trust. For many years the Dragon Project has been studying energy effects at ancient sites by instrumental monitoring as well as the use of dowsers and psychics. He has conducted his own research at sites in Britain, the USA and Egypt. His lecturing and broadcasting commitments in Britain, America and Europe bring him in contact with other researchers on a worldwide basis. He currently lives and works with his wife, Charla, at their home in Cornwall.

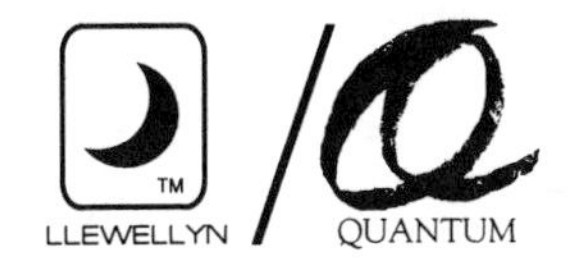


# EARTH MEMORY

*Sacred Sites—Doorways into Earth's Mysteries*

*Paul Devereux*

1992
**Llewellyn Publications**
**St. Paul, Minnesota 55164-0383, U.S.A.**

First U.S. Edition, 1992
First Printing, 1992

Cover art by Tom Canny

Unless otherwise stated, photographs
were provided by the author.

Library of Congress Cataloging-in-Publication Data
Devereux, Paul.
Earth memory: sacred sites, doorways to Earth's mysteries /
Paul Devereux. — 1st U.S. ed.
p. cm.
Includes bibliographical references and index.
ISBN 0-87542-188-1
1. Parapsychology and archaeology. 2. Sacred space.
3. Geomancy. I. Title.
BF1045.A74D48 1992 92-2922
CIP

This Llewellyn/Quantum edition produced for
U.S.A. and Canada under license by:

Llewellyn Publications
A Division of Llewellyn Worldwide, Ltd.
P.O. Box 64383, St. Paul, MN 55164-0383, U.S.A.

# ACKNOWLEDGEMENTS

Ideas for a book providing a thorough, genuinely-informed and 'systemised' account of the area identified as 'Earth Mysteries' were long in their development. For starting the process in the early 1980s I thank Michael Cox, then with Turnstone Press at Thorsons. For its continuation, I am grateful for the interest and input of Ian Jackson and Nick Eddison at Eddison Sadd Editions Ltd. Their belief in the project helped me to keep it alive. And it is with gratitude I acknowledge the role of Bill Anderton at Foulsham in providing the opportunity to bring the matter to fulfilment. I thank John Michell for putting Bill and myself in touch in the first instance.

My much-respected colleague, Nigel Pennick, was jointly involved with me in the earlier approaches to what has ultimately become this different piece of work. I value his excellent work in the field of Earth Mysteries, and the inspiration it provides. Indeed, I am grateful to all those dedicated researchers whose work is reported herein. Together, they are assembling a mosaic of knowledge and insight forming a picture we can as yet barely glimpse.

It was a dozen years ago that John Steele informed me of the existence of General Systems Theory, which is so relevant to the nature of Earth Mysteries work. I am grateful to him for that initial nudge.

Many people have helped me in a variety of ways in the assembling of the material in the following pages. I appreciate and acknowledge all their generosity and kindness.

Most of the photographic illustrations are my own, but I thank the various named photographers for their additional material. Every effort has been made to contact all the copyright holders, and I acknowledge with thanks any that might have slipped through the net.

My wife, Charla, and my son, Solomon, have my love and gratitude for their support and for just being there.

# CONTENTS

# FOREWORD

This book is about a *way of looking* at ancient sacred sites. It suggests how we might approach them, think about them, in a more whole manner than is allowed by separate disciplines or particular attitudes and beliefs. The view is presented here that archaeology as it is currently framed cannot *by itself* ever really understand the full nature of sanctified places, and has to be seen as a part of a wider-ranging set of descriptions of such sites. By the same token, no other single approach or description of an ancient site is adequate in isolation.

Although the material in this book does update and thoroughly describe key approaches to the understanding of ancient monuments, it would take a set of encyclopaedic tomes to fully plumb all the topics involved. References are therefore given to guide readers to more extensive sources on various subjects. The main purpose of this work is to present the wider description of the nature of sacred sites; to allow the process involved to be seen as a whole for the first time. The book engages in 'a new way of ordering the information' as Ervin Laszlo put it in his *The Systems View of the World* (1972). It will be seen that there is no such thing as an 'alternative' approach to the problem or mystery that ancient ceremonial sites present to us: there are simply *many* approaches, each describing an aspect of such places. By considering a number of them together we can come to see links between them as well as an understanding that the ancient monuments and sites of sanctity are themselves a summation of these many factors, and, indeed, are 'greater than the sum of their parts'. In probing into what that greater characteristic might be, we are led to face profound possibilities about the nature of our planet, of consciousness, of ourselves, and the relationships between all these.

The following chapters therefore cover many areas of human knowledge. I urge readers not to select those parts which they think appeal most to them and skip the rest – that defeats the question of wholeness this book addresses. There are those, I know, who shy away from technical matters. Well, there are no technical matters here, only essential ones. Everything is presented, I hope, in comprehensible fashion, if only because I am no 'technician' myself! On the other hand, some people avoid what they consider to be 'airy-fairy' topics. My appeal applies equally to them. Nor should a sense of 'I know what this bit is about' encourage piecemeal reading. The context presented here is unfamiliar, and brings out unexpected aspects of certain subjects, quite apart from the fresh material that abounds in these pages. To the reader I say, 'Give your mind permission to spin; start at the first page and read through to the last at the fastest pace you can.' In that way a sense can be garnered that no author can actually put on paper.

The subject of this book is therefore not antiquarianism: it is the unravelling of perennial verities that can be reapplied in the world today; becoming conscious again of ancient world views that might help us realise our future.

*Paul Devereux*

# INTRODUCTION

## WISDOM FOR THE GLOBAL TRIBE

The human race is now emerging as a global tribe. Our electronic telecommunications act like planetary senses, bringing us instant information about all kinds of events from anywhere on Earth. We watch ourselves. We talk to ourselves. We can look down at where we live from outer space. Increasingly, we tend to react as a single organism. It is a condition that was predicted half a century ago by the French visionary, Teilhard de Chardin: he called it the 'planetisation of humanity'.

This changing of state is fraught with danger and confusion. It is a *crisis* – which means a turning point, the word deriving from the Greek term for decision. We are in a global state of political, environmental and spiritual turmoil. The feedback from our space-age technology tells us of the dangers we are creating with our Western (effectively global) cultural behaviour. We are poised to destroy our habitat. At the same time, political blocs are crumbling, and though people are being freed from appalling oppression, confusion is on the increase.

But political and environmental issues are the outcome of inner states. Political turmoil is the product of mental and emotional confusion, and the many forms of environmental decay worldwide mirror a matching erosion of our spiritual condition, of our inner knowledge of ourselves. The global tribe finds itself without an understanding of, or a relationship with, its own psyche. All traditional tribes had a model that allowed them to place themselves harmoniously in the world, that allowed them access to direct spiritual experience. Our uneasy, milling global tribe does not have such a model. The great religions, which undoubtedly encode eternal spiritual truths, have by now become largely externalised structures, rote systems of belief. We sense this spiritual erosion. Some people try to counter it by going back to crude, fundamentalist versions of the great religions, which inevitably leads to high emotion, intolerance, extreme political postures and violence of expression. The chemistry that occurs in religious fundamentalism, of whatever variety, produces the antithesis of spiritual insight. Others embrace New Age pseudo-spirituality, pinning their faith in channelled messages from supposed entities, the coming of the Space Brothers or newly-formed etheric energy patterns on the face of the globe. In reality, such notions express a spiritual bankruptcy. Spiritual rejuvenation is sought by yet other people in far more valid, but hence more demanding, oriental and other exotic systems of meditation or spiritual practice. Few are up to meeting the demands. Ironically, as Westerners seek Oriental spiritual wisdom and methods, the East moves increasingly towards Western materialism.

The spiritual crisis is dealt with in some philosophies by denouncing spiritual realities altogether and replacing them with a firm belief that modern science and technology will triumph over the problems we face; that there will be a technological fix. But this attitude is rapidly losing its appeal for many people who are seeing with increasing clarity the environmental mess our technology, our applied science, is creating under the present worldview.

Unfortunately, the reaction against science has led some New Agers into a rejection of all rigour and discrimination (faculties not necessarily synonymous with science, in point of fact) so a good deal of spurious misinformation gets bandied around and confusion develops logarithmically. But, like science, in amongst the dross and the harmful aspects, the New Age in its saner guise of the Human Potential movement has a core of validity, particularly in the attempt to resurrect the intuitive, *gestalt* dimensions of the human being. Brilliant new work in consciousness studies, from research into lucid dreaming to ethnobotany, the study of plants used by traditional cultures to achieve profound altered states of consciousness, is a powerful beacon of hope.

Another positive offshoot of human potential awareness has been the development of complementary medicine or alternative health. A necessary adjustment of the body-as-machine view has started to come about, and many implications will flow from this. As we learn more about the ecology of our bodies, of energetic life fields and meridians, of the interactions between mind, brain and body, so too we may learn about the health of our planet's body, and what place consciousness has in the landscape.

Taking all these matters together, it seems that we have come to a certain crisis point where the total abilities of the human being – physical, spiritual, analytic, intuitive – need to be brought into a synthesis, a new focus. But if not to mainstream science, some automatic golden age, or our political and religious institutions, where we can turn for guidance to achieve this?

It is the instinct of a child to seek counsel, wisdom and healing from its mother, and that in a sense is what is beginning to occur. There is an involuntary turning back to nature, which, as far as human beings are concerned, means to our planet, Mother Earth. This is a realistic human reaction, not merely symbolic. *Mater*, the Latin for mother, gives us matrix, a womb or place in which something is developed. Nature is thus our matrix, our mother. Nature, after all, nurtures. Earlier peoples on this planet thought of the Earth, of nature, as being alive, and referred to the world in maternal terms.

This return to earth is taking numerous forms. One form is ecological awareness, a concern for the incredibly interactive and interdependent web of life on this planet: the biosphere. Some people prefer direct action, taking great personal risk, interfering with the slaughter of creatures such as the whales, or attempting to prevent the destruction of forests, seas, rivers. They seek ways to raise public awareness of the damaging processes of industry. They have all met with considerable success. There is increasing public debate and concern on environmental issues, which is prompting some areas of First World commerce into a faltering improvement in its behaviour and has extended into politics with the various Green movements.

Then again, there is the New Age version, which is usually presented as a diffuse need to 'heal the Earth', though further consideration would show that the direction of the healing has more likely to be in quite the reverse direction. The Earth is being damaged by human action, it is true, but that damage simply makes the planet less likely to keep providing the conditions that sustain human and most animal life. We are killing ourselves, not the planet. Our very actions will terminate the problem, which is ourselves, and Earth has geological ages in which to heal itself and spawn other lifeforms. *It is our mentality, literally our worldview, which needs healing in the first instance. The environmental healing will then be a natural consequence.*

Many people feel the way to learn to live on Earth again is by attempting to absorb the wisdom of traditional cultures. So contact with Australian aboriginals, rain forest Indians or Amerindians is actively and increasingly sought. The destruction of the rain forests is seen not only as a great disaster affecting weather patterns, but one that will also destroy many species of life, and remove the natural habitat of the indigenous peoples, thus closing a whole chapter of ancient human awareness. This is undoubtedly true, even if only from the relatively narrow perspective of pharmacology: many Western medicines derive from the botany of the rain forests, and it is the Indians who guide the pharmacologists. There is also the loss of native knowledge of psychoactive plants and herbs. Hallucinogens, while seen as a social problem in fragmented Western-style cultures, were part of the spiritual life of many traditional peoples, their use providing the shamans and their people with great insights into the workings of mind, body and planet, thus keeping them in harmony with the Earth and their inner lives.

Of course, as with any other attempt to remind ourselves of lost ways of Earth harmony, the need to receive wisdom from indigenous peoples can become superficial. So quite a bit of the tribal wisdom of, say, the Amerindians, belies what they themselves have forgotten, and bears uncanny resemblance to the psychobabble of New Age expectation. There are mysteries in the ancient American landscape, for instance, as we shall discover further on in this work, that no current Amerindian tribal memory seems able to reach back to.

Another form of Earth memory is being adopted by growing numbers of Westerners: the resort to nature for the practice of various forms of pagan practice. Rituals now employed are effectively a synthesis of mimicked traditional material and relatively modern invention. Goddess worship is a prominent element in this kind of return to nature, the Goddess being synonymous with the Earth Mother: *Ge* or *Gaia* to the ancient Greeks, Isis in ancient Egypt and, essentially, the Blessed Virgin to Christians. The modern pagans (from the Latin *pagus* meaning 'country district') seek to contact the soul of nature. Some of this modern practice is wishful thinking, some of it theatre, but it is also a manifestation of a profoundly deep memory within humanity: the essentially universal Earth religion. Contrary to the mutterings of contemporary society that such goings on are Satanism, modern neo-paganism is essentially a wise and harmless activity. The horned god of the pagans is not the Devil: that association was a politically astute piece of conceptual engineering by the medieval Christians who branded everything prior to Christianity as being by definition evil. Some contemporary Christians, however, such as the American Dominican priest, Matthew Fox, are attempting to forge a new theology that combines paganism and Christianity. The difficulty is, of course, that nature worship is seen as essentially evil by the Church, so it is a profoundly explosive alchemical process. Indeed, Fox has already run foul of Church authorities.

The only actual weakness of modern paganism is that, whereas true Earth religions in traditional societies derived from an intimate knowledge of and companionship with nature, the modern varieties are inevitably attempts to copy this within a considerably different social context and world experience.

What seems to be required is an authentic Earth Wisdom for the gathering Global Tribe, a wisdom that can lead to a more harmonious living with the Earth, to a greater contact with our inner selves (the two sides of the same coin) and one that will transcend cultural and national boundaries. It will need to maintain the wisdom that has manifested itself in archaic cultures the world over with some of the insights that our culture has also managed to achieve. It would need to be not merely multidisciplinary, but also multimode, appealing to both analytical and intuitive mind frames, to intellect and direct human experience. Such a spiritual awareness, based on the ultimate common denominator of nature itself, would perhaps be the most holistic and satisfying one ever to be adopted by humanity. It will be required to underpin the growing Green and eco-pagan awareness.

But is this not some forlorn hope? Surely there need to be teachers and guides who might help in such a development?

Well, there are.

We need to go to the moors, deserts, forests and mountains, the remaining wild places of our world, to find them: they are the mysterious sacred places of antiquity. Some have been built, actually engineered, in appropriate locations: the temples, great stone (megalithic) structures and so on. Others are the caves, springs and mountain peaks recognised and selected as natural places of power by traditional peoples. Many sites are destroyed or lost, but thousands still survive, in varying degrees of structural order. These places embody *perennial* knowledge, which means that it is both old and new simultaneously; a wisdom for all seasons. However long ago this perennial knowledge or wisdom was encoded and used, it is forever relevant. We can access it now at these ancient places, and bring it into our contemporary stream of consciousness where it can fuse with what is good and wholesome in modern thought and knowledge. We need to start thinking of ancient monuments as *memory banks* in the landscape: after all, as consciousness researcher, John Steele, has pointed out, the very word 'monument' derives from a Latin term meaning 'to remind'.

Although it has barely been perceived as a phenomenon in its own right, there is an increasing return to these ancient sacred places by human beings. This is happening not only in the conscious forms of neo-paganism mentioned above, but in the more prosaic forms of tourism. Hundreds of thousands of people can visit a well-known ancient monument such as Stonehenge or the Great Pyramid in the course of a single year, while thousands of lesser-known places also receive numerous visitors. This is not without its problems, and most such visits are superficial. Yet it does manifest a need to touch base on the part of vast numbers of human beings. It represents an involuntary requirement to come in contact with the strangely powerful places of Earth.

The most significant way in which people have begun to return to the Old Places, however, is through the agency of a multidisciplinary and multimode study area that has no real name and has developed of its own volition, outside the vision or scope of any individual. It has no name because it is too holistic for anyone to find an adequate and sufficiently succinct descriptive title. Presumably out of desperation, an unknown sub-editor of the early 1970s called it 'Earth Mysteries', but others prefer the term 'geomancy'. Neither are adequate, but they provide handles of sorts.

The background to this curious emergence goes back over a century, when Victorian missionaries brought back news to Europe of strange landscape-scale practices by the Chinese called *Feng shui* in which the siting of homes and tombs was conducted in strict accordance with certain principles relating to the energies, *ch'i*, of land and air, and which sometimes involved extensive modification of the topography. The word 'geomancy' properly relates to a system of divination using the patterns created by pieces of soil cast on the ground, but these missionaries applied the term to describe this Chinese sacred geography of Feng Shui. In the 1920s, the English inventor and businessman, Alfred Watkins, produced books on his disscovery of similarly large, linear schemes laid out in the British countryside: his famed 'leys' or alignments of ancient sites. In the 1960s the works of both Watkins and the Victorian missionaries were rediscovered and led to an upsurge of weird and wonderful ideas about the mysteries of prehistoric monuments, energy lines, UFOs, Atlantis and much else. It was a juxtaposition of naivety and esoteric ideas typical of the psychedelic decade. But although there may have been more enthusiasm than rigour at the outset, a potent alchemical mixture was created which has matured in the ensuing years (though there are still plenty of enthusiasts who prefer to invent ancient disneylandscapes than to learn from actual archaic landscapes).

The problem with this Earth Mysteries area has been its scope: Watkins warned that students of leys would come into contact with 'many -ologies', and the modes of its expression. It is really a combination and further sophistication of all the other modes of returning to Earth; a new crucible of consciousness, so diverse that many of those working in contiguous areas, such as consciousness studies or ecology, have not been aware of it, or think it to be something else. Booksellers and librarians do not know which shelf category to put Earth Mysteries books in. (For example, I have seen each of my own titles placed variously under the headings of 'archaeology', 'geology', 'UFOs' and, the most popular catch-all, 'occult'. Insofar that occult simply means 'secret' I suppose this is to some extent appropriate!)

While leys were being rediscovered in the Sixties, archaeology itself was undergoing traumas of its own. Archaeological radiocarbon dating methods (Chapter 2) were found to be in need of recalibration, and suddenly it was found that ancient sites were even older than had been thought. New, powerful research was simultaneously being published that showed that there had been a sophisticated degree of astronomical and geometrical knowledge on the part of the megalith builders, and the research area of archaeoastronomy (or astro-archaeology) came to full recognition. It was not long before students of the esoteric were showing that arcane knowledge was encoded in the groundplans and measurements of prehistoric (and other) monuments. More material on leys and traditional geomancy was published, and people began to look at the sites in Western Europe, and later in the Americas and elsewhere, from these points of view. Dowsing (water divining or witching) underwent a renaissance. Its functions were extended to the search for unspecified 'earth energies' and ardent researchers were soon visiting sites using what they hoped was direct, primary sensing as well as intellectual analytical study. The more people visited the sites with these new perspectives, the more they saw. Unusual phenomena were noted: strange lights, electric-shock like effects from standing stones, and so forth. New works on the folklore of prehistoric sites began to appear.

# *PART ONE*

# **TREE**

CHAPTER 1

# SITES AS SYSTEMS OF KNOWING

We call places like Stonehenge, Machu Picchu, Serpent Mound, the Great Pyramid and the thousands of other monuments worldwide 'sacred sites'. But what, exactly, *are* they?

In simple terms, they are essentially those locations or structures that were used for other than domestic or secular, utilitarian purposes – though in some cases there was a synthesis of roles. Archaeologists use terms like 'ceremonial' or 'ritual' to describe sites whose function is unclear or can definitely be ascribed to magico-religious practice. Great burial sites and temple remains were obviously for this purpose, though only sketchy knowledge is now possessed as to the actual rites and practices carried out there. Many other sites are totally mysterious.

For our modern culture, the European megaliths – which include standing stones, dolmens (box-like structures made from slabs of stone), underground chambers, chambered mounds and stone circles – are particularly important to understand because they tell us something about the roots of Western consciousness, which has put its stamp on the whole globe and is, for good or ill, the basis for the emergent Global Tribe. The great stone monuments started to be erected in the Neolithic ('New Stone') age, which in Britain ranged between about the fifth and second millennia BC, and considerably earlier in parts of Eurasia. Something quite obscure happened during this period. For countless generations human beings had roamed the land in nomadic cycles. They lived lightly, hunting and gathering. They doubtlessly had what they regarded or recognised as sacred spots on their routes of travel, but they did not monumentalise them. Consciousness was soft-edged, merging with the whole environment. It has been suggested in various ways by different writers that this period might have been akin to a dream state. Then people began to stop their wanderings; they began to develop more permanent settlements and practise farming and animal husbandry. Out of this phase came megalithic building, and the great stone and earthen sites of European prehistory were constructed.

These monuments thus result from a shift in consciousness. They represent some balance point between a deep association with nature and the emergence of technology and, as we shall see, what we can recognise as a form of scientific thought. The old stones fossilise a 'moment' in the history of consciousness, when it seems that the intuitive and intellectual properties of the human mind hung in a delicate symbiosis. But the balance was not maintained for long. After the Neolithic period, metallurgy was introduced, more monument building went on and societies became more organised, or, at least, more hierarchical. And, it would seem, more warlike. Some people maintain that what was happening was a shift from a goddess-oriented religious mentality to a male, god-oriented one, a move from a feminine to masculine principle in the dominant tone of culture and thus of consciousness. This may be a simplistic reading of events, but must have some validity.

So an understanding of the European megaliths would allow us to begin perceiving some process of consciousness that has led to the present highly technological, materially successful Western culture which is bringing about the crisis in ecological condition and an erosion of living spiritual reality. Perhaps, too, we may learn from the mysterious monuments ways in which technology can augment the needs of the psyche and environmental nature rather than negating them, for the sense from these places is that we are in the presence of intellect still bound close to Nature. We see monumentalised in them the interaction of the human psyche with the land. The very act of building a ring of stones amidst wild nature is a potent symbol of this.

Apart from constructed, engineered monuments, there are the natural sites, or slightly modified natural places, that were used for visions and other purposes of the spirit in antiquity: sacred springs and wells, holy trees, hill and mountain peaks, caves, sacred groves. We know of some of these, but many must now be lost to us. But these natural sites were, by definition, only identified by human beings: they were made by nature. So while there are aspects about them that we can identify with, find relevant, there are non-human facets too. So a natural site has a wider spectrum of effect than an engineered site, which probably accounts for differing responses in modern humans to such places. A constructed monument, on the other hand, already contains a selection process: it is built by humans for humans. In many cases the constructed sites seem to echo natural forms: a dolmen, for example, is reminiscent of a cave. Elements present in nature are abstracted and marshalled in such structures. They are adaptations of nature for human usage. Nevertheless, they are still close to natural processes, and focus on rather than depart from the natural world. Nature has provided human beings with the equipment, the mentality, that not only allows them to do this, but virtually assures that they *will* build on nature. Indeed, this may be nature's way of extending its own work. That is why it is unwise and thoughtless to reject completely the role of technology, one of the first flowerings of which is represented by the Neolithic monuments. The morality of technology is bound up with whether it adapts natural principles or supports a worldview that is fundamentally anti-nature. That is the real argument.

In whatever form, there was conspicuous human activity in the past that recognised the value of place, of sacred space; a concern with the interaction of the psyche and the environment that seems alien to us today, an alienation, perhaps, that is at the root of our problems.

The 'sacred' is important in ancient sacred places because it involves areas of awareness that have become stultified in contemporary consciousness. We need to return to first principles. The words 'holiness' and 'health' both derive from a Germanic root word that means *whole*. As we shall shortly see, wholeness is the key to it all.

Sacred, yes – but why 'ancient'? How old is 'ancient'? It cannot be accurately defined, in fact. In their most potent form, ancient sacred sites are *prehistoric*. But prehistory is equally variable: European prehistory has different dates to, say, prehistory in the New World, which starts when Europeans arrived there. Prehistory simply means before written history: in other words *prehistory is a definition of another cultural status, another kind of collective state of mind to that now prevailing*. Archaeology uses the perspectives of the current historic worldview to study the remains of prehistory. Hence there is a dissonance between what Gregory Bateson called 'logical types' (*Mind and Nature*, 1979).

The human race has much more prehistory than it has history. The human brain carries that prehistory in its various structural parts; the mind carries it in the subconscious. The conscious mind is a small island in the ocean of the subconscious in just the way that history sits bobbing like a cork on the sea of prehistory. Human consciousness has lived through prehistory, so to study a prehistoric sacred place is analogous to peering into the depths of mind. We are *unearthing* our subconscious. A site is a fragment that survives from prehistory, like a dream is a fragment of the subconscious that survives into our waking consciousness. And how difficult it is to properly recall our dreams! By studying such places, being at them, listening to them, we are bringing into consciousness states of mind that, by definition, began to fade at the dawn of history.

But ancient does not necessarily mean prehistoric. To a lesser degree, sacred places originating in the historic period, but prior to about the seventeenth century in Western societies, also display characteristics no longer recognised by modern scholarship. The very concepts of sacred space, of spiritual numinosity, of holistic methods of thinking (called in arcane language 'correspondences') no longer figure as viable in modern intellectual awareness. Thus such aspects of, say, a great Gothic cathedral are *invisible* to modern scholarship.

In short, the label 'ancient sacred sites' refers to those places appropriated or built for the purposes of the spirit before the Newtonian world-view emerged, before nature was seen as a machine, before the Age of Reason arose and became dominant. At these places, we sift through the layers of time to uncover the founts of wisdom, of spirituality and, indeed, science and technology.

So it is appropriate that ancient sites are the focus for an attempt at returning to Earth, a return to the understanding of ourselves and our world, and the relationships existing between mind, body and planet.

But words like 'site', 'mind', 'body' and 'planet' do not refer to simple, single items. Each is a great complex of its own, and none has clearly defined boundaries. Prehistoric peoples left great structures that even today are interacting with the sun and moon, the local geology and meteorology, and with people who visit them. Where do the guiding concepts behind such places find their boundary? When a person visits a ceremonial monument, is it their intellect, their five senses, their intuition, or the electromagnetic fields around their bodies that perceive the place? If the monument is built of rocks giving out gamma radiation, and if this creates certain physiological effects in the brain which in turn trigger an altered state of consciousness, where is the boundary between inner and outer, between mind, body and site? Where are the boundaries of perception?

If a site is visited on one particular day in the year, it may show an aspect of itself that is not perceptible at other times: the midwinter rising sun shining down the passage of Newgrange, for instance. At another time this aspect will not be seen, but other facets may assume greater prominence. In 1985 the British government banned the observance of the midsummer sunrise from Stonehenge, and bloody riots ensued, a pattern that has been continued with variations up to the time of this writing. Stonehenge is a still-functioning astronomical observatory of the past, a ritual centre for a lost culture, a mnemonic that encodes universal measures, and it is also a modern icon symbolising conflicting political attitudes and social values. When does the function of a sacred site cease?

To try to understand how we interact with these places means we have to broaden the terms in which we think. It is no longer sufficiently informative for us to think in simplistic building block ways. We have to take into account *relationships* too, and orders of relationships. As a simple analogy, when I was a student at art college, we were taught to draw a group of still life objects, such as a row of bottles, not by drawing outlines around the objects themselves, but around the *spaces in between* the objects. If one correctly noted the spaces, the placing and shape of the objects took care of themselves.

This type of thinking is called 'holistic', a term which tends to get bandied about more frequently than it is actually used. It is a process of thought that needs to be adopted consciously to some degree, otherwise the most nonsensical misjudgments arise. People who prefer an intuitive approach at sites tend to denounce any form of mental rigour in other people's attitudes, while those who have a predilection for analysis and measurement tend to deprecate the 'vibers'. In fact both camps are cutting out part of the valid perception of a site, part of what it is about. One may individually respond in a limited set of ways to a site, but it is crucial to know that one's preferred reactions are only part of a *network of knowing* that is involved in the more complete description of the place.

A sacred site of antiquity, as distinct from a domestic or utilitarian site or a modern building, is a *whole.*

Ironically, there is also a growing need for science and technology to think in wholes, too, and in these contexts this is sometimes referred to as 'the systems approach' or 'general systems theory'. When I first heard of these terms I visualised cogs and wheels and mechanical processes of the most soulless kind. In fact, a systems approach is the framework for holistic thinking, and no more belongs to science and technology than any other area of human activity. Nature itself works in systems. The builders of, say, Stonehenge thought in systems terms, in correspondences. Stonehenge is a monument to systems thought processes. That is why an ancient sacred site can yield information on physical, intellectual, intuitive and spiritual levels *simultaneously*. That holism is lost by those who fail to see the site *as a system*, or, at least, their interaction with it in systems terms.

Modern systems thinking emerged around the middle of this century. One of the key pioneers of General Systems Theory was the German biologist, Ludwig von Bertalanffy. Marilyn Ferguson sums the theory up by saying that it:

> . . . sees all of nature – including human behaviour – as interconnected. According to General Systems Theory, nothing can be understood in isolation but must be seen as part of a system . . .
>
> Science has always tried to understand nature by breaking things into their parts. Now it is overwhelmingly clear that *wholes cannot be understood by analysis* . . . In relationship there is novelty, creativity, richer complexity. Whether we are talking about chemical reactions or human societies, molecules or international treaties, there are qualities that cannot be predicted by looking at the components.[1]

Systems theory celebrates the truism that the whole is greater than the sum of its parts. In the case of ancient sites, we need to be aware of what some of the parts are that make the greater whole, or, to put a different emphasis on that statement, to understand that a particular approach is but one aspect of the greater whole the monument embodies.

Bertalanffy wrote his first piece on General Systems Theory in 1945, though he had been working towards it in earlier years. A Society for General Systems Research was formed in 1954. Modern technology, as it became more complex, requiring teams of different specialists to work together on certain projects, had to develop systems approaches. But Bertalanffy pointed out that this way of thinking had to be applied to even the 'most esoteric' subjects too: it was 'a change in basic categories of thought . . . In one way or another, we are forced to deal with complexities, with "wholes" or "systems", in all fields of knowledge,' he wrote.[2] He quoted R.L. Ackoff who stressed that while systems have been studied for centuries, 'Something new has been added . . . the tendency to study systems as an entity rather than a conglomeration of parts.' The aura of sanctity of an old holy place, the feeling of it being 'a place', is this sense of entity, an aspect we will take almost literally later on.

Bertalanffy referred to Herman Hesse's Nobel-prize-winning novel, *Das Glasperlenspiel (The Glass Bead Game)*, in which a multimode and multidisciplinary game linking mind and matter is played, as an expression of systems thought. While he saw General Systems Theory as a way of enhancing human understanding, Bertalanffy was also aware that soulless versions could be developed in society and industry in which the human individuality was minimised. As with all powerful modes of cognition, from magic to science, there is a gamble with positive and negative outcomes.

General Systems Theory is a 'general science of wholeness which up till now was considered a vague, hazy, and semimetaphysical concept,' Bertalanffy stated. Moreover, the basically same models of relationships and organisation were found to apply to many problems in subject areas as diverse as biology and engineering, or sociology and physics. Systems thinking is the search for what Gregory Bateson called 'the pattern that connects'. The pattern is a greater entity, is other, than the specific elements that comprise it. In this way, General Systems Theory is an antidote to the stultifying specialisation that has developed within the sciences especially, to the degree that one researcher looking at one aspect of a particular subject can barely communicate with someone else dealing with another facet of the same area of inquiry! A remarkable thing was how the systems approach developed independently in separate areas: it was as if Mind needed a new way of functioning. Bertalanffy and other researchers were looking for 'universal principles applying to systems in general'.

An example of an area that has to be approached in a systems manner is ecology, the science of the interrelationships of living organisms and their environments – hence we have 'ecosystems'. Without systems thinking, *ecology could not even be perceived.* Bertalanffy observed that the world showed independently occurring 'traces of order' at all levels and realms. Or as Bateson put it, enlarging on his 'pattern' thesis:

> The *pattern which connects is a metapattern.* It is a pattern of patterns. It is that metapattern which defines the vast generalisation that, indeed, *it is patterns which connect.*[3]

'The unifying principle,' Bertalanffy observed, 'is that we find organisation at all levels.' This view of organisation stands opposed to mechanistic concepts. Bertalanffy perceived that the mechanistic philosophy, 'found its expression in a civilisation which glorifies physical technology that has led eventually to the catastrophes of our time.' General Systems Theory is essentially a general theory of organisation, badly needed because the classical modes of thinking fail in the case of interaction of a large number of elements or processes.

Systems thinking is not reductionism. As Laszlo puts it:

> How can we speak of many different kinds of things in reference to a common concept, such as a system? Is this not the ancient fallacy of reductionism in modern guise? Instead of reducing phenomena to the concourse of atoms, we now reduce them to the behaviour of systems.
>
> In fact, there is no such fallacy involved in systems thinking. To speak of systems *per se* is, of course, a simplification, but it is not a reductionist one. Whereas traditional reductionism sought to find the commonality underlying diversity in reference to a shared *substance,* such as material atoms, contemporary general systems theory seeks to find common features in terms of shared aspects of *organisation.*[4]

There are various types of system, two of the most fundamental being 'open' and 'closed' systems. Basically, closed systems are those which are considered to be isolated from their environment, while an open system is defined as that which is in exchange of matter with its environment, presenting import and export. Thus a living organism is an open system; it is also a *steady state* system. That is, its inner components and processes many change but the whole is maintained. For example, the human body is said to change all its cells in cycles of about seven years, but the 'person' is maintained.

Normally, that which is exchanged between an open system and its environment is matter or energy, but it can also be information. Information is an interesting case of interaction. It need not use energy, the 'currency of physics':

> . . . examples can easily be given where the flow of information is opposite to the flow of energy, or where information is transmitted without the flow of energy or matter. The first is the case in a telegraph cable, where a direct current is flowing in one direction, but information, a message, can be sent in either direction by interrupting the current at one point and recording the interruption at another. For the second case, think of the photoelectric door openers as they are installed in many supermarkets: the shadow, the cutting off of light energy,

informs the photocell that somebody is entering, and the door opens. So information, in general, cannot be expressed in terms of energy.[5]

Bateson observed that, 'in the realms of communication, organisation, thought, learning and evolution, "nothing will come of nothing" without *information*.'[6] He observed that even zero can carry information, can convey a message, like the letter you never sent, the apology you did not make.

(Biochemist Rupert Sheldrake has invoked fields of information in his hypothesis of formative causation, or morphic fields.[7,8] Sheldrake has proposed that species memory can be accessed in general by individuals of that species because memory is a field effect, located *outside of the individual brain.* A field itself is a mysterious entity, being sometimes defined simply as 'a state of space'. We know a magnetic field exists around a magnet because an iron filing will leap through space to the magnet, but no one can actually define what that field is comprised of. So a field of information is doubly enigmatic. 'What is information?' Sheldrake asks. 'Is it physical or is it mental? Is it essentially mathematical? Is it some kind of conceptual abstraction? If so, an abstraction from what?'[9] His morphic fields are accessed by 'morphic resonance'. This does not involve a transfer of energy as in electromagnetic fields, but a 'non energetic transfer of information'. These morphic fields, 'like the known fields of physics, are non-material regions of influence extending in space and continuing in time.' They themselves change with the increase of information obtained by the species.)

Pattern and information can be readily blurred by the random. Messages stop being information when nobody can read them, as when a means of decoding a message is lost by some accident, or if a means of decoding information remains unfound. But randomness is a good thing, Bateson argued, because in all manifestations of the creative – art, learning, evolution – processes of change feed on the random. He used the idea of the *stochastic process* which is one that contains a random element with a selective function so that only certain outcomes of the random are allowed to endure. An artist might consider an accidental splash on the canvas a fortuitous addition to the composition, and work it into the painting or, conversely, find it unhelpful and simply remove it.

Systems models can be technical and mathematically precise, but they can also be what Bertalanffy called 'empirico-intuitive'. While this approach 'lacks mathematical elegance and deductive strength and, to the mathematically minded, will appear naive and unsystematic,' he argued that, 'the system idea retains its value even where it cannot be formulated mathematically, or remains a "guiding idea" rather than being a mathematical construct.'[10] He felt it was preferable to start with a non-mathematical model expressing some unnoticed aspect rather than going for the apparent precision of mathematics at the outset, which could possibly restrict the field of vision. (The present book uses the systems approach to ancient sites only in the form of a 'guiding idea', for example.)

The parts of a whole combine to produce new or *emergent* characteristics that are recognisable only when the whole is perceived. Look at ourselves. Each of us is built up of a set of systems and subsystems. Elementary particles which form atoms which form molecules which form cells which form tissues which form organs which combine into organ systems which constitute the whole organism. Then we recognise Joan or Joe, and they have 'personalities' and 'intelligence', the emergent characteristics of their organisms. And the systems go on: Joe and Joan are part of the local community which is part of a national population which is part of the human race which is part of the biosphere which is an aspect of the planet which is a member of the solar system which is, etc . . .

If we delve away into the structure of our own bodies we will find that the molecules, or cells or atoms, each operate in their own right, that they have their own characteristics, identities and goals. Yet they also work together to add up to larger wholes, wholes within wholes like a Russian doll. But at no stage can you find the presence of your personal sense of self, your identity, your consciousness. These factors are emergent from the whole formed by the many-tiered systems comprising the larger system of the body. Teilhard de Chardin referred to these changes of level as 'a change of state'.[11] From a preceding state it is impossible to know the nature of the next state until the state change occurs. A gate is a gate as one goes through it, but on looking back there is no gate. Author, Peter Russell, finds there are crucial numbers involved in reaching certain state changes. For instance, there are no known forms of life containing less than $10^9$ atoms: 'in terms of sheer numbers, there would seem to be a threshold below which life does not readily emerge.' He goes on:

> A similar threshold appears to exist for the emergence of self-reflective consciousness from life. The average human brain contains about $10^{11}$ nerve cells, of which $10^{10}$ are in the cortex, the area associated with conscious thought processes. Brains with

> cortices containing $10^9$ or fewer neurons, such as the brain of a dog, do not appear to show the phenomenon of self-reflective consciousness. Only when you reach the size of the human cortex does this faculty emerge, and with it the development of thinking, language, the intellect, knowledge, free will, science, art and religious experience.[12]

With these matters, though, we are not just dealing with number and quantity, piles of beans or grains of sand, but with what Bertalanffy called 'organised complexity' or 'connected complexity' to use the phrase of another systems pioneer, Ervin Laszlo. The non-corporeal mind is able to shimmer into manifestation within the human brain, for example, because of the billions of synaptic connections between neurons in the cortex. Teilhard de Chardin likewise stressed 'the number and quality of the *links* established between the atoms . . .'[13] The more complex their structure, and the greater variety of mechanisms within living creatures, 'the more living they are,' the French Jesuit declared.

In a similar manner, the emerging Global Tribe will be a different order of civilisation to any preceding it. Humanity is becoming increasingly connected by information: it is claimed by some that the global telecommunications network could equal the complexity of the brain by the end of the millenium. We can see the apparent contradiction in the involuntary movement towards a global consciousness and the ragtaggle attempts at nationalism and 'holy wars' as the last ditch responses of an old state of mind; a perturbation at the threshold of a state change. What is known and conceptualised by people this side of the state change are the smaller systems of nation states, but what is *actually* happening is the globalisation of culture. People fear losing sense of place and identity, of being controlled by some larger bloc. In the end, only a systems approach can deal with this: one can be connected intimately with one's immediate region, but see that as part of a global whole, like an organ within the body. An effective systems method of regional interaction would reduce the habit of centralisation, which is so damaging and is *really* what people fear. Countries will need to think of themselves as regions of the globe as a whole, operating as a subsystem of the Earth's body, the health of each region and the people within it being seen as essential to the health of the whole world.

Bateson realised that our knowledge at any given moment is a function of the thresholds of our available means of perception, and as these thresholds are crossed and perception is improved (as it was, for example, by the inventions of the telescope and microscope) there will be disclosed 'what was utterly unpredictable from the levels of perception that we could achieve before that discovery.' This is really another way of describing a change of state. As Laszlo points out, 'The systems approach does not restrict the scientist to one set of relationships . . . he can *switch levels* . . . A system in one perspective is a subsystem in another'[14] [My emphasis.]

Paiakan, the leader of the Kayapo tribe of the Amazon rain forest, expresses systems thinking, even though he would not understand such a term, in this statement:

> The forest is one big thing; it has people, animals and plants. There is no point saving the animals if the forest is burned down; there is no point saving the forest if the people and animals who live in it are killed or driven away. The groups trying to save the animals cannot win if the people trying to save the forest lose; the people trying to save the Indians cannot win if either of the others loses . . .[15]

There is still a long way to go before Westerners can think easily in whole terms about the world. We are strongly locked into certain worldviews. One reason for this, Bertalanffy was convinced, was because of our language. He concurred with Benjamin Lee Whorf who held that linguistic patterns determine how a person perceives the world and thinks about it. Thus people using different linguistic systems can hold basically different world views.The Indo-European languages, for example, stress things that do not occur in other cultures. They separate a thing from its properties, so in English we may say, 'a light' flashed, or 'it' flashed, whereas a Hopi Indian would say simply 'flash' (occurred). Or, again, the Indo-European languages powerfully emphasise *time*. Whorf contended that Hopi does not make the same temporal distinctions we do. In his *Language, Thought and Reality* (1956) Whorf wrote: 'The Hopi language is seen to contain no words, grammatical forms, constructions or expressions that refer directly to what we call "time".'

However, Ekkehart Malotki has strongly contested this (*Hopi Time: a Linguistic Analysis of the Temporal Concepts in the Hopi Language*, 1983), showing that Hopi language does contain concepts relating to the passage of time. But Malotki did only have access to sources who were average Hopi from the communities of Third Mesa, and did not include Hopi who were 'experts, such as sun watchers, society leaders, and others,' as these were unwilling to share 'esoteric knowledge'. One only has to see how an ancient language like Welsh can become heavily anglicised to realise that the conceptual integrity of an ancient worldview can become eroded by close contact with a dominant culture. However, there is no doubt that the Hopi Indians did have temporal concepts, because they had sun watchers and solar horizon calendars (see Chapter 4). Perhaps the real difference is that the ancient Hopi thought of time in natural cycles, whereas we today have a powerful mechanical concept of linear time, with ever-increasing divisions of time (can an ancient Hopi Elder be imagined requiring a watch that measured to a hundredth of a second?). Modern Western culture has such a dominant concept of linear time that individual members feel that they 'have no time' for this or that, often the more basic human matters of their lives. This ruling concept of time spills over into other perceptions entirely: time is measured in spatial ways ('long' or 'short' periods of time) and we 'buy time' for advertising, and 'time is money'. We are a culture that worships the transubstantiation of time. No other culture ever had such a perspective on the world.

It is unfortunate that Whorf used an only partially valid interpretation of language, Hopi, as the basis for his thesis of cultural relativity in which language determines worldview. But common sense tells us that something like this has to be the case.Language is not neutral. It encodes cultural attitudes by its definitions, scope and structure, and these are passed on to each generation, so that thought itself is conducted as an inner commentary in the learned langauge mode. Language is bound to affect worldview, and the direction taken by a culture is thus both expressed and created by language. Language and worldview thus share a symbiotic relationship.

Even more intriguingly, cognition is also dependent on an organism's organs, senses, and so on. If we were able to share other animals' worldviews, many characteristics of the environment we are used to would become startlingly unfamiliar. The perception of time, for instance, is variable and dependent on metabolic rate and other physiological factors. In the human being the smallest unit recognised as an 'instant' is about one eighth of a second, which means impressions shorter than this are not separated out, but flow together and fuse. This 'flicker fusion' allows us to see motion pictures, which are 18 still pictures thrown onto the screen every second. The fighting fish *(Betta)* on the other hand, cannot recognise its image presented in a mirror at 18 times a second. At 30 times per second, however, it attacks its own reflection.

If we could obtain a glimpse of the time perspective of small and very active creatures, it would look like a slow-motion world to us. This is because small animals are able to distinguish shorter 'instances' than we are. (Similarly, a slow-motion camera takes *more* frames per second than a normal-speed camera.) A fly can discern intervals of time as short as one hundredth of a second, so fast movement to us would appear quite slow to it. Birdsong is found to have great detail when recorded and played back at slow speed. To a creature like a snail, though, time is pixillated compared to our human sequence: it distinguishes longer instances. A stick vibrating at four times a second appears at rest to a snail because it is distinguishing less images per second.

Even within the lifetime of a single human being, the perception of time is variable. Time seems to fly if it is filled with many impressions, but lingers when we are bored. When body temperature and metabolic rate rise in fever, time also seems to go slowly, because we suffer the slow-motion effect of increased frequency of 'instances'. This is apparently related to the frequency of certain brainwaves. In emergency situations, adrenalin is produced allowing the brain to process information more rapidly, thus a car accident, say, is typically remembered as a slow motion sequence. It is common experience, too, that as one gets older, time seems to pass more rapidly. This is related to the slowing down of our metabolic rate with age.

Drugs can likewise affect perceptions of space and time. Amphetamines and cannabis for instance can create a higher sequence of discernable instances so time slows down and brief thoughts or sensory impressions can be experienced in depth: eternity can be had in an hour. Alcohol and barbiturates have a reverse effect. Psychoactive substances can blur the distinction between self and not-self. One's awareness can slip into what is 'normally' perceived as the environment, and be mobile there.

Language may also be connected with drug usage. Magic mushrooms, (psilocybin) can liberate spontaneity 'that is not only perceptual, but linguistic.'[16] Some researchers have proposed that different ethnic temperaments and religious symbolism, and perhaps even language, arose from early humanity's interaction with various psychoactive elements in the botanical environment. One group using a particular psychotropic plant may have developed cultural traits that related to the specific langauge/perceptual stimulus of that plant. It is the case that some hallucinogens do seem to act on the language centres in the brain's temporal lobe region, which is also the area containing the organs associated with memory, dreaming and emotion. The temporal lobe thus integrates several sense modes, and its association with language is therefore probably of profound significance.

Bertalanffy suggested that biological relativism in the experience of time is likewise worth relating to similar relativism of categories from the standpoint of culture and language. 'Thus what is seen depends on our apperceptions,' he concluded, 'on our line of attention and interest which, in turn, is determined by training, i.e. by linguistic symbols by which we represent and summarise reality . . . Technical language, including the symbolism of mathematics, is, in the last resort, an efflorescence of everyday language . . .'

These are the sorts of problems facing our approach to ancient sites. They have been built by people with a different, archaic language, with a different worldview, with a different state of consciousness and even perhaps with different perceptions of time and space, in a world which was infinitely more wild and natural than our own, and with tribal values different from our own. A site cannot therefore be understood solely by the single frame of archaeology, which is anchored to our present state of cognition, to our language structures and thought processes. In fact, the very subject of archaeology, 'the study of the past', is an outcome of the cognitive processes engendered by our culture and language structures. In a way, archaeology only compounds the difficulties encountered in the modern attempt to understand these monuments, for all the reasons hinted at in the foregoing paragraphs.

There simply is no doubt that for archaeology to cope with its enormously difficult job, it has to broaden its frame and be flexible in its perspectives. Only in such a manner can an ancient sacred site be adequately approached and understood.

A broader archaeology would have to be *systems archaeology*, and that in effect is what the nameless subject we are calling Earth Mysteries or Geomancy is. Modern archaeology is systems-based to some extent, but its frame is still defined by modern cognitive prejudices.

But what is true of the archaeological problem is true, more or less, of *any* narrowly-framed approach to a ceremonial monument. Bateson found the matter of *description* to be most important. He defined information as 'the news of difference'. Human sense organs can only perceive difference, and the differences must be coded in events into time (into *changes*), Bateson argued. 'Ordinary static differences that remain constant for more than a few seconds become perceptible only by scanning,' he pointed out.

'Similarly, very slow changes become perceptible only by a combination of scanning *and* bringing together observations from separated moments in the continuum of time.'[17] Even when we are looking at a static object, say a brick wall, our eyes have a continual tremor called 'micronystagmus' causing the optical image to vibrate on the retina allowing the sense organ to test for difference or change.

And so it is with our understanding of anything. Whatever the things we come in contact with may actually be in their unadulterated thingness, we only – *only* – know about them from the report of them we get from our senses and through the conceptual filters we place on that information. In communication they are only names, which are ideas using the language structures or notation appropriate to our culture. Thus Bateson stressed the truism 'two descriptions are better than one'. The more ways one can describe something, he argued, the more information is garnered: 'A bonus or increment of knowing follows from *combining* information from two or more sources.'

He gave stereovision as a parable. We have two eyes that provide binocular vision, and only because of that do we perceive depth in space – three dimensions. With a single eye one has to work from various cues or other senses to attempt to assess depth in space; it cannot actually be seen as with two eyes. The brain, and hence mind, is able to note the *difference* between the two sets of information provided by each eye. The combination of that information provides an increment of knowledge of a different logical type – a new dimension is literally added by the synthesis of the two sources of information. Just try to think what exactly has been added by binocular vision to the monovision version. Think of describing the visual sensation of depth in space to someone who has never experienced it (someone blind or single-eyed from birth), or to two-dimensional entities. One has to describe something which has the prime characteristic of being nothing! Stereo acoustic systems likewise give 'depth' to sound, and a 'ghost' loudspeaker is created between the two physical speakers. Quadraphonic systems, by giving more description of sounds, produce an even more realistic effect. Another example given by Bateson in *Mind and Nature* was of interaction of two superimposed patterns, as occurs when moving past two wire mesh fences: the moiré effect. A ghost pattern appears as a result of the combination. Something that was not perceptible becomes so because of the combination of more than one source of information.

Information in the 'two or more' descriptions may even be in different languages or modes. Information that might be disregarded in one description can take on new or extended meaning when placed in juxtaposition, in relationship, with information in another description. Bateson summarised the value of increased description thus:

> The combining of information of different sorts or from different sources results in something more than addition. The aggregate is greater than the sum of its parts because the combining of the parts is not a simple adding but is the nature of a multiplication or a fractionation, or the creation of a logical product. A momentary gleam of enlightenment.[18]

My argument here, then, is that an extended frame of reference, an increased range of description, is necessary for sacred monuments of antiquity to be apprehended 'in the round'; to be more fully understood.

If the sites have survived in sufficiently good order, we can consider them as systems. We need perhaps to make an initial differentiation between engineered, constructed, sacred places and those natural ones which were merely selected: the former contain the input of human awareness to a greater degree than the latter, and so are more amenable to human decoding.

We can think of engineered sites as being systems in various ways. They can import and export energy, information, or both. A chambered mound might receive a sunbeam into its darkened interior on certain key days of the solar year. This light might interact with carvings on the stone facing-slabs inside the mound, or informative shadows might be thrown, pointing to specific ancient carvings. An observer will thus receive information left encoded in the site that only the sunbeam activated (we will consider precise examples of this in later chapters). Actual energy has been imported into the site, and exported, along with information. Or, for example, an observer might receive an energy shock of some kind from a megalith. This may be static electricity gradually collected by the stone from its environment in various ways, which is discharged by the touch of a hand. In time past, this energy may have been used for healing or mind-change techniques, and our increasing knowledge of the effect may cause it to be similarly used in the future. In such a case, a monument is a recording device that stores information which can be accessed as energy (a static electric shock) or as information (the shock may have healing or mind-changing effects). The information only exists if it is perceived and decoded.

Yet again, energetic displays at sites, ranging from static electrical effects, through magnetism and radiation to bizarre light phenomena, can sometimes be instrumentally measured, and this in turn yields information which can be placed in larger contexts of processes in the natural world in general, or about the use of specific types of sites in prehistory. Some energy effects encountered at ancient sacred sites interact with human physiology in various ways, and as we shall see, may occasion altered states of consciousness in certain cases.

Sites can thus provide information at sensory, spiritual, intellectual and technical levels. They can receive energy from the sun, moon and geophysical sources, as well as from the human body. They can output energy as light (see later chapters), as magnetism, as static electricity, as radioactivity, as pressure waves (sound), and perhaps in forms not currently measurable.

In terms of information alone, sites were built for specific effects known about at the time of their construction, or to encode information as a recording device (as we shall see occurred in terms of metrological information at Stonehenge, for example). Later visitors or investigators at a site can receive that information if the method of accessing it is understood. Thus we can access information put into the site involuntarily by the builders as well as specific information they intended to pass on.

So sites import and export information and energies. Sites are, therefore, open systems. But there is another way in which their systems nature can be perceived, and that is in their *interaction* with the human mind: how we can learn from them. To arrive at as useful a description as possible of a sacred monument, to receive the widest range of information from it, we need to have a multidisciplinary and multimode approach. In other words, a systems approach is the only one which can access the information embodied by a site. And this is precisely what has developed as if by itself in recent decades in the form of Earth Mysteries studies.

Any set of approaches will contain a marginally arbitrary element whoever makes it. I present here only a guiding idea, merely an initial, preliminary system. It is bound to reflect personal biases to some extent, but if it at least allows us to start comprehending the systems attitude towards ancient holy places, it will serve its purpose.

The front-line approaches I define as: archaeology; 'being and seeing'; archaeoastronomy; sacred geometry and metrology; folklore; and the sensing and monitoring of effects at sites.

*Archaeology* in its presently circumscribed academic form is seen here simply as part of a greater descriptive potential. *'Being and seeing'* is my term for just being present at a site and being open to the receipt of whatever information the site might be yielding. We will deal with some concrete examples of this in later pages. *Archaeoastronomy* is the study of ancient astronomies left encoded in ceremonial monuments. Like archaeology, this emerged as an academic study area through folklore, antiquarianism and primitive early scholarship. *Sacred geometry,* and measure, can be deduced from groundplans of sites and sometimes in the elevations and ratios between their integral structures. *Folklore* is the memory of those generations who have intimately shared the landscape with ancient sacred monuments. Like a secret phone message, it is scrambled, but information is in folktales and traditions awaiting decoding. *Sensing and monitoring* involves the use of direct, human sensitivity, and the employment of instrumental means to gather information about the numinous quality and energetic properties of sites.

These feed into second-line, more integrated approaches which I would list as: geomancy, correspondence and use.

*Geomancy* is being used here in the sense defined by the Victorian missionaries in China – the orientation and relationships of sites with one another, and with topographical and astronomical factors. Sacred geography, in fact. In systems terms, geomancy provides a perspective in which a site's information potential is extended into the local landscape and ambient conditions. Astronomy, sacred geometry, metrology and aspects of folklore can be integrated into the greater context of *correspondence,* an ancient form of systems thinking common to arcane practices such as magic, alchemy, and sacred architecture. It is essentially the exercise of symbolism. Sacred sites were *used,* and this requires us to look at what forms this took in the past and what usage can mean today.

It will be discovered that consideration of geomancy, correspondence and site use brings us in turn to fundamental questions related to *energies* at sacred sites. What was the nature of the Chinese *ch'i* manipulated by the Feng shui geomants, and the *prima materia* of the old alchemists? What other traditions and ideas about a universal force exist? Do any of them mix in with known energies? If so, what energies, and how are they present at ancient monuments? What were they used for?

The presence of energy phenomena at sites leads us ultimately to ideas relating to the Earth as a living entity. But how can we envisage the Earth, a planet, as alive? What is the history of the idea, and how can we relate to it today? If the Earth is alive, is it sentient? If it is sentient, can we communicate with it?

All these various and interrelated topics can be seen in two ways – as approaches we make to the site, or, conversely, as resulting from the site acting as a catalyst in drawing out these various approaches from our consciousness. This is an animistic view of the site, but perhaps a useful model to use. In either case, we are dealing with a human-site *interaction*.

This interfacing system could be depicted in various ways, but perhaps the most appropriate would be as a form of 'systems tree' (Figures 1 and 2). The 'top' of the tree shows the seven initial approaches to a site. They blur into one another, and yield a second row of the three larger areas. The final point, where the branches emerge from the trunk of the tree, is where the whole matter seems to originate or dissolve (depending on whether one is climbing up or down the tree). The site is effectively the trunk of the tree, and these various areas can be seen as its fruits. The trunk, the site, is rooted in the living Earth itself. It was built by people who would have thought of the planet as literally alive, as a Mother Goddess. It is only our modern times that considers such an idea as being superstitious or bizarre. In actuality, the modern global culture is the eccentric one in this respect. All previous cultures have held the idea of the living Earth in one form or another.

A systems tree is an appropriate conceptual structure to use, as Fritjof Capra has explained:

> As a real tree takes its nourishment through both its roots and its leaves, so the power in a systems tree flows in both directions, with neither end dominating the other and all levels interacting in independent harmony to support the functioning of the whole.[19]

We can envisage our tree, then, as an 'Earth Mysteries tree'. The exact form suggested here is, I re-emphasise, preliminary and necessarily biased. I would not only expect but hope that the system would develop or become modified the more it was used. What I present here is *a* systems approach, not *the* systems approach.

In each of the chapters in Part Two there will be a demonstration as well as a discussion of the areas involved. The site selected for the demonstration is Castlerigg, a stone circle in England. *Any ancient sacred site anywhere on Earth could perform the same role.* The fact that I am using Castlerigg here is simply for the sake of convenience: I happen to be writing in Great Britain, the site happens to be known to me, and I happen to know of various factors concerning it. There is nothing otherwise special about this particular monument. Indeed, I encourage readers to go out to the nearest sacred place of antiquity known to them and to employ a systems method to describe it, to understand it.

It is time to plant a tree.

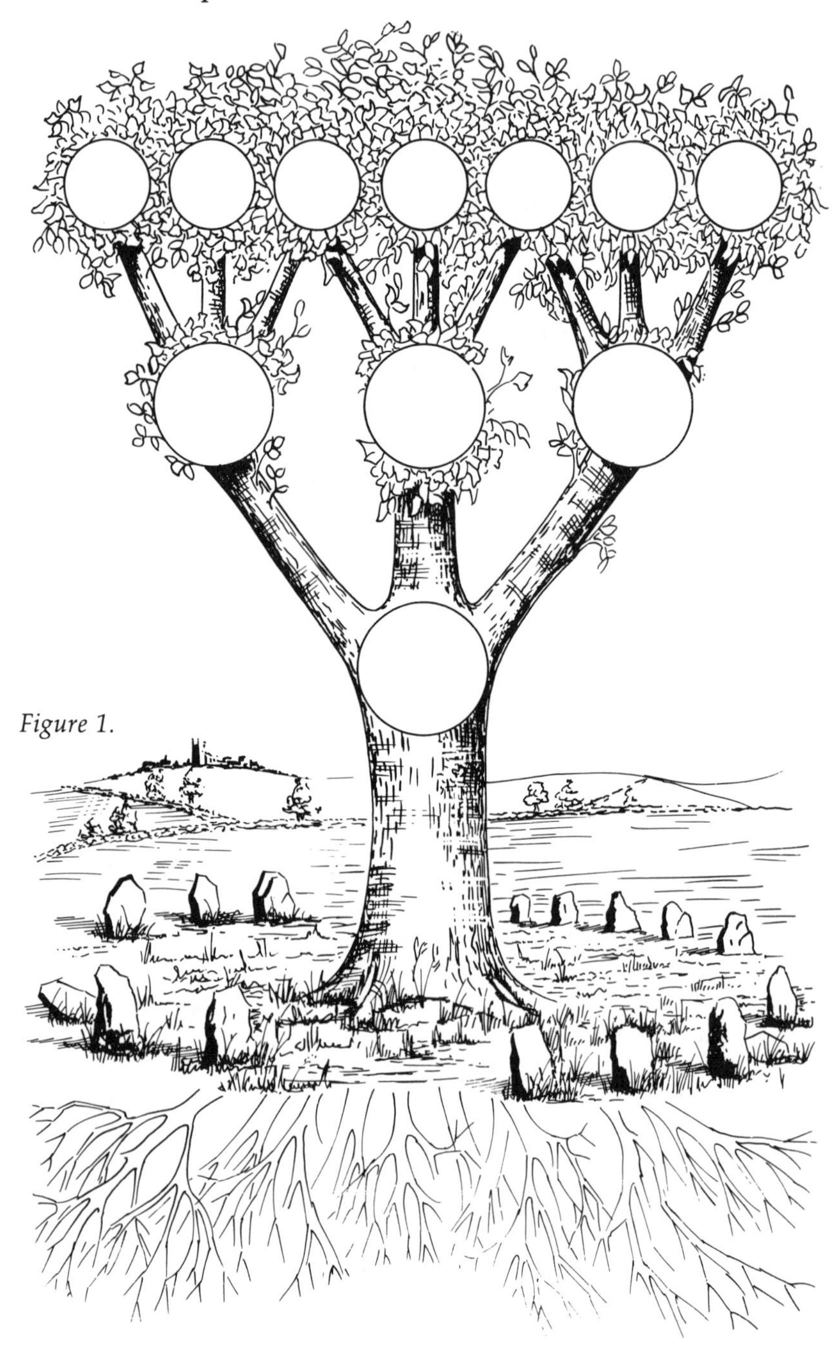

*Figure 1.*

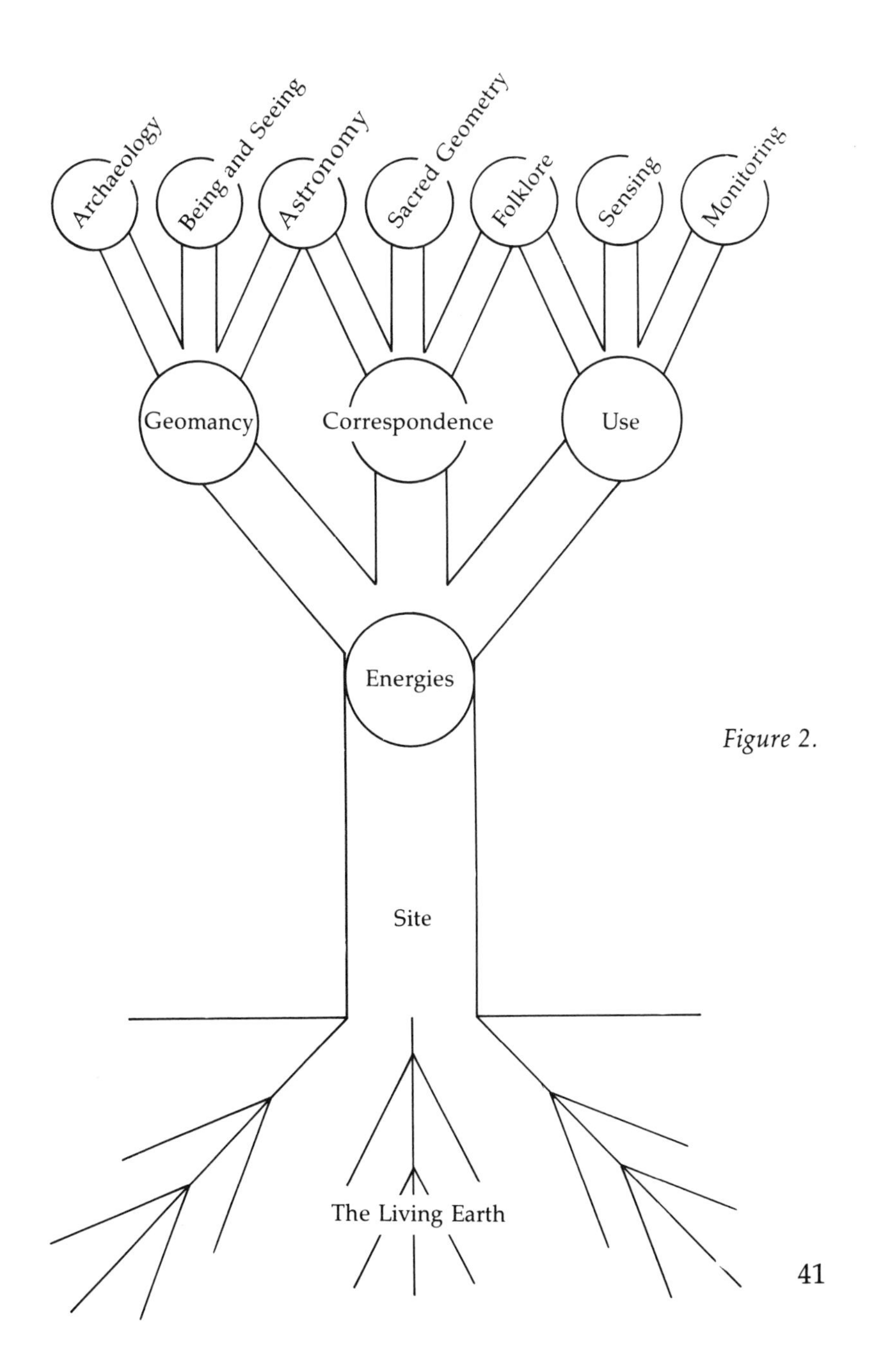
Archaeology
Being and Seeing
Astronomy
Sacred Geometry
Folklore
Sensing
Monitoring
Geomancy
Correspondence
Use
Energies
Site
The Living Earth

*Figure 2.*

*PART TWO*

# BRANCHES

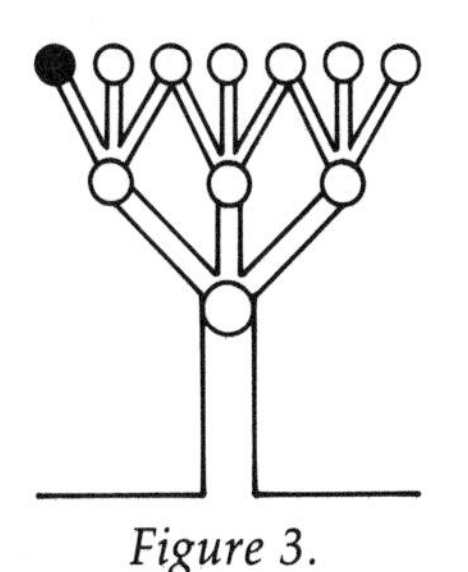
Figure 3.

# CHAPTER 2
# ARCHAEOLOGY

## Demonstration

The ancient sacred site selected here, purely for the purpose of example, is Castlerigg, a well-preserved stone circle less than two miles east of Keswick in the Lake District of northwest England. It is in a beautiful mountain setting, and has panoramic views.

The archaeological information is limited. There are 38 extant stones at the site, virtually all in their original position, and all but five still upright. They mark out a slightly flattened circle which has a longer diameter of 110 feet (33.5 m). There is an 11-foot (3.5 m) gap on the north side of the ring flanked by two large stones which suggest that it was an entrance. Ten of the 38 stones form a roughly rectangular enclosure within the main circle. This is usually referred to as 'The Cove' and its purpose is not known. The stones are from the local region. The tallest stone stands at almost seven feet (2.1 m) and weighs about 15 tons. Slight traces of

Figure 4.

possible banking have been found on the SSW of the circle, just outside the ring of stones: this may indicate that the site was once a henge (a circular enclosure of ditch and bank), but this is by no means certain. There have been a couple of excavations in the nineteenth century – an unpolished stone axe was uncovered, but this may not be directly associated with the stone circle: archaeologist Aubrey Burl has called it 'a stray find'. A deep pit containing charcoal was discovered at the west corner of The Cove. This may have been the trace of a burial, but no one can be sure, and its association with the circle may be secondary (i.e. the circle was not built for the purpose of the burial; rather, the burial may have been added later.)

Archaeologists tentatively associate Castlerigg with a number of other circles in the English northwest, and it may date from around 2000 BC.

The archaeological information on the circle is thus useful but limited. As we shall see in following chapters, the site itself can tell us much more.

## Discussion

Archaeology is a European invention, projected onto the remnants of antiquity worldwide. It is a product of the Indo-European cognitive framework. Other cultures with other worldviews do not have archaeology as we understand it. Australian aborigines, for instance, have the Dreamtime, a time of origins, yet also a time of another order contiguous with the everyday world. They would visit places on the defined route of their cyclic wanderings over the vast Outback where the mythic beings of the Dreamtime emerged from the ground, made camp, defecated and so on. The mythic origins were celebrated and recreated at periodic intervals of current time. To such peoples living myth was their archaeology, and it totally informed their lives.[1]

The type of archaeology a people may have is tightly bound up with their perception of time, or, at least, their cultural image of time. Bronislaw Malinovski observed that the Aborigines:

> . . . do not conceive of a past as of a lengthy duration, unrolling itself in successive stages of time. They have no idea of a long vista of historical occurrences, narrowing down and dimming as they recede towards a distant background of legend and myth . . . This view, so characteristic of the naive, historical thinking among ourselves is entirely foreign to the natives . . . Any idea of epochs of time is absent from their mind; the past is one vast storehouse of events . . .

> Again, they have no idea of what could be called the evolution of the world . . . We, in our religious and scientific outlook alike, know that the earth ages and that humanity ages, and we think of both in these terms; for them, both are eternally the same, eternally youthful.[2]

The famous French anthropologist and philosopher, Lucien Lévy-Bruhl, similarly observed that to us, 'the background of time past which we call history is an institution of the mind so familiar, it is almost impossible to imagine any human intelligence lacking it.' He noted that the African Bushmen had a:

> . . . complete lack of interest in the past as such. What is over is done with; no longer matters . . . And so the Bushmen preserve nothing that even distantly resembles history. They live entirely in the present . . . Yet they possess a multitudinous stock of myths and legends. Moreover the events they report take place in a setting of ancient time. But . . . it is not time at all in any rational sense; it is a special kind of time, itself as mythical as the events it embraces or the beings who have their existence in it.
>
> That is what appears to us to be so strange: instead of the myths fitting into a certain epoch of historical time, the epoch itself participates actively in the identity of the world of the myths . . . It is our habit to think of the past as though it were a vast, coloured stage-set against which our present life acts itself

*Plate 1.*

> out; it is the great panorama against which we trace the outlines of our perceptions and formulate our thoughts. It provides for us the very proportions of space and time.[3]

Lévy-Bruhl used the fascinating term 'extra-temporal phase of time' to refer to this mythic concept of time held by primary peoples. He further noted that, 'Australian and Papuan myths conform to certain generalizing perceptions governing the interpretation of time *and place*.' (My emphasis.) The sacred place in the landscape also recreated mythic time. They were not merely locations but events, reconstituted in a cyclic fashion.

Our Western cognitive frames can be changed by means of psychedelic agents. These substances, we may recall from the previous chapter, can alter perception of space and time and possibly affect language centres in the brain. In some cultures this fact was used traditionally – knowledge of the history of a tribe was entrusted to the shaman who would use psychoactive plants to assist in the task. Maria Sabina, who was a Mazatec Indian shaman of Central America, said that when she ate the sacred psilocybe mushroom she could, 'look down to the very beginning. I can go to where the world is born.' German ethnopsychologist Holger Kalweit notes that it was necessary for a shaman to have 'visions of the mythical past'. The South American Tukano, for example, 'consider the drinking of yajé to be equivalent with a return into the cosmic uterus, the primordial source of all things . . . the flow of time is, as it were, reversed: one . . . returns to and re-experiences the beginnings of mankind . . .' When the Huichol Indians of Mexico chew peyote or mescal, 'time assumes a mythical duration for them.' When the Amazonian Yebamasa take caji they meet the mythical heroes and gods who take them through the universe revealing its secrets.[4]

We should not, with typical Western arrogance, automatically assume that such experiences are somehow 'unreal' and do not represent actual knowledge of the past. Stanislav Grof, a Czechoslovakian psychologist and psychotherapist with immense practical experience in the use of psychedelic substances and techniques, both in eastern Europe and in the West, warns that while transpersonal information gained in altered states of consciousness challenges our standard Newtonian/Cartesian worldview, it may nevertheless represent actual knowledge:

> Persons who report transpersonal experiences [under the influence of psychoactive substances] often obtain access to detailed and relatively esoteric knowledge about . . . the material universe which vastly exceeds their general level of education . . .

> experiences of collective and racial unconscious in the sense of Jung, and memories of previous incarnations often contain quite astounding details concerning specific historical events and costumes, architecture, weaponry, art or religious practices of the societies concerned. Persons who relive phylogenetic memories or consciously identify themselves with a living species of animal not only report on the unusual authenticity and convincingness of these events, but also obtain in this manner unusual insights into animal psychology, ethology, species-specific habits, complex reproductive cycles, and the mating customs of the most diverse species.[5]

Archaeology in our sense of the word is therefore a product of our worldview, a worldview that is dominating the planet. It is thus important for us to at least have an outline idea of how Western archaeology arose; how we developed our particular cultural relationship with the past. We can then perhaps better judge how we need to adjust the perspectives of that archaeology in order to extend our descriptions – enhance our understanding – of ancient sacred sites, which were built and used by people operating more closely to a mythic worldview than our own.

Our Global Tribe will only survive with such an understanding, such a sufficiently broadened archaeology, because it will underpin our entire sense of living with the Earth.

In the West, history was for many centuries understood in the terms of the classical writers, the Bible, legends. The sites in the landscape were known (and resorted to) by country folk. This latter aspect represents the secret history of the sites, and may link more closely to the human dimension of prehistoric places than any archaeological thesis. But the stirrings of archaeology as we know it today, as the systematic study of the remains of the past, really began around the fifteenth, sixteenth and seventeenth centuries, when the beginnings of science (also as we know it today) were 'in the air' – the early dawn of the Age of Reason.

The Renaissance created a fresh interest in the classical period, and scholars and artists became more conscious of the surviving remains of the classical world which still stood in Italy, Greece, Egypt and other parts of the Mediterranean world. The first private collections of removable items of antiquity commenced.

One of the first signs of antiquity being identified as a specific area of study manifested in England in 1533, when John Leland was appointed as the King's Antiquary. A society for the preservation of national antiquities was founded in 1572. One of the members of this society was William Camden, who produced his

*Britannia* in 1586, an illustrated guide to the visible antiquities of Britain, the first work of its kind. Camden called the study of antiquities 'the back-looking curiosity' in which 'there is a sweet food for the mind'.

In Scandinavia, which was to dominate the early period of modern archaeology, an excavation was carried out on a dolmen near Roskilde in 1588. Only a few fragments of pottery and other items were found, not the bones of a giant that legend had suggested and which the diggers had hoped to uncover.

Prehistoric flint arrow heads and stone tools that were turned up by ploughing had been assumed to be thunderbolts or to originate from fairies. The accounts given by the explorers of America concerning the living Indians using stone tools, however, made some scholars, like the Vatican's Michel Mercati in the sixteenth century, wonder if there had been similar stone-age people in Europe.

The seventeenth century saw an expansion of antiquarian activity on a number of fronts in several countries. The revived interest in the classical writers had lured numerous Europeans to Egypt: the early Greek and Arab travellers had described many of the standing antiquities of Egypt. The Europeans for a long time

*Plate 2. The description of the great fallen statue of Ramasses II by the classical writer Diodorus Siculus inspired Shelley's poem* Ozymandias. *This great stone figure measures 7 metres across the shoulders, and was fashioned from a block of granite weighing 1000 tons*

rarely ventured further south than the Pyramids of Giza, but by 1638 a fairly accurate drawing of the interior of the Great Pyramid had been produced (by the Englishman, John Greaves).

Probably the first excavation report (of urns in Norfolk) was published in 1658, and the excavator, Sir Thomas Browne, showed touching respect to what he thought were the remains of the Roman invaders (they were Anglo-Saxon), stating that, 'we mercifully preserve their bones, and pisse not upon their ashes.'

Much early archaeological activity developed in Sweden. John Bure toured Sweden studying runic inscriptions. He published some material but his *Monumenta Runica* went unpublished. In 1662 a Chair of Antiquities was created at the University of Uppsala, and its first holder, Olof Verelius, was appointed Royal Antiquary in 1666, and a college of Antiquities was founded. British archaeologist Glyn Daniel considered that at this time, 'Sweden led all Europe in pioneering archaeological studies.'[6]

Antiquarian John Aubrey, author of *Monumenta Brittanica*, was the first to recognise the mighty henge monument at Avebury, Wiltshire, as a single, vast complex. He felt somewhat unappreciated, stating that, 'This searching after Antiquities is a wearisome task . . . for nobody els hereabout hardly cares for it, but rather makes scorn of it.' Like Browne, he would not take human remains away from a site: 'I never was so sacralegious as to disturbe, or rob his urn.' The Ashmolean Museum in Oxford was opened in 1682, its basis formed by the collections of Elias Ashmole and John Tradescant's 'Closet of Curiosities'. The museum's first curator, Robert Plot, produced natural histories of Oxfordshire and Staffordshire in 1677 and 1686 respectively, which contained details of antiquities along with other matters of regional interest. His method of investigation was direct: he would make field visits to the area under study, and circulate questionnaires to local notaries asking them if they new of 'any ancient sepulchres hereabout . . . What memorable places . . . What fortifications, camps?'

In 1685, a French megalithic site of the long, slabbed *allée couverte* type, was discovered at Cocherel and excavated, producing another early excavational report.

Edward Lhwyd, who succeeded Plot as curator of the Ashmolean, visited antiquities throughout the British Isles and Brittany. At Ireland's Newgrange he displayed one of the first recorded examples of chronological reasoning by deducing from the position of a Roman coin near the top of the mound that the site had to be older than anything since Roman times.

*Figure 5. The seventeenth-century Cocherel excavation*

The seventeenth century was one of contrasts, of key Western attitudes locked in struggle. It was the century of Newton and Bacon, the 'New Men' of rationalism, logic and deduction, of the last blossoming of the occult revival, and also of Christian fundamentalist dogma which stated that the world was barely 6000 years old. Churchmen were, indeed, arguing over which day in October 4004 BC the Creation had occurred! This claustrophobic cosmology was to hinder the acceptance of the developing findings of the pioneer archaeologists and the new geologists which remorselessly spoke of vaster periods of time. In 1655, for instance, the French scholar Isaac de la Peyrère published a book which added to the view that 'thunderbolts' were in fact tools belonging to a stone-age people who lived *before Adam.* The Inquisition obliged him to recant and his book was publicly burnt. A year later William Dugdale in England discussed the finding of a stone axe and wrote of 'the native Britons' who worked in stone prior to the discovery of metallurgy. Both Plot and Lhwyd were aware that such stones were prehistoric artefacts.

The eighteenth century saw another upsurge of interest in Classicism, and archaeologist David Miles describes the period as one of 'Gothic Romanticism' when prehistoric mounds 'were opened either in a spirit of awed mysticism or as a field sport.'[7] Fortunately, England had a great antiquarian in William Stukeley, who, in the first half of the century visited and described in text and sketches numerous prehistoric sites. Two of his works dealt with individual complexes, *Stonehenge* (1740) and *Abury* (1743). His work was based on careful and close inspection, and his record of what he found has been of great use to modern archaeologists and Earth Mysteries researchers. Like Aubrey before him, Stukeley carefully replaced any human remains and artefacts he found in excavation.

Brittany, an area dense with megalithic remains, naturally attracted antiquarians. In the 1720s and 1730s, de Robien described the stones of the Carnac area and employed an artist to depict them. Later in the century antiquaries correctly ascribed the monuments to pre-Roman origins.

A society was founded in England in 1732 for those who had done the Grand Tour of the classical sites of the Mediterranean world. Many books about travels in these parts were published, and it became fashionable for artists to make the tour. There was some studying, measuring and drawing of sites, and these results were duly published. Robert Wood and James Dawkins journeyed to the Near East studying sites such as Baalbec. The Dane, Carsten Niebuhr, visited the ruins of Persoplis (Iran) and discovered cuneiform inscriptions which he copied and analysed. Excavations began at Pompeii and Herculaneum. In his *Travels in Egypt* (1755) Richard Pococke described sites further south than Giza, giving the best account of the stepped pyramid at Sakkara of his

*Figure 6. One of Stukeley's drawings of Stonehenge*

*Figure 7. Two of the many Carnac stone rows*

day. The most significant event in Egyptian archaeology to happen this century was the work done by over 150 savants of the scientific and artistic commission brought to Egypt by Napoleon Bonaparte. The French-Egyptian Institute was based at Cairo, and an enormous amount of work was accomplished in a three-year period. A key find of this period was what came to be called the Rosetta Stone, a basalt slab with inscriptions on it in Greek, Demotic and hieroglyphics. This was ultimately deciphered by Jean Francois Champollion, rendering Egyptian hieroglyphics readable for the first time.

*Plate 3. The Step Pyramid of Djoser, Sakkara*

The mutterings of scholars convinced that there had been a stone age in Europe of great antiquity continued through the 1700s. Antione Gouguet in France declared in a book of 1738 that there had been a stone age preceding one of bronze which in turn came before an iron age. This was the first clear modern expression of a three-age system to prehistory. It was not taken up at the time, but the Bishop of Carlisle wrote in 1765 that he agreed with Dugdale that stone tools were 'by far the most ancient remains existing today of our British ancestors.' In 1797, John Frere discovered what today we recognise as palaeolithic (Old Stone Age) hand axes over 12 feet (3.5 m) down in a gravel pit in Suffolk. In making the observation that these objects had to belong to a most ancient stone age people because of the thick layer of gravel lying above them, he had glimpsed the principle of stratification which was to become a vital guide to archaeological dating.

The period saw pioneering archaeology in America, too. When the first settlers arrived from New England to the banks of the Muskingham River at what is now Marietta, Ohio, they found extensive earthworks consisting of truncated earthen pyramids, mounds and ritual ways, laid out with geometrical precision. One embankment encloses an area of over 40 acres, and the tallest mound, which the settlers called *Conus*, is some 30 feet in height.[8,9,10] The people of Marietta took up a public subscription

*Plate 4. The great Indian mound in Marietta, Ohio, called by the settlers 'Conus'*

to keep and preserve the sites, and Brigadier General Rufus Putnam surveyed the earthworks – thought to be the first map of an archaeological site in America, representing 'the genesis of the science of archaeology in the Americas'. Putnam's agent, the Reverend Manasseh Cutler, observed workmen cutting down trees on the earthworks and counted the growth rings of the felled trees. One had over 460 rings, and counting one year per ring, Cutler assumed, correctly, that the earthworks were earlier than 1300 AD. (It is now known that the sites are around 2000 years old, belonging to what is called the Hopewell culture.) Putnam went on to excavate the remarkable Serpent Mound in Adams County, Ohio. No burials or artefacts were found in it. The mound, about a quarter of a mile long and just under five feet high, depicts a serpent with rippling body, spiral tail and either an open mouth or one carrying an egg-shaped object. It is thought to belong to the Adena culture, who were a little earlier than the Hopewell. It was through the persistent efforts of Putnam that the site came to be protected and, moreover, caused the first law to be passed in the USA for the protection of archaeological monuments.

There was argument amongst American antiquaries whether the mounds were built by indigenous Amerindian peoples or a 'lost race' – the lost tribes of Israel, early Old World travellers, survivors from Atlantis and so on. The 'lost race' thesis allowed the white Americans to consider the Indians as savages, incapable of belonging to a race which could have built the mighty earthworks, and many of these remarkable structures did not fare as well as those at Marietta. Putnam was strongly opposed to the Lost Race idea, but Thomas Jefferson, who was to become the third president of the United States, was unsure. He investigated a mound in 1784. What was remarkable was that he employed a sophisticated

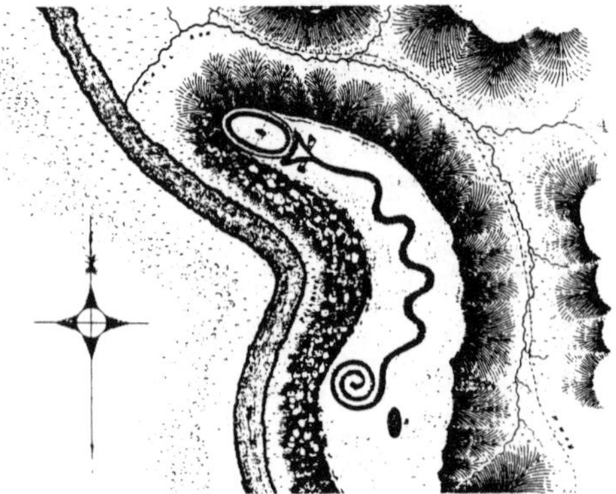

*Figure 8. Squier and Davis' survey of Serpent Mound, Ohio*

approach to digging, anticipating by many years the later, careful and scientific approach to archaeological excavation. He dug a trench into the mound, and noted many bones lying at different levels. He perceived that these related to inhumations of different periods, and also noted children's bones amongst the remains. He was unable to come up with an answer as to the identity of the mound's builders, however. In 1799, Jefferson sent round a circular to learned men urging that 'accurate plans, drawings and descriptions' be made of ancient sites, and that 'cuts in various directions may be made into many of the Tumuli, to ascertain their contents; while the diameter of the largest tree growing thereon, the number of its annulars and the species of the tree, may tend to give some idea of their antiquity.' This showed that Jefferson, along with Cutler, was a pioneer of tree-ring dating – dendrochronology – which was to become a major dating technique in modern archaeology.

In Europe, the matter of dating came to a head in the nineteenth century, primarily through the development of geology. From the seventeenth century onwards, it gradually became apparent that the ground was not a random heap of soil, but layered in *strata*. By 1762, John Michell, a geology professor at Cambridge, was able to provide a clear written description of the appearance of strata, and to have a good working knowledge of it in England and abroad. In a book of 1785 James Hutton recognised that much of the present land surface had once been sea. He felt this had occurred naturally over vast periods of time, in contrast to those who preferred a biblical 'universal deluge' idea of sudden change. This was seen as an argument between 'uniformitarians' and 'catastrophists'.

Another proponent for uniformitarianism, for the gradual laying down of strata, was William 'Strata' Smith. In 1816 he started publishing his findings in which he drew up a table of different strata, using the fossils within them to assign relative ages to the rocks. The unformitarianists finally won out with the publication of Sir Charles Lyell's *Principles of Geology* (1830–33), which was to have a great effect on Charles Darwin. It was clear that the world was much older than the Biblical 6000 years. 'From now on, in archaeology as well as geology,' Glyn Daniel has written, 'Moses and the Flood were dead. The archaeologists who were working in the post-Lyell years were no longer cabined in their interpretations by diluvial catastrophes.'[11] Archaeologists had been finding human bones in association with ancient geological deposits and the bones of extinct animals, but because of the resistance of Biblical dogma, the fear of undermining the Christian faith and perhaps sheer awe at accepting the vast prehistory of humanity and the age of the Earth, the implications of the findings were resisted for a long time.

In Denmark, Christian Thomsen was appointed as the first curator of the National Museum of Denmark in 1816. Looking at the mass of artefacts in the collection, he began sorting them on the basis of their material – stone, bronze and iron. In 1836 he published a book, translated into English ten years later, in which he clearly set out that prehistory in Europe had been first a stone age, then one of copper and finally iron, and that the materials indicated a chronology. He was clearly aware, however, that the various 'ages' overlapped, that there were not distinct boundaries between them. Thomsen's assistant, J.J.A. Worsaae, was able to demonstrate the relevance of the 'Three Age' system in excavations, and also practised the careful 'peeling away' of layers at a site. Worsaae has been called the first professional archaeologist.

The nineteenth century was full of major discoveries and extensions of knowledge in archaeology, far too many to catalogue here in such a brief review. Perhaps the most colourful event was Heinrich Schliemann's discovery of Troy at Hissarlik in the 1870s. He took the writings of the Greek poet Homer literally, and confounded his critics. This was one of the finds that helped to create great public interest in archaeology. Another was the discovery of the ancient Nineveh (Iraq). This was partially excavated by the French, but the big discoveries of fabulous palaces, statues and a library of thousands of cuneiform tablets were made by Sir Austen Henry Layard.

But there was also much to deplore in nineteenth-century archaeology. To some degree it degenerated into little more than treasure hunting in Europe and by Europeans elsewhere. William Cunnington and Sir Richard Colt Hoare, for instance, while having some admirable scientific aims, nevertheless managed to 'dig too many barrows and too quickly'.[12] Hoar reported digging 379 mounds. Dean Merewether was no better, cutting into 35 barrows in 28 days in Wiltshire in 1849. The first archaeological conference ever held was at Canterbury in 1844, and involved the entertainment of unwrapping a mummy and opening eight barrows before the audience of delegates, supervised by Lord Albert Conyngham 'dressed in an explorer's costume'.[13] Egypt, with its exotic and visible remains, became a target for European archaeological tomb robbers. The most infamous of these was Giovanni Belzoni who left England for Egypt in 1817. He described breaking into many tombs, of falling amongst mummies and 'being covered with bones, legs, arms and heads rolling'. Gone was the respect for the ancient dead shown by the likes of Browne, Aubrey and Stukeley.

The idea of excavating with care and precision for the purposes of knowledge instead of for loot or as a sport came only gradually. The example of people like Worsaae set the tone which was ultimately to prevail. Adjustments came to the Three-Age system of prehistory, as finer subdivisions were noted and catalogued. Towards the end of the century figures like General Pitt-Rivers and Flinders Petrie in England and Montelius in Sweden hauled archaeology into the era of rigorous excavational standards. Michele Arditi in Italy conducted the first large, planned excavation at Pompeii. Auguste Mariette in Egypt had some rough and ready excavational techniques himself but he did stand up fiercely for the principle that antiquities in Egypt should not be removed to other countries. Thus began the first glimmerings of morality in archaeology regarding the integrity of a site and of the right of individual nations to their own heritage, their own memory.

In America, archaeological awareness continued to develop. The American Antiquarian Society was founded in 1812. One of its papers, by Caleb Atwater, described mounds near Circleville, Ohio. In 1817 James McCulloch made the statement that the mounds were built by American Indians, not by any lost race. In 1848, E. G. Squier, a journalist, and E. Davis, a doctor, both from Chillicothe, Ohio, produced a huge compendium of material called *Ancient Monuments of the Mississippi Valley*, giving textual description, drawings and plans of a great many mounds and earthworks, as well as of finds of bones and artefacts in some of them. This work was the first publication of the new Smithsonian Institution. In 1837, Samuel Haven wrote a work on the archaeology of the United States and implored that speculations be replaced by the results of evidence found at sites. Scotsman Daniel Wilson, who had made the first attempt to apply the Scandinavian Three Age system to British archaeology, emigrated to Canada and provided a considerable influence on North American archaeological studies. George Peabody founded the archaeological and ethnological museum at Harvard.

Central America began to be opened up archaeologically speaking during the nineteenth century. American and European archaeologists began to encounter mysteries such as the great Mayan cities.

Archaeological developments have crowded the twentieth century, and only a tiny handful can be touched on here. Not only had there been a new geology showing undreamt vistas of time in the

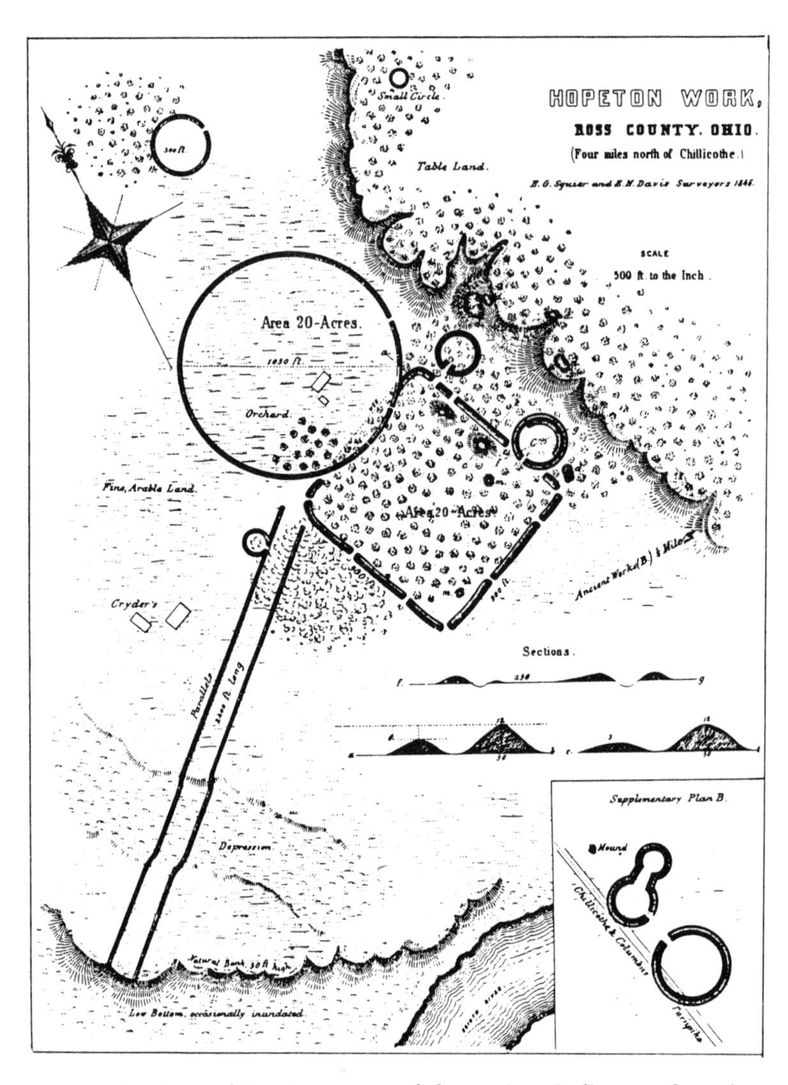


*Figure 9. Squier and Davis' survey of the ancient Indian earthworks at Hopeton, Ohio*

nineteenth century, there had, of course, been Darwin's theory of evolution. This further supported the idea of ancient man in the archaeological field. But evolutionary theory became almost a new religion, and the search for the supposed 'missing link' between ape and man was obsessive in some people. Thus it was that the 1912 Piltdown Man hoax could be perpetrated and believed in so long by learned men. 'Learning' is relative to the obsessions and perspectives of a time.

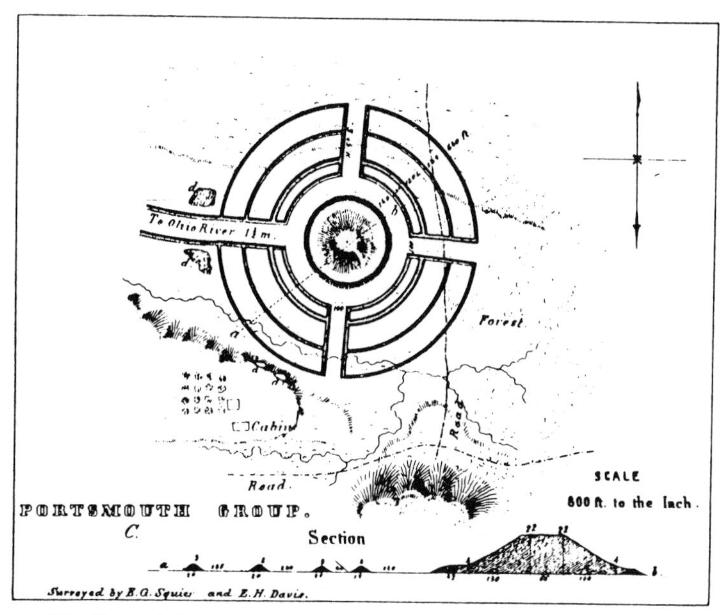


*Figure 10. One of the curious ancient Indian earthworks on the Kentucky side of the Ohio River, near Portsmouth, Ohio, as depicted by Squier and Davis*

Archaeologists agonised over the way language and cultural information got around the Old World. The problem had first presented itself back in the nineteenth century. The Danes Thomsen and Worsaae wondered how the stone age changed to bronze, and Worsaae tended to the idea that the change had been so abrupt on the western fringe of Europe that there must have been influence from some outside group of people. But others argued parallel development, and pictured civilisations rising and falling, slowly disseminating their culture.

The contest between the concepts of independent invention and diffusionism (cultural information brought from elsewhere by travel, war or trade) spilled over into the twentieth century. In 1911, Grafton Elliot Smith set out his belief that settlers from ancient Egypt had civilised barbarian Europe. This came to be known as 'hyperdiffusionism'. There was also the problem of language. The use of this avenue of research was commenced by Sir William Jones in 1788. As Glyn Daniel put it:

> If languages from Ireland to Central Asia and India all came from one parent source, who were these people and with what archaeological material could they be identified? What was the homeland of the Aryans (or the Indo-Europeans)?[14]

Today, the source of the Indo-European languages is identified as the Russian steppes, from where the linguistic roots diffused 'largely through folk-movements in the second millennium BC, into Europe, the Near East . . . Iran and India.'[15] 'Indo-European' is used as a linguistic category, not a racial one. Some archaeologists such as Marija Gimbutas and Riane Eisler see a more dramatic role for these steppe people, or 'Kurgans', as Eisler describes:

> The Kurgans were what scholars call Indo-European or Aryan language-speaking stock, a type that in modern times was to be idealised by Nietzsche and then Hitler as the only pure European race. In fact, they were not the original Europeans, as they swarmed down on that continent from the Asiatic and European northeast. Nor were they even originally Indian, for there was another people, the Dravidians, who lived in India before the Aryan invaders conquered them.
>
> But the term *Indo-European* has stuck. It characterises a long line of invasions from the Asiatic and European north by nomadic peoples. Ruled by powerful priests and warriors, they brought with them their male gods of war and mountains . . . they gradually imposed their ideologies and ways of life on the lands and peoples they conquered.[16]

According to this view, the feminine, goddess, archetype of the indigenous European societies was disturbed and ultimately terminated by the Kurgan influx.

Gordon Childe, a British-based Australian archaeologist, proposed that a barbarous Europe was infiltrated by cultural diffusionism from southwest Asia, but which then created its own cultural identity out of such contacts. It was a sophisticated version of diffusionism, but it was to prove too simplistic in the light of the development of radiocarbon dating, a key element in twentieth-century archaeology.

Because of finds in Egypt, Greece and other parts of the eastern Mediterranean, a dating based on cross-referencing was possible, and a reliable chronology for the region was developed. But other areas such as northern Europe could not be brought into the scheme so readily. Childe's vision of ethnic groups moving westwards and northwards, of cultural diffusionism, held great sway and attempts were made to identify links between northwest Europe and the east Mediterranean. Faience beads found in the north were assumed to have been made in Greece, and Baltic amber was found in Mycenae, so trade links were discerned and embellished upon in support of the theory. But less creditable links were championed too – the spirals at Newgrange were like those on Mycenaean grave slabs; the form of the northwestern megaliths showed Greek influence, and so on. Even as late as 1960 leading British archaeologist R.J.C. Atkinson could speak of Stonehenge being a Mycenaean concept.

But the late 1940s marked the beginning of the end for such notions because of the pioneering work on radiocarbon dating by American scientist Willard F. Libby. The process relies on the fact that organic matter contains traces of C-14, a radioactive isotope of carbon absorbed from its environment by a living thing during its lifetime. When the organism dies, the C-14 is not replenished and the radioactivity decays at a known rate. This allows a procedure in which the time elapsed since death of the organic sample can be deduced. Radiocarbon dates from samples sent to the now many laboratories doing the process have 'bp' dates, which means 'before present', the 'present' being established as 1950. However, it was gradually realised that radiocarbon dates were themselves somewhat awry due to geophysical factors, and radiocarbon dates were checked against sequences of tree ring dates from the incredibly ancient Bristlecone Pines of California (which had allowed dendrochronology to be extended to 8000 years). In 1967, the American chemist, Hans E. Suess, published a paper which showed that radiocarbon dates would have to be recalibrated. The results of this were, simply put, that the older a sample was, the greater the discrepancy became. It began to be seen that some of the sites in western Europe were very ancient indeed, older than the pyramids of Egypt or the ziggurats of Mesopotamia. Radiocarbon dating rang the death knell for simplistic visions of diffusion of civilisation from the east.

The twentieth century has seen the application of many techniques and disciplines to the purposes of archaeology in addition to radiocarbon dating. Air photography reveals evidence of sites invisible from ground level, and geophysical aids like magnetometers and resistivity meters can reveal below-surface disturbance of the ground. Analysis of pollen grains buried in ancient times gives archaeologists an idea of what the environment of a site might have been like. Sophisticated methods of trenching in excavations have been developed. Meticulous care in salvaging all objects at a dig is shown in methods such as sieving, which also increases the amount of organic matter to produce information about what plants and animals might have been there as well as a source for radiocarbon dates (only organic matter can be dated by this method). Techniques from physics now allow the material in some objects found in excavations to be traced to their source.

Simple methods such as fieldwalking have also been developed to a high art, so whole areas can be scanned by teams of archaeological workers for artefacts turned up by ploughing, worms and so on. Computers have been adopted by archaeology for analysing and statistically quantifying data and other functions. New dating techniques have come onto the scene.

Writing of the developments in British archaeology since the 1960s and 1970s, David Miles has written:

> At times archaeology seemed like a magpie of a subject, lifting ideas from geography, biology, cybernetics and mathematics . . .
>
> A growing interest developed in systems as a whole, including the interaction and feedback between them . . . This encouraged more rigorous collecting and recording of artefacts on sites, together with the search for patterning . . .
>
> As diffusionist explanations became discredited, interest grew in taking regions as units of study. These gave statistically definable populations; appealed to the systems theorists; and coincided with a similar interest on the part of geographers, whose work began to make an important impact on archaeology. Another area of research which developed rapidly among archaeologists in the late 1960s was trade, a subject which linked local, regional and wider systems.[17]

Sometimes getting away from the 'single site syndrome', as archaeologist Peter Fowler has put it, has produced work in contemporary archaeology that is indistinguishable from what Earth Mysteries researchers would call geomancy, as we shall see. This shows that the more flexible, *systems approach* of modern archaeology enables it to derive a wider description of a site, which inevitably must involve its relationship with its environment. It is important to note that it is the changes in archaeology that has brought it closer to a geomantic view of ancient sites rather than changes in the 'alternative' viewpoint. Geomancers are being validated by modern archaeologists, who tend nowadays to fudge issues by saying, 'What was all the fuss about?' as though their subject area has not been the one to move. The 'fuss' was promoted solely by an archaeology that was providing an inadequate description of ancient sites.

Clearly, modern archaeology is a complex area of its own, and is a subsystem of our Earth Mysteries 'tree'. No meaningful, comprehensive approach towards the understanding of the nature of ancient sacred sites can afford to ignore the work of archaeology, and fail to make use of it. It has transcended many of its earlier limitations, it is no longer a treasure-seeking, barrow-bashing pastime, which some critics of archaeology still think. Modern archaeology seeks only knowledge.

But despite its development, archaeology still tends to dismiss the study of sites if it occurs outside the frame of what is perceived as academically acceptable.

This attitude used to be based on arrogance and prejudice, only marginally justified by the over-enthusiastic ideas of early Earth Mysteries researchers. The late Glyn Daniel, quoted a number of times above, who was editor of *Antiquity* for many years and Disney Professor of Archaeology at the University of Cambridge (1974–81), was the arch-enemy of 'alternative' archaeology. To him it was *all* crazy, Von Daniken-type rubbish (*some* of it was). Ley hunters were 'dotties at random'. Daniel was also profoundly sceptical of archaeoastronomy. To him, 'one of the tasks of archaeology and archaeologists in the 1980s . . . is to see that the lunatics are exposed.' There was much acrimony between the orthodox and the 'alternative' camps, as there had been on and off ever since Alfred Watkins discovered leys in the 1920s (Chapter 8). Yet Daniel also stated, 'To my mind the best theoretical position to adopt in archaeology is to use all possible means to make the fullest reconstruction of the past from the surviving material remains.' Had he thought, he might have realised that the 'alternative' researches he so reviled could provide such further 'possible means'.

But Daniel is gone now, as are, to a limited extent, the attitudes he was spokesman for. Today there are some archaeologists prepared to at least debate with Earth Mysteries researchers, with the modern geomants, and to listen. Indeed, there is now a corp of undergraduate archaeological students and young archaeologists, who come from an Earth Mysteries perspective.

There are still problems, however. Archaeology as a whole still fails to see that the geomantic approach to ancient sites is not 'alternative' at all, It is simply *an extension of the descriptive process.* Archaeology is moving in part towards the position of the geomants, but does not recognise it. Archaeologists do not know of the geomantic literature, or of Earth Mysteries research in any depth, and too many still have a Pavlovian response to such matters. This is because archaeology ultimately has an Achilles heel; it cannot extend its role beyond defined limits because it *cannot perceive* certain ways in which ceremonial sites can be approached. This is because it is itself the product of Indo-European cognitive processes – archaeology, remember, was a European invention. It is secular. It belongs to the rationalist structure of science. But ancient sacred sites were not constructed in that same milieu, thus there are factors about such places that are not perceptible to archaeology used on its own, however skilled and complex it is within its own parameters.

The other branches of the Earth Mysteries tree explored in the following chapters are facts – they are not inventions. It is simply a matter of whether archaeologists see them as relevant, if they can see them at all. In other words, the cognitive processes that gave it birth, also limit archaeology in its task of *fully* understanding monuments that come from other times, other cognitive processes, other perceptions of reality. The numinosity of a site comes out of magic, religion, spiritual understanding, altered states of consciousness and lost or overlooked principles of natural science; out of a way of placing the human psyche in relationship with the land.

If the worldview of modern archaeology can be massaged by the addition of extended descriptions which belong to other facets of human consciousness and experience, then we will have a powerful tool indeed. So powerful, it might enable us to regain our memory as a species before we fall into a night of the Western psyche that will banish us from our planet.

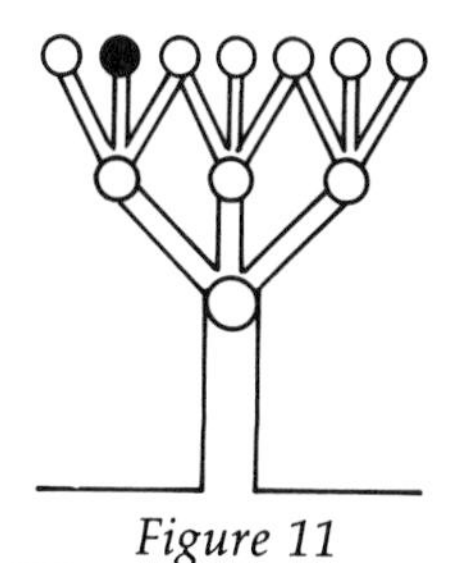

Figure 11

# CHAPTER 3
# BEING AND SEEING

## Demonstration

Earth Mysteries researcher John Glover has made a special study of the Castlerigg circle. In a way, it could be said that Castlerigg adopted him! Glover, an artist and photographer, visits the site at any time – dawn, dusk, summer, winter. He sits, walks, looks, feels. He allows the site to present to him what it will. One aspect so revealed was that certain stones in the circle seemed to possess a curious association with parts of the skyline: they visually echoed the contours of the horizon when viewed in a particular direction, as if they were subtle direction marker.[1] Over time, Glover has become aware of several instances of this skyline coincidence at Castlerigg. One cannot bluster into a site and see this sort of detail: it comes as a result of being and seeing at a place.

A more dramatic, though more fleeting, example of this occurred when Glover was preparing to photograph the midsummer sunset at Castlerigg. The sun on this day slips down behind a ridge called Latrigg, to the northwest of the circle. Glover set his camera and tripod up, and awaited the moment when the sun's disc would descend to the ridge, so he could obtain dramatic sunset pictures. 'I became more and more intent, concentrating to get the photographs I wanted, when, for no apparent reason I turned round,' Glover recalled. 'There at my feet was a wide, dark shadow extending for hundreds of yards in the direction of the notch marking the Candlemas rising sun. I was utterly amazed by this and my first reaction was to run down it as fast as I could; I felt projected into one of those fairytale situations when, if you are at the right place at the right time, a secret path appears to show you the way to a treasure.'[2] The setting sun was causing the tallest stone at Castlerigg to throw a long and regular 'shadow path'.

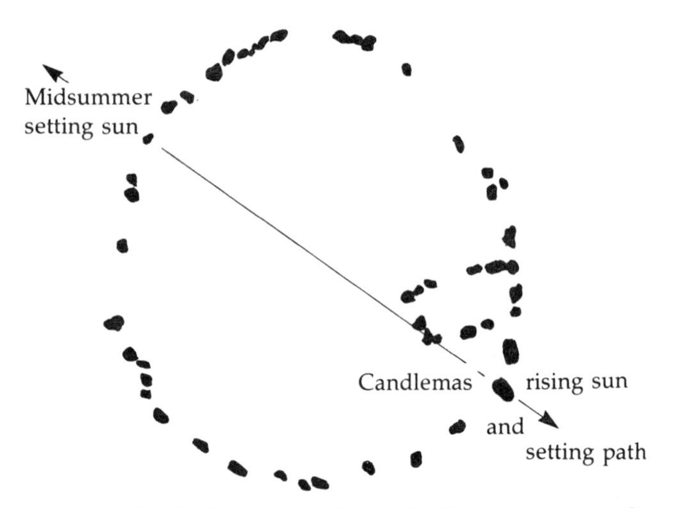


*Figure 12. Castlerigg groundplan and midsummer sunset line*

## Discussion

It was mentioned in the previous chapter that archaeologists who try to avoid Peter Fowler's 'single site syndrome' can sometimes engage in work that is effectively geomantic study. For instance, during an archaeological survey of Dorset in 1970 Fowler himself noted that some barrow groups 'appear to be deliberately sited so that a complex system of intervisibility is created . . . a considerable degree of control and deliberation must be postulated.' In 1983, archaeologist David Fraser studied intervisibility between Bronze Age cairns (mounds of boulders) on the islands of Orkney off Scotland's northern coast. He found cairns on different islands to be sometimes visible one to another as well as being intervisible within individual islands. 'Intervisibility is not a simple reflection of proximity,' Fraser observed, 'and is influenced by subtle changes in the landscape.'[3] He found sightlines up to 11 miles (17.5 km) long, and concluded that cairns which showed evidence of being special in some way or other tended to be 'located, with purpose, in places which are relatively dominant.' There was tentative evidence that fires had been lit at these cairns. In America in the early 1980s, archaeologists studying the mysterious, thousand-year-old Anasazi straight-road systems around Chaco Canyon in New Mexico (see Chapter 8) walked the almost invisible fragments of these old straight tracks, observing the subtle characteristics of their relationship with the local topography, how the features were aligned to distant points or across interven-

*Plate 5. Skyline coincidence at Castlerigg (Courtesy John Glover)*

*Plate 6. Shadow path at Castlerigg (Courtesy John Glover)*

ing ridges maintaining their line even when sites were not intervisible. They also carried out experiments involving flares placed at Anasazi cairns to test intervisibility amongst them, and to compare those sightlines with the straight road system on the ground.[4]

In the case of ceremonial landscapes, such observations are dealing inevitably with sacred geography, with geomancy, and can only be made by the observer becoming immersed in the sites, their positioning and their ambient topography. Site visits have to be either prolonged or frequent, and, equally as important, the observer has to be *open* to what the site or its landscape has to say. To go looking just for visible remains, just for astronomical alignments, just for weird and wonderful 'energies', is already to prejudice and restrict the description that might be revealed, the new increment of information that might be presented. It can stop the seeing of that which is already visible: it engenders cognitive blindness.

This was the lesson that John Glover was aware of, as we have seen above. Figures 13 and 14 show two other examples of his stone-skyline observations at Castlerigg, while Figure 15 shows a particularly interesting example. In this instance, the view is across the circle and incorporates the tops of stones on opposite sides of the ring. It can be seen that each stone respectively echoes the two distant ridges. Moreover, this alignment also indicates the most southerly rising moon at Castlerigg, an event that occurs as part of a lunar cycle taking 18.61 years to complete (see next chapter). The distant ridges 'slope towards each other and cross at a point above the centres of the stones and immediately below the notch where the moon is seen to rise,' Glover observed. 'Thus one can easily find the exact position from which to view the event by

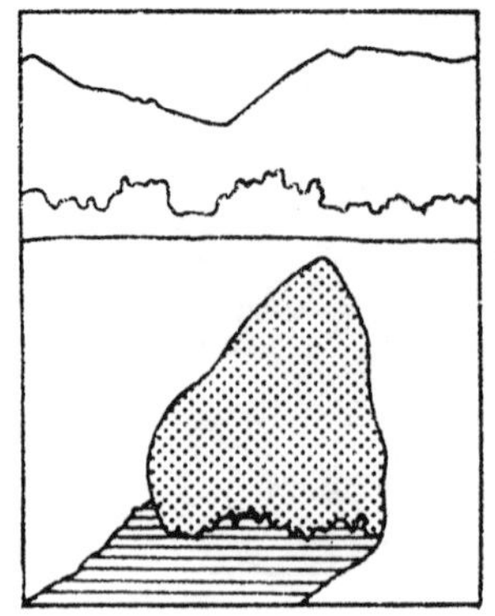

*Figure 13. (After John Glover)*

*Figure 14. (After John Glover)*

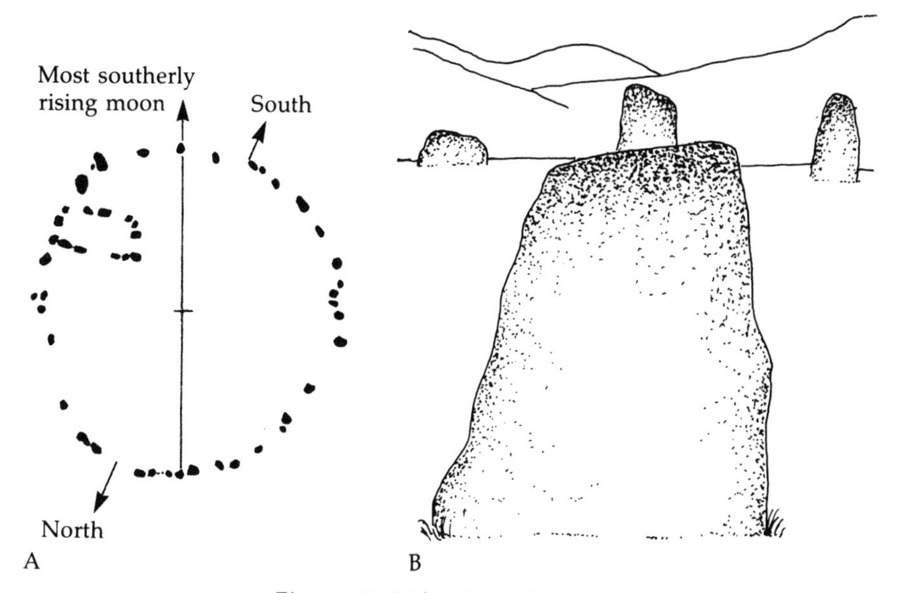


*Figure 15. (After John Glover)*

crouching down behind the stones and lining up their top edges with the hills under the notch. It is an exact fit, and provides stunning visual evidence for deliberate intention on the part of the builders.'[5] While such an astronomical alignment from the circle could be calculated from a survey (which indeed it was, by Alexander Thom), the involvement of the stones in depicting the precise point of the skyline could only be obtained by being and seeing at the site.

Helen Woodley, another Earth Mysteries researcher, has also noted skyline coincidences at Castlerigg as well as at other sites. Figure 16 shows three at Castlerigg she has published.[6] Figure 17 depicts her finding at the Greywethers circle on Dartmoor, where one of the stones in the ring echoes Bellever Tor on the skyline. Woodley argues that while the preservation of sites in themselves is commendable, it is nevertheless inadequate. The failure to note the geomantic aspect of sites means that the various 'heritage' committees overlook the fact that the landscape surrounding a ceremonial monument is likely to be *an integral part* of the place. Site and environment cannot be divorced: the very essence of thinking of sites in systems terms. It is thus no good preserving a stone circle, which may have had sightlines and other connections with the local region, and allowing afforestation to go on all around it, hemming it in and suffocating its geomantic dimension. To do so is to limit the description of the site. Valuable

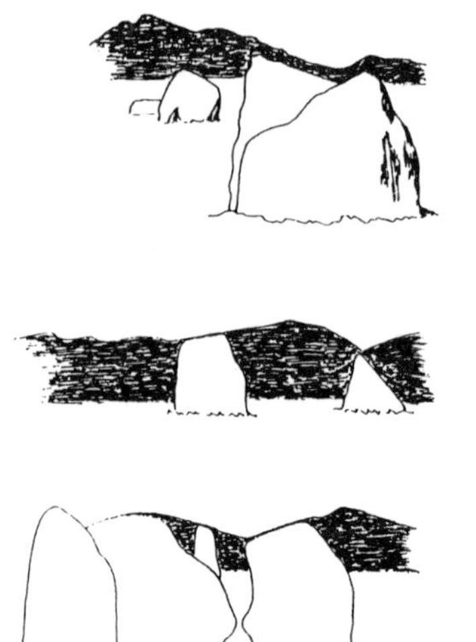

*Figure 16. (After Helen Woodley)* *Figure 17. (After Helen Woodley)*

information is lost – permanently inaccessible in cases where environmental obstruction has occurred before observation has taken place.

Archaeologists are becoming more aware of this aspect. For example, one can read in the archaeological guide to the Brecon Beacons National Park, an area of hill country in southern Wales, that the top of a standing stone at the village of Bwlch 'may have been shaped to represent the profile of the Sugar Loaf mountain to the east-south-east.' Or, again, in the same leaflet, that the top of the Maen Llwyd monolith deep in the mountains 'may have been shaped to represent the skyline to the south-east. A man-made notch near Mynydd Llysiau aligns on this stone.'[7] But there is still a long way to go before the occasional observations of archaeologists who have allowed themselves to see at sites become part of a general archaeological understanding and the full geomantic significance of the site-landscape relationship taken on board.

I was personally engaged in a prolonged series of being and seeing sessions at the great Avebury complex in the latter half of the 1980s, so can report directly from inside the process, as it were. I invite the reader to come along with me to see how that process commenced and developed – the material discussed has not previously appeared in book form.[8]

Avebury is one of the great prehistoric sites of the world. It is situated in Wiltshire, in southern England, about 80 miles west of London. It is not just a site, but a whole complex; a Neolithic

*Plate 7. Part of the outer ring of stones at Avebury henge, southwestern sector*

landscape, in fact. Avebury is the name of the village which actually sprawls into the interior of the 28-acre henge. This vast site was hewn out of the solid chalk ground by means of deer antler picks. The ditch was originally about 30 feet (9 m) deep and has an external bank. On the inside rim of the ditch are the remains of a ring of massive megaliths. Within this great ring are the remnants of two smaller circles, the centre of the northern one is marked by the stones nowadays called The Cove, and the centre of the southern circle was marked by a great standing stone called the Obelisk, surrounded by a setting of small stones.

The now-destroyed Obelisk was fallen but visible in Stukeley's day, and he did a drawing of it (Figure 19). It was over 20 feet (6 m) tall and several feet thick, much taller than the other stones at the site. (The position of the Obelisk is now marked by a large concrete plinth. This was erected by Alexander Keiller who restored and partially reconstructed the Avebury complex in the 1930s; he used smaller concrete markers for other missing stones.) Two avenues of stones, one to the south and another to the west, converged on – or diverged from – the henge, and parts of the southern one, Kennet Avenue, are still visible. In all, it is estimated that some 600 megaliths, weighing up to 70 tons apiece, were used in the site, and some archaeologists reckon that it must have taken 500 years to construct. John Aubrey, who we noted in

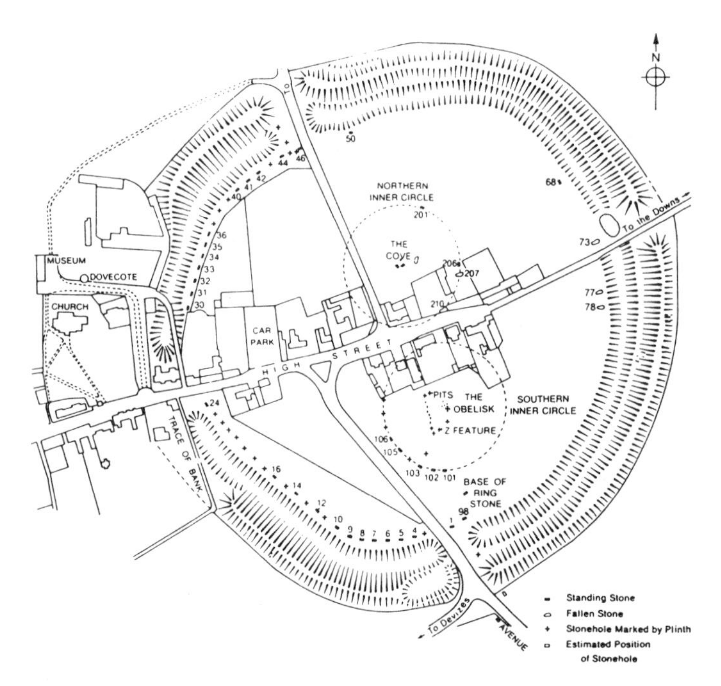


*Figure 18. Plan of the henge at Avebury (after I.F. Smith)*

the last chapter was the first of the learned men of his time to recognise the Avebury site for what it was, stated that Avebury 'does as much exceed in greatness the so renowned Stonehenge, as a Cathedral does a parish Church.'

*Figure 19. Stukeley's 1723 drawing of the fallen Obelisk*

But the greatness of Avebury does not end with the henge and its avenues. Scattered around the surrounding landscape are other major monuments, some even older than the henge (which is dated to around 2700 BC). A mile to the south-south-west is the mighty Silbury Hill, an artificial mound standing 130 feet (40 m) high, the tallest monument of prehistoric Europe. It was probably built contemporaneously with the henge. To the northwest of the henge is Windmill Hill, a natural eminence that was earthworked in early Neolithic times. It was some kind of gathering place for hundreds of years prior to the construction of Avebury henge. To the southeast is The Sanctuary, a circular site built from stones and posts at the terminus of the Kennet Avenue. It is marked now only by concrete plinths. Elsewhere in the landscape are great long barrows, pre-dating the henge. Scattered amongst all these are later Bronze Age round barrows and the locations of lost sites.

The Avebury landscape is a zone of ancient sanctity, and to view the sites separately from that landscape is to lose vast amounts of information. I had visited the complex for nearly two decades and was always awed and impressed by it. I realised it looked much as it had in the late Neolithic period, and that it therefore must contain geomantic information. And yet I couldn't see it. This depressed me, but did not give me a psychological complex because no one else had seen it either! The sheer scale of the Avebury complex has always rendered it susceptible to cognitive myopea, as Aubrey had shown.

In 1984, the frustration got too much: I dropped to my knees in Kennet Avenue (when no one else was around!) and implored the *genius loci*, the spirit of the place, to help me *see*. There was no immediate, blinding flash of inspiration, but I decided to have a closer look at the Avenue when circumstances allowed. The following year a group of friends and colleagues assisted me in conducting a careful study of the Avenue. We saw what archaeologists had already noted: that the avenue, while apparently sinuous, is in fact made up of straight lines of stones articulated together, and that there was a distinct tendency for pillar- and lozenge-shaped stones to face one another across the Avenue. British prehistorian Aubrey Burl has suggested that these stones may symbolise masculine and feminine respectively.[9] But what else? We completed an accurate survey of the Avenue, and photographed all the stones from various angles. Some tentative alignments to outlying barrows were noted, but even if authentic, these would be difficult to confirm as the barrows were Bronze Age, more recent than the Avenue. Any alignments could at best have

*Plate 8. Pillar and lozenge stones facing each other in the Kennet Avenue, Avebury*

been merely afterthoughts, developments, in Bronze Age times. (There is, in fact, little doubt that Bronze Age peoples added to the geomancy of the Avebury landscape – for example, in the way Bronze Age barrows are visible on the exact skyline as viewed from Avebury henge. But this is controversial ground on which to base an argument promoting Avebury geomancy.) I recall walking along Kennet Avenue with archaeologist John Barnatt, who had supervised the survey. He pointed out that if it were alignments I was after at Avebury, they did not seem in plentiful supply. I had to agree. It began to appear that Avebury's *genius loci* was the unhelpful type.

Racking my brains for an angle, I shortly afterwards recalled that we had noted that Silbury Hill, one of the greatest monuments in the complex, was invisible from virtually the whole course of Kennet Avenue, as it would also have been from the no longer extant Beckhampton Avenue to the west of the henge. Where the course of Kennet Avenue and Silbury were intervisible, however, was where the rows of stones would have come up to The Sanctuary, which is on the eastern, bounding ridge of the sacred landscape. I went to The Sanctuary and saw that Silbury was indeed visible from it, its upper half protruding above the limb of Waden Hill, a natural ridge a quarter of a mile to the east of the monument.

Many people have commented how strange it is that Silbury Hill, a tremendous achievement of Neolithic engineering, should be located in such a low position, tucked away alongside Waden Hill. A superficial, imposing display had clearly not been the intention of its builders. As I looked at the great mound, it suddenly dawned on me that the focus of the Avebury complex was *not* the henge, where everybody went, where the village, pub, shops and big stones were, but Silbury Hill instead. It was a pretty modest insight perhaps, but it was not apparent to most people any more than it had been to me. I suddenly felt as if the *genius loci* had whispered in my ear.

I wanted to know from which other Neolithic sites in the complex Silbury was visible. Archaeological wisdom has it that Silbury is not visible from the henge. This piece of folklore was trotted out in an archaeologist's book as recently as 1989.[10] But it isn't true. The top of Silbury Hill can be seen from the northern part of the henge around The Cove, and is *just* perceptible from next to the Obelisk plinth position. The Obelisk, so huge and at the centre of the South Circle, can surely be thought of as having been the major position in the henge, so it was this view which particularly intrigued me, and I return to it below. In addition to The Sanctuary and selected points in the henge, I found Silbury to be additionally visible from the long barrows of Beckhampton, West Kennet and East Kennet, as well as from Windmill Hill, which overlooks much of the complex, like a mother keeping an eye on her children. So Silbury Hill was the pivot of a ragged circuit of Neolithic sites, of selected points in the ceremonial landscape (Figure 20).

The *genius loci* had got me to look at the complex in the right way, but what was I supposed to be looking for?

My first instinct was to seek some astronomical significance. According to some commentators, the name Silbury can be interpreted as Sol-bury, 'sun hill'. An association with the sun is also a possible interpretation of the legend associated with the monument. This states that the great mound covers the body of a king – Sil, Zil or Sel – mounted on horseback and clad in golden armour. The 'golden king' could be a metaphor for the sun. Indeed, there had been various astronomical speculations by different researchers over the years. So I undertook a programme of visiting the Avebury complex at the key solar dates of the year – solstices, equinoxes and the cross-quarter dates between them – looking at Silbury from one of the surrounding sites whenever I felt the sun might rise or set behind the mound, accompanied by my long-

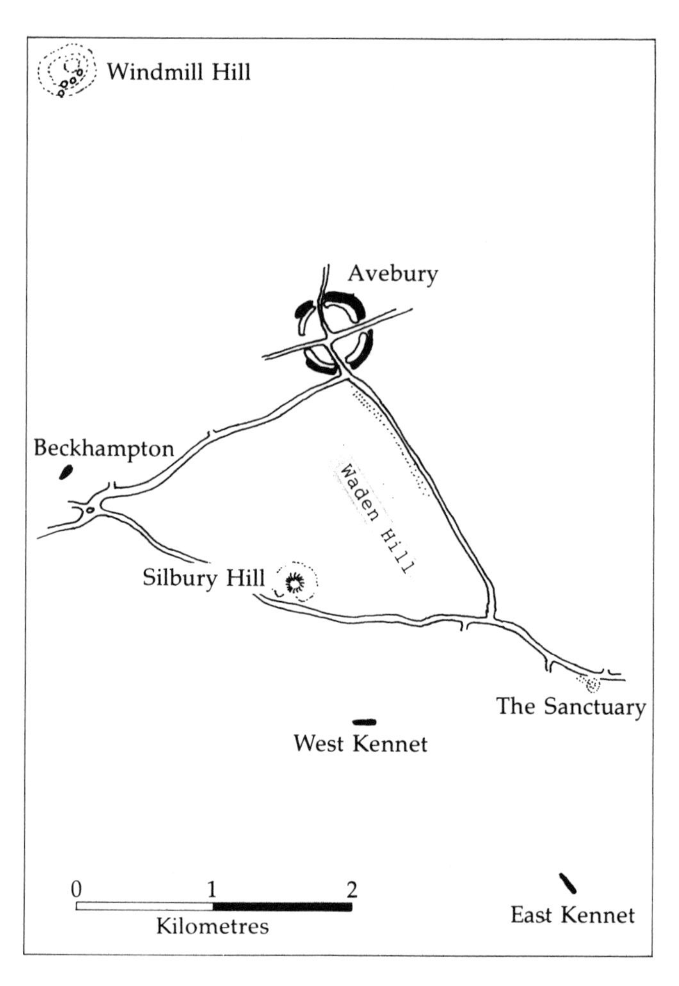


*Figure 20. Key surviving features of the Neolithic Avebury landscape, showing position of the natural Waden Hill*

suffering wife, Charla. Dawns and sunsets, rain, shine, overcast, heat, cold. We journeyed to and fro between our Welsh home and the Avebury complex whenever we could.

We never witnessed a significant solar event with regard to Silbury from any of the vantage points I had identified. I was cluttering my perception with preconceived ideas.

But something subtle began to happen during these visits: I developed the distinct sense that Silbury Hill was communicating in some way. I slowly began to think of it as a teacher – a living, sentient, teacher. Such an animistic idea would of course make any archaeologist, any Western rationalist, wail in despair. I felt uneasy about it myself to begin with, but soon learned to adopt the attitude with ease. Whether or not the idea is taken literally, is it a good mental model to have regarding the site? I found it was. It opened me up to the complex; it put me in receptive mode. I was Silbury's pupil, in the classroom formed by the sacred landscape of the Avebury complex. I waited patiently for the rest of the lesson – I did not want to interrupt the teacher with my rowdy, Western-rationalist classroom behaviour.

I did not have to wait long. On West Kennet long barrow I found Silbury Hill had indeed been communicating with me – at a subliminal, visual level. West Kennet is the longest barrow in Wiltshire at 330 feet (100 m). The eastern end has a facade formed by large stones, and there is a short passage which has side chambers and ends in a larger chamber. All this takes up only a small volume of the whole mound. Many bones were found in the mound, but it is thought that it was not merely a grave, but also some kind of ritual centre in which bones had ceremonial use. There were probably several phases to the barrow, whose origins are dated to around 3700 BC. It must have been one of the first monuments to have been built in the Avebury landscape, contemporary with activity on Windmill Hill, or shortly thereafter. But

*Plate 9. Silbury Hill viewed from West Kennet long barrow. Note that the skyline, formed by Windmill Hill three km to the north, cuts the mound's profile at the height of the ledge or terrace on the eastern slope*

why did the Neolithic people of Avebury make the barrow so long, apparently for no functional purpose? Archaeologist Richard Bradley has suggested that some long barrows may have had earthen 'tails' added to turn them into extra long mounds, and cites West Kennet as an example. But there is still the 'why'. Silbury Hill is visible from all parts of the long barrow, but I felt that the west end of the mound must be significant, otherwise why had the feature been extended? I stood there and looked at Silbury. Then I saw the open secret.

Silbury has a 'step' interrupting its profile about 17 feet (5 m) down from its summit. This is a deliberate feature. The monument was built as a stepped cone (Figure 21), made from a honeycomb of chalk walls filled with rubble. The whole was covered with soil, creating a smoothed profile. But the topmost step was left, presumably as some kind of terrace on the eastern side. On the western side the terrace is only slightly visible, and there is disagreement as to whether it has been filled and disfigured by erosion (the prevailing winds affect that side of the great mound) or was simply not left with the deliberation of the eastern terrace. As I looked at Silbury, I saw that not only did the horizon intersect the shape of Silbury at the level of the ledge, but that the horizon from this viewing point was, of course, formed by Windmill Hill – the Bronze Age round barrows dotted on it were clearly visible. This meant that the West Kennet – Silbury – Windmill Hill

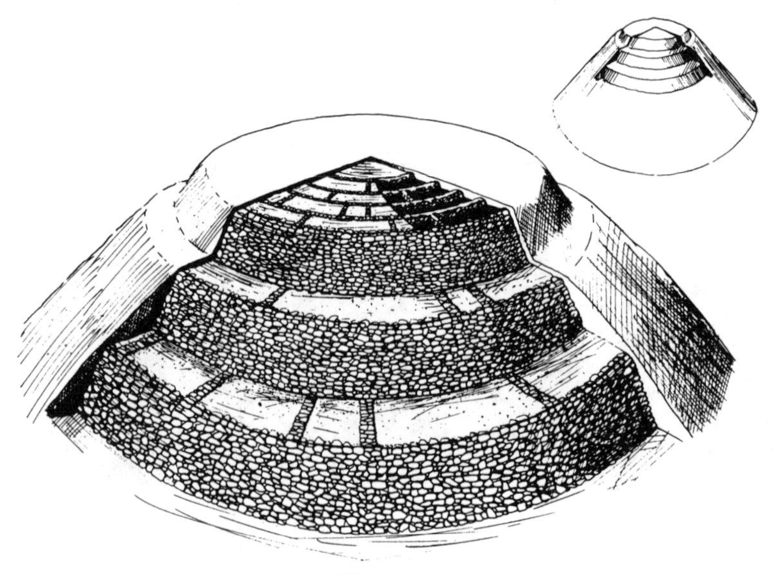

*Figure 21.*

*Plate 10. View of Silbury Hill from the east, showing the ledge or terrace below the summit*

alignment, three miles (4.8 km) in length, not only worked as a line drawn on a map, but that it also worked in elevation! A three-dimensional alignment. Precision geomancy. It was further found that from East Kennet long barrow, The Sanctuary and Beckhampton long barrow, the skyline also cut Silbury's profile between the summit and the ledge (see Figure 22 a–d). The same pattern affected Silbury when viewed from the henge, a matter I shall return to. It was clear that the summit-terrace segment of the monument was significant. But what could that significance be?

Little is known about Silbury Hill. Archaeologists had assumed that it was simply a particularly big Bronze Age burial mound – Glyn Daniel made the point almost dismissively. But R.J.C. Atkinson's excavations in the late 1960s changed that view. Atkinson's team, with the BBC's new colour TV cameras waiting to pounce, tunnelled into the centre of the mound, expecting to find a rich Bronze Age burial. No burial of any kind was found. Moreover, Atkinson discovered that Silbury Hill was not Bronze Age at all, but Neolithic. It appeared that Silbury was built in stages, on a natural spur several feet high. At first a circle of closely-positioned stakes was produced, and this was filled with turves. On top of this were laid consecutive layers of soil, clay, chalk and gravel (the 'orgone' arrangement – see Chapter 11). This made a drum-like

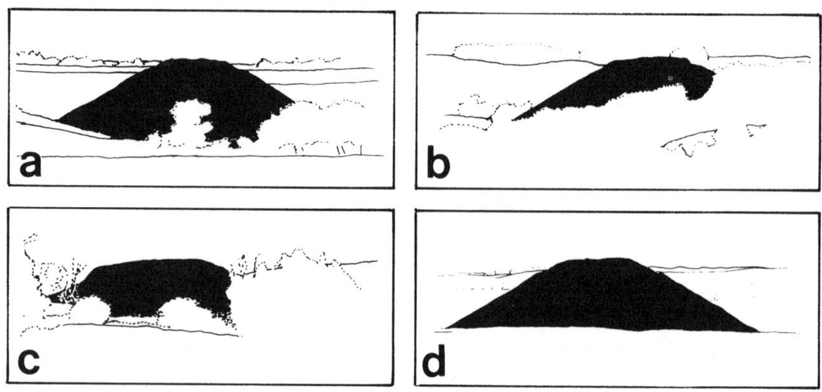


*Figure 22. The relationship of Silbury Hill (depicted in silhouette) with skylines viewed from key Neolithic locations: (a) from East Kennet long barrow (b) from The Sanctuary (c) from Beckhampton long barrow (d) from West Kennet long barrow – in this instance the skyline is formed by Windmill Hill. It can be seen that the far horizon always intersects the profile of Silbury Hill between the monument's summit and terrace. These views are derived from telephotographs. Broken lines depict foliage*

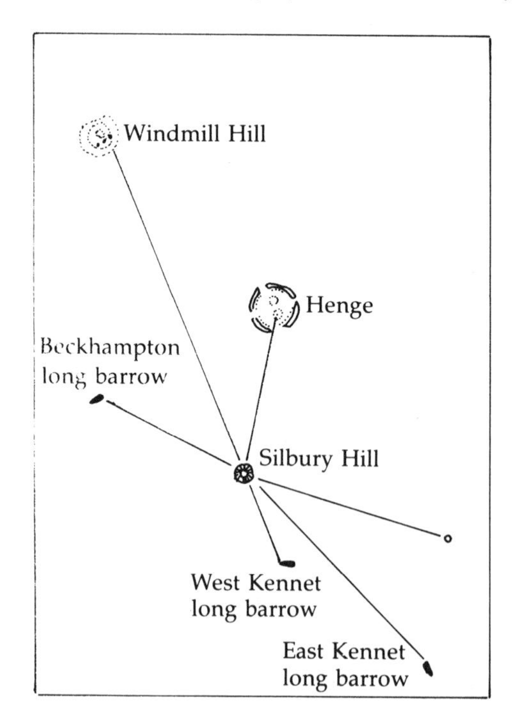


*Figure 23. Neolithic sightlines in the Avebury complex. The line between West Kennet long barrow and Windmill Hill to the north is three miles long*

mound 15 feet (4.5 m) high. In the next stage the mound was enclosed in a larger conical mound composed of chalk blocks. Stage three enclosed the previous two mounds and was skilfully constructed in the honeycomb-walled stepped pyramid already described. The walls were constructed with an inherent tension in them so that the form of the mound has been kept with minimal decay for nearly five thousand years. It was a remarkable piece of engineering, and indicates that the monument was of great importance to the people of the day. Former Avebury curator Caroline Malone has said of Silbury that it is 'unique and unexplained . . . the single most impressive engineering feat of prehistoric Britain.'[11]

Although there was no burial, Atkinson's team did find something remarkable in the centre of the mound: the original turves were exceptionally well preserved, with the grass still green and recognisable, and the insects that had been in it still identifiable. From this it has been possible for ecologists to determine that the monument began to be constructed at the end of July or the beginning of August. This, we shall see, is most significant.

The Avebury mystery centres on Silbury, and its solving would yield clues as to the consciousness of Neolithic peoples in general. Archaeologists have tacitly assumed that the enigma of Silbury will never be known; others have come up with theories, the most persuasive being Michael Dames' suggestion that Silbury represents the Great Mother Goddess[12,13] – which must be true at some level.

I knew that the builders of Silbury Hill had to be aware that they were constructing the mound on the line of sight between the already existing West Kennet barrow and Windmill Hill. This was certainly part of the explanation why the great mound had been placed in its otherwise inexplicable position in the lowest part of the Kennet valley.

It was becoming clear that Silbury's height must have been tied to some function as a platform. So I began visiting the monument at key solar dates throughout the year to watch sunrises and sets from the summit. Some of these positions linked to skyline features, but not in any definite, obvious manner. I knew I was still missing the point. One dawn, I arrived at Silbury to find it in a thick, grey mist. I clambered to the top from where the sky was clear overhead, but the low mist hung like a shroud over the landscape around. It was like sitting on an island of grass in a cottonwool sea. As I sat, awaiting the sunrise, a clear, bell-like phrase rang out in my mind. It jolted me as much as if someone had spoken in my ear. The 'voice' said, 'In this mystery shall we dwell.' It was definitely something from outside my conscious mind – it was not the sort of thing one thinks up in order to pass the time. My immediate sense was that it was somehow Silbury itself communicating, but my rational self saw it as a product of my subconscious being projected into my quiescent, waking mind as a result of being in a strange place at an odd time in rather disorienting circumstances. Plus the fact that I had been mulling over the Avebury problem for a long time. But whatever the strange mechanism causing the startling effect might have been, I wished that the 'message' could have been a bit more informative!

In early May 1987, I watched from the top of Silbury as a glorious Beltane sun rose majestically out of the horizon several miles to the east, formed by the Marlborough Downs. It was only after the sun had risen some way that I *saw* what I had merely looked at so many times before: the horizon to the east of Silbury was double. In other words, the far horizon formed by the Downs exactly echoed the contour of nearby Waden Hill. From Silbury's summit there was only a narrow visual difference between the two lines formed by the ridge of Waden and the distant skyline. I slithered down the steep slope to the terrace, and stood looking eastwards. The Marlborough downs skyline had moved downwards along with my eye level, and now visually just grazed the top of Waden Hill. At one point it dipped behind the bulk of Waden for a short distance. I was pretty sure that the Beltane sun had risen from that area of the horizon, but I could not be sure unless I saw it again. There was a further, obvious implication of the double horizon. If the far horizon could be visually replaced by the near one formed by Waden simply by changing viewing position between summit and terrace on Silbury, then surely the sun could be seen to apparently rise *twice* at the appropriate time of year from the monument?

It was not until 1989 that the opportunity arose where this idea could be tested. I was taking part in a BBC Radio 4 series[14] in which various people – archaeologists, latter-day druids, historians and myself – discussed ancient sites from our respective viewpoints. For each of the programmes we were at a different prehistoric site. On the last day of July we happened to be at Avebury. The weather had been superb all summer: dawns and sunsets were clear. I realised that we would be staying overnight near Avebury during Lammas, the Christian term for the early August harvest festival which in the Celtic calendar was called Lughnassadh. The Lammas sun rises at the same point on the

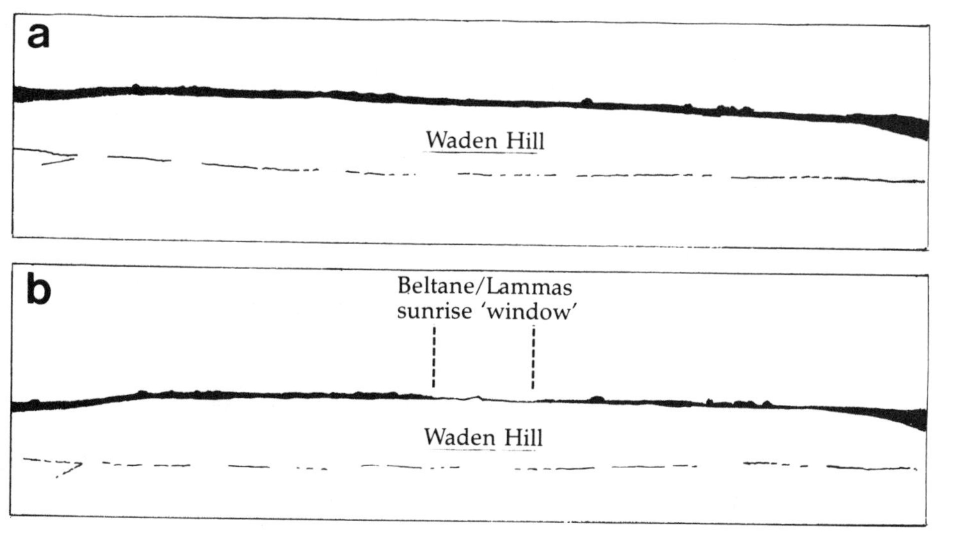


*Figure 24. The eastwards view from Silbury Hill: (a) the view from Silbury's summit across Waden Hill to far skyline (depicted in silhouette) showing the 'double horizon' effect (b) the view from Silbury terrace showing how the far skyline 'dips' behind the bulk of Waden Hill forming a 'window' in which Waden's crest provides the only horizon. This 'window' coincides with the sunrise position at Beltane and Lammas; changing viewing positions between Silbury top and terrace allows a 'double sunrise' to be seen at those times*

horizon as at Beltane. Atkinson's findings had shown that Silbury had started being built at this time of year (see above). I informed the archaeologists present that I was going to Silbury at dawn the next day, August 1, and they were welcome to come if they wished. Getting up later than intended, I drove at speed from the hotel and managed to make Silbury's summit before sunrise. Christopher Chippindale, who took over the editorship of *Antiquity* after the death of Glyn Daniel, arrived shortly afterwards. The sky was crystal clear. I felt uneasy, realising that if my guess was wrong, I would look rather foolish. A pink glow tinged the far horizon, and the sun's disk broke into view. Chippindale timed the event as I slid down to the terrace. A little over a minute later, I saw the sun rise again, this time over the back of Waden Hill. It was a powerful moment.

The east-west position of Silbury Hill had been determined by it being on the sightline between West Kennet long barrow and Windmill Hill. Its north-south position was determined, it now appeared, by it catching this curious skyline coincidence. The height of the mound and the position of the terrace were determined by the need to allow the view of the double sunrise phenomenon. This segment of the hill also was made to relate to the skyline when viewed from a number of other Neolithic sites, as I had already determined. Some incredibly sensitive and accurate landscape perceptions had been made by the Neolithic geomants of Avebury.

Silbury Hill itself, then, encoded by means of its location, size and shape, information about the geographical distribution of sites in the immediate ceremonial landscape, about the plan and elevation of that landscape, and about an astronomical (time) event in that landscape. Silbury Hill was a Lammas mound, a harvest monument, from bottom to top. The monument is a pure, crystallised piece of geomancy. It symbolises the union of the sacred heavens with the holy Earth. Its designers could not resist making the great gesture of having the harvest-period sun rise twice in celebration of the gathered crop.

Michael Dames has presented evidence to suggest that Silbury Hill was a harvest hill, which this present evidence further supports. He also thought that Silbury was a representation of the Earth Goddess. The new double sunrise finding could also support such an idea. Waden Hill means Hill of Woden. In Norse and Lombard mythology, the wife of Woden was Frigg (Frija, Freya), whose name means Lady. This Lady was the Earth Goddess, the Earth Mother. The German Meresburg Charm similarly links Frigg and Wodan: 'Thus chanted Friia and Volla, Then chanted Wodan, as he well knew how . . . ' Woden and The Lady – Waden and Silbury – are intimately linked by the double sunrise. It is popularly assumed that the Earth Goddess is more associated with the moon (who knows what lunar secrets Silbury encodes?[15]) but there are also powerful solar associations with her. This is suggested, for example, in a twelfth century herbal treatise (British Library, Harl MS 1585 12a f.):

> Divine Goddess Earth, Mother of Nature, who generates all things, and brings forth ever anew the sun which you alone show to the folk upon the earth: Thou guardian of heaven and sea, and arbiter of all the gods . . . you are she who restores day and puts the darkness to flight . . . you send forth the glad daylight . . .

The Lady has many manifestations, including that of the grain goddess. Frazer reminds us in *The Golden Bough* (1922) that the last sheaf of corn was known as the Great Mother or the Harvest

Mother in some north European traditions.

The harvest connection was further emphasised by the sightline to Silbury from the Obelisk position within the Henge. This is a particularly dramatic example of the skyline relationship with the top segment of Silbury. Only the very top of the Silbury is visible from the Obelisk in the notch formed by the background skyline swooping down to meet the northerly slope of Waden Hill in the foreground. When the crops are high on Waden, Silbury is barely perceptible; invisible, in fact, to anyone not knowing exactly where to look. It is known that cereals were grown on Waden Hill in late Neolithic times, and ancient types of cereals grew taller than modern varieties, which have been developed to allow for mechanical harvesting. I realised that a taller crop would blot out sight of Silbury from the Obelisk when it was ready for harvesting. *The sightline was harvest dependent.* (When I later showed Peter Fowler some of these sightlines at Avebury, I commented that what we were looking at was geomancy. 'I'd prefer to call it good archaeological observation,' he retorted. I replied that what *we* were doing might be described as that, but what we were observing, what the Neolithic builders of the Avebury complex had been engaged on, had been geomancy. Fowler took the point.)

As Chippindale and I turned to climb down off Silbury Hill, we noted in the field immediately to the north a set of five crop circles,

*Plate 11. Mystery crop circles in a field immediately north of Silbury Hill. Photographed from Silbury's summit in 1989*

laid out with geometric precision. These mysterious features have caused a storm of controversy and interest in recent years. Hundreds of them have appeared, mainly in southern England, in a variety of precise patterns. Hoax has been ruled out, at least as a major cause, and opinion centres on some unknown energy effect causing the circles.[16,17,18,19] The crop within these features is swirled clockwise or anticlockwise, bent at ground level but not broken. In 1988, a large number of the enigmatic features had appeared in the field to the south of Silbury Hill. I could not escape the feeling that Silbury the teacher was still giving lessons. I was later to learn that strange balls of orange light had been seen by local people to descend into the very field sporting the crop circles Chippindale and I were observing (see Chapter 11).

Light phenomena of another kind caught the attention of Charla and I on August 2, when we went to photograph the double sunrise effect. It was another pristine dawn, and we got our pictures. As we turned round to climb down the hill we marvelled at the almost surreal effect the light of the rising sun was creating on the golden fields to the southwest. The shadow of Silbury was cast onto a sloping field below (this slope may have been used by the builders of Silbury initially to observe the double-skyline feature they made such use of). The gauge, or movement, of Silbury's shadow is said to be the same as that of the Great Pyramid at Giza. Another odd coincidence between Silbury and the Great Pyramid is that the mean slope of the pyramid is a little under 52 degrees, extremely close to the latitude on which the Avebury complex sits, while the mean slope of Silbury is about 30 degrees, and the Great Pyramid sits on the thirtieth parallel. But it was not such coincidences which held us fascinated: out of the top of Silbury's shadow we noticed a flare of light. As we moved, the glow of light on the field far below also moved. What on Earth was it? Later enquiry revealed the nature of the phenomenon.

There is an effect sometimes reported by mountaineers called 'the Brocken Spectre': if one stands with, say, a couple of companions atop a mountain at sunrise, and there is a cloud on the opposite side to the rising sun, two, not three, shadows will be seen by any one of the people. Where the viewer's shadow should be is only a patch of light – the Brocken Spectre. This is due to a refractive effect in the droplets of moisture forming the cloud. The 'glory' is a related effect. The shadow of a person standing in a field at sunrise will have a glow of light around the head. This is a similar optical effect caused by dew on the grass. In the case of Silbury, the shadow of the viewer's body as far as the shoulders is

*Plate 12. The shadow of Silbury Hill cast by the rising Lammas sun. Note the 'flare' of light coming off the top of the shadow – the Silbury Glory, a dramatic phenomenon to the naked eye*

cast across the summit area, but where the head should be is lost in the shadow of the great mound itself, thrown on the field below. A greatly enlarged glory is thus formed. A unique Silbury Glory. This effect can only come about by the presence of a person on top of Silbury, of course, and as one reader of *The Ley Hunter* magazine commented, when he read an account of the effect there, 'Do you realise that you have seen a human soul? (Metaphorically speaking.)' It felt that way.

That same day Silbury revealed a number of other potential sightlines. I now cannot help but refer to the great Neolithic mound other than in animistic ways. If it makes rationalists uncomfortable, then they should recall the systems approach to sites, and the need to get outside our Indo-European cognitive framework at times. The animistic mental model yields more information, extends description, and that is what counts. Being and seeing, free of preconceived concepts, is an essential mode to employ in the wider understanding of ancient sacred places, and that means being open to feelings as well as to observations – indeed certain observations may rely on the appropriate feelings being present in the observer.

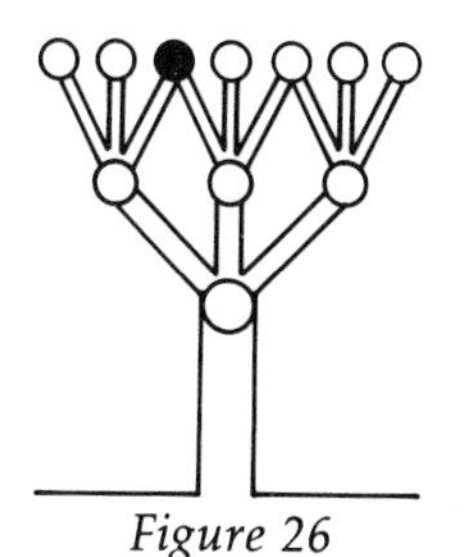
*Figure 26*

CHAPTER 4

# ANCIENT ASTRONOMY

## Demonstration

Alexander Thom surveyed Castlerigg as part of his great work in studying the astronomical and geometrical properties of megalith sites. Castlerigg was remarkable in a number of ways. Astronomically, Thom found that the stones indicate a total of seven solar or lunar declinations (see figure).

Witnessing one of these astronomical events at the site is a profoundly moving experience, not the cerebral, dry effect created by looking at surveys and calculations which archaeoastronomers are obliged to produce in order to identify possible astronomical alignments at sites. The on-site event itself is an experience of the heart, not the head. I witnessed midwinter sunrise at Castlerigg, one of the lesser astronomical phenomena at the ring, with John Glover and other colleagues in 1978. It was the calculations of Thom that allowed us to know where to look and place our cameras, but it had been the site in turn which had instructed him. The culmination of our vigil was heralded by the rays of the sun, still hidden behind the mountains, casting an exquisite violet light on the surrounding snowy peaks. When the wan solar disk broke over the far mountain ridge it was as if time had been swept away, and we all felt a close kinship with the circle's builders and original users. It was so cold even the weak beams of the midwinter sun felt warm. These crucial beams, at the dark turning of the year, seemed as if nurtured at Castlerigg, as the orientation was effectively marked by two of the lower stones creating a visual channel, a sort of cradle, across the ring.

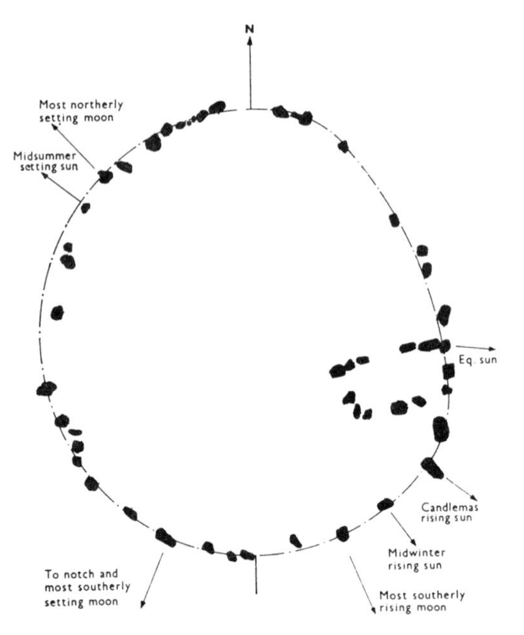


*Figure 27. (Modified after Alexander Thom)*

*Plate 13. Midwinter sunrise at Castlerigg*

## Discussion

Two of the main examples of 'being and seeing' given in the previous chapter, the Castlerigg shadow path and the Silbury double sunrise, are related to astronomical events interacting with sites. This relationship is thus yet another aspect that has to be covered in providing comprehensive descriptions of sacred monuments.

The association of astronomy and sacred place is a traditional one, and survived in Europe as a folkmemory, usually in the form of seasonal fairs and games. At Stonehenge, famous for its midsummer sunrise over the outlying Heel Stone, there were 'vile and indecorous games' at the solstice period, as the Bishop of Salisbury described them in 1223. These games very possibly harkened back to pagan attendance at the site. Sports were held at Stonehenge even as late as the eighteenth century, as a newspaper notice of 1781 confirms. The dates given in the paper for the event were July 4 and 5, not the traditional Midsummer Day of June 24 (the astronomical solstice is June 21), an interesting piece of evidence supporting a greater antiquity for the gathering, as folklorist John Goulstone has pointed out:

> Popular gatherings tied like this to the old style calendar were almost invariably traditional events originally celebrated eleven days earlier in the calendar year. Thus before the official changeover from Julian to Gregorian reckoning in 1752, when September 14 immediately followed September 2 – thereby provoking public outcry over the "lost" eleven days – the two days July 4 and 5 were June 23 and 24, the original Midsummer Eve and Midsummer day.[1]

Midsummer games were held at many places, including prehistoric monuments, landmark hills and so on. In effect, astronomy was celebrated in the landscape. Indeed, fairs, festivals and games punctuated the year at the solstices, equinoxes and the cross quarter times of early November (Celtic Samhain, Christian All Saints, following Hallowe'en), early February (Imbolc, Candlemas), early May (Beltane) and early August (Lughnassadh, Lammas). The ancient eight-point year. There occurred merriment with cakes and ale, licentious revels, morris dancing, bottle kicking, races, football, bull baiting, 'jingling', 'Whipping Toms', and a whole variety of activities, some quite violent. Almost certainly some modern games such as football came out of these seasonal activities, and the Olympic games may have derived from calendrically-related fertility festivities.[2]

The folk traditions thus gave the early antiquarians their cue, so it is not surprising that they sometimes looked for astronomical aspects at the places they visited and studied. In 1740, William Stukeley noted that the axis of Stonehenge and its earthen avenue align to the northeast 'where abouts the sun rises when the days are longest' and referred to Classical writers on the ancient practice of orienting temples to face the sunrise on foundation day. Stukeley had also made astronomical allusions in earlier work. His contemporary, John Wood of Bath, surveyed both Stonehenge and the Stanton Drew circles near Bath. He saw Stonehenge as being concerned with lunar and calendrical events. In 1770, John Smith wrote that the Heel Stone, viewed from the centre of the monument, marked the midsummer sunrise. He further suggested that the sarsen and bluestone settings at Stonehenge recorded astrological information. At about the same time, William Chapple wrote that the shadows thrown by the Spinster's Rock dolmen and surrounding megalithic emplacements in Devon had been used by the Druids in their astronomical and geodetic work.[3] In Ireland, Colonel Charles Vallencey declared in 1786 that Newgrange had been a kind of sun temple, and he also felt that various Irish stones had been used to 'mark the cycles'. As researcher Martin Brennan has commented, 'What cycles they marked and how the cycles were recorded is not entirely clear, but it is clear that Vallencey believed the stones and other monuments to have astronomical functions.'[4]

So, like archaeology, the study of ancient astronomy arose out of early antiquarianism, and its growth from heresy to accepted academic discipline has more or less coincided with the course of the twentieth century. The modern study has come to be called 'archaeoastronomy', a term that was coined by Scottish archaeologist Euan MacKie and which has largely replaced the earlier 'astroarchaeology'.

The 'father of archaeoastronomy' was Sir Norman Lockyer, a renowned scientist of his day, and editor of the prestigious scientific journal, *Nature*. While travelling in Greece in 1890, he was struck by the changes in the axes of some of the ancient temples there and wondered if they had aligned to foundation day sunrises. He set out to test his ideas on Egyptian temples and published his findings in *The Dawn of Astronomy* in 1894. At Karnak he found two alignments to the midsummer sunset and one to midwinter sunrise. One of the sunset lines formed the axis of the Great Temple of Amun (Amen-Ra) in the Karnak complex. The sunbeam would have been able to penetrate to the inner

*Plate 14. Looking west down the axis of the temple at Karnak, Egypt. Lockyer claimed this line indicated midsummer sunset*

sanctum. He also felt that certain temples were aligned to stars. Inscriptions at Edfu and at Denderah referred to the 'stretching of the cord' at the temples' foundation ceremony along an astronomical line. In the case of the Temple of Hathor at Denderah, the King oriented the stretched cord to a star in the 'Bull's Foreleg' (Ursa Major – our Plough or Big Dipper). Lockyer calculated that the Temple of Isis at Denderah was oriented on the rising of Sirius, the brightest of the stars in our skies, in 700 BC. The first appearance of a star or constellation in the eastern predawn sky is termed its heliacal rise (after *helios*, sun), and the heliacal rise of Sirius warned of the midsummer sunrise which coincided with the Egyptian New Year and the rejuvenating annual Nile flood (only stopped by the building of the Old Aswan Dam in 1902). So Sirius

*Figure 28. 'Stretching the cord'*

was a key star in Egypt, and Lockyer found seven temples oriented on it. Denderah also had a zodiac ceiling (the original is now in the Louvre).

Lockyer's book was greeted unenthusiastically by archaeologists, but, undeterred, he started an astronomical study of Stonehenge, the monument that has been most closely implicated in the development of archaeoastronomy. To appreciate properly some of the astronomical findings at Stonehenge there are a few facts about the site that need to be borne in mind.

The monument as we now see it was not built all at the same time. The first feature on the site, at around 3300 BC, seems to have been a wooden building almost 100 feet (30 m) across. It had an entrance at the northeast and a narrower aperture at the south. Prehistorian Aubrey Burl thinks that it was a charnel house, and may also have housed astronomer-priests making the first prolonged lunar observations at the site. A century or so later came what is known as *Stonehenge I*, comprising a ditch and bank circular enclosure (the actual henge), a ring of 56 filled-in pits known as the Aubrey Holes inside the inner bank, and the Heel Stone and a possible companion stone a short distance to the northwest (to the left of the Heel Stone when viewed from the centre of Stonehenge). Three holes (F,G,H in Figure 29) also shared the circumference of the Aubrey Hole circle. It was thought these

*Plate 15. The outlying Heel Stone at Stonehenge, viewed from the centre of the monument, approximately along the midsummer sunrise axis. The shorter standing stones are bluestones*

were post or stone holes, but the general archaeological opinion now seems to be that they are tree holes.

The entrance to the henge was on the northeast, on the axis of the original timber building. Two stones stood in this entrance gap 'like a gunsight straddling the axis of the henge,' as Burl puts it.[6] (Holes D and E in Figure 29.) Numerous small post holes were found in the entrance causeway, and these probably belong to this phase of the monument or even preceded the earthen henge. There were another set of larger postholes in a line near the Heel Stone (A in Figure 29). In the next phase, *Stonehenge II*, about a thousand years later, the axis was shifted slightly, and on this an earthen avenue was built, approaching the henge entrance. The two stones here were transferred to the mouth of the avenue, on its centre line, between the henge and the Heel Stone (holes B and C in Figure 29). Either during this phase or at sometime in phase I, the Station Stones, or positions, were put in place, forming what is virtually a rectangular setting (91, 92, 93, 94 in Figure 29). These Station Stones are the key to Stonehenge astronomy, rather than the more famous Heel Stone midsummer sunrise, as we shall see. Only two Station Stones survive today, and one of those may not be original, but the other two positions are known. During this

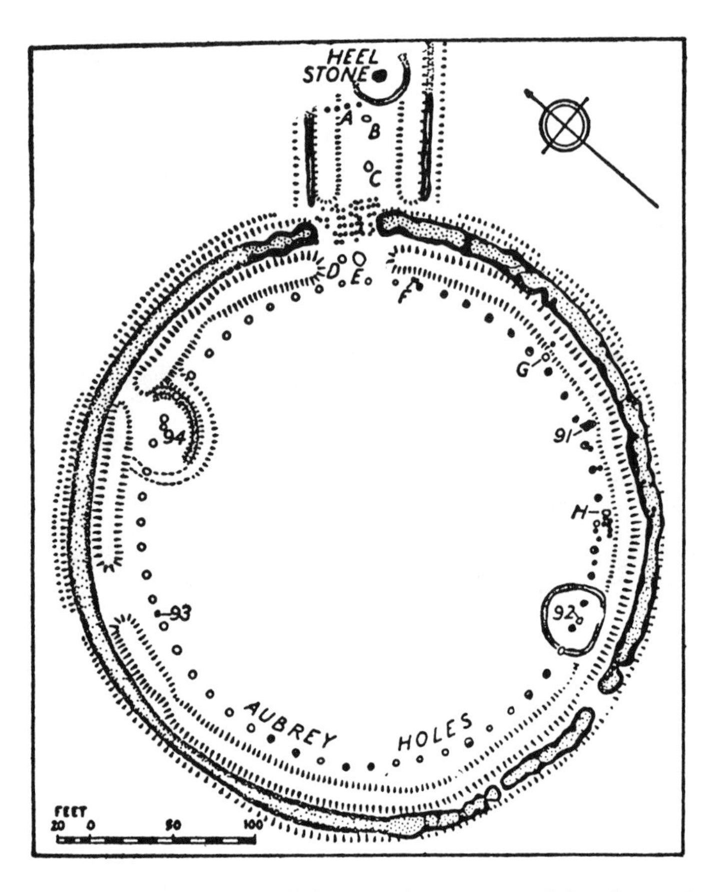


*Figure 29. Selected features of the Stonehenge groundplan from Phases I and II. See text. (Modified after R.J.C. Atkinson)*

phase the first setting of bluestones was arranged within the henge. (The bluestones are the smaller, darker stones the visitor sees at Stonehenge today.)

Figure 29 shows Phases I and II combined. *Stonehenge III* dates from around 2000 BC and marks the erection of the huge, lintelled sarsen stones that most people identify with Stonehenge. The bluestones were carefully removed and stored no one knows where, and ten massive, shaped sarsens were set up as the uprights of five freestanding trilithons (a term invented by Stukeley, meaning 'three stones' in Greek – two uprights and a lintel) arranged in a horseshoe configuration. An outer circle was formed from 30 slightly smaller sarsens topped with lintels forming a smooth, level ring of stone 16 feet (5 m) above the ground.

*Plate 16. Stonehenge viewed from Station Stone 91*

The centre of this outer sarsen circle differs from the centre of the original henge and Aubrey hole circles by about three feet (1 m). Two stones were erected by the entrance, one survives today as the fallen 'Slaughter Stone'. Archaeologists divide Phase III into a series of subdivisions stretching over the following centuries, when various changes were made to the monument: the bluestones reappeared, a large stone, the Altar Stone, which may have also been present in Phase II, was erected within the trilithon horseshoe, and, around 1100 BC, the avenue had a longer addition made to it but on a sharply different axis to the east. Stonehenge is a complex site suffering the depredations of time, and there are obscured or lost elements of the structure. It also helps to have a basic grasp of a few astronomical factors.

Two aspects of the Earth's celestial mechanics have particular relevance to archaeoastronomy. One is called the 'change in the obliquity of the ecliptic', which means the varying angle of the tilt of the Earth's axis to the plane of its annual orbit around the sun. (We here on Earth have the daily illusion that the sun goes round us, and over a year it cuts a specific swathe through the firmament called the ecliptic, the constellations along which give us the star signs of the zodiac. The ecliptic is the geocentric view of the plane of the Earth's orbit.) The value of the angle between the Earth's tilt and plane of solar orbit is known as the obliquity, and this varies slowly over the centuries due to complex gravitational effects on the Earth by other planets. Over a human lifetime this movement is undetectable, but over the thousands of years involved in the study of ancient sites astronomers have to calculate exactly where the sun or moon would have risen in a given year millennia ago. So a very accurate orientation of stones in, say, 4000 BC, when the obliquity was a degree or so greater than at present (about two solar disc widths different) would be less accurate today. Questions about whether the top, bottom or centre of the rising or setting solar or lunar disc was aligned to by a monument's builders becomes another problematical area that can drastically affect dating attempts.

The other factor affecting the Earth's axis is precession. If the change in tilt can be visualised as rocking action, then precession

*Plate 17. One of the Stonehenge trilithons*

can be seen as a rotating, wobbling effect, like that on a spinning top. Fortunately, the Earth's wobble takes 26 000 years each time so we do not feel it! Nevertheless, in only 50 years the rising point of some stars can actually be seen to change. So possible stellar alignments at sites are difficult to determine as deliberate, but in theory would allow a site to be quite accurately dated if one could be certain of an engineered stellar orientation there.

At midsummer the sun rises and sets at the most northerly positions on the horizon it ever reaches, thus giving the longest day, and at midwinter it rises and sets at the most southerly. This variation is due to the tilt of the Earth's axis relative to the sun (towards it in summer, away from it in winter in each hemisphere). These are the solstices. 'Solstice' means literally 'sun stand still', because the movement of the sun's rise or set points at these times is barely apparent for a few days. At the equinoxes, in March and September, the tilt of the Earth's axis is 'sideways on' relative to the sun and its effect is temporarily negated. So the sun rises and sets due east and west, and day and night are about equal (equinox means 'equal night').

The moon is more complex, its total cycle being not a single year but 18.61 years, sometimes called the Metonic cycle. This is due to the moon's orbit around the Earth being at an angle to the plane of the Earth's orbit around the sun and also at another angle to the plane of the Earth's equator. The moon's path crosses the plane of the ecliptic twice a month and the two points where these intersections occur are called the nodes of the moon's orbit. These in turn move their positions and are key components in the celestial mechanics causing eclipses.

At what is called the Major Lunar Standstill, the moon reaches its maximum northern and southern rising points on the horizon. Solstices of a kind, though this analogy is not really accurate. In the year of a major standstill it is the winter full moon which achieves the northerly rising extreme, and the summer full moon the southerly extreme. Also in a major standstill year, the arc of the moon across the sky can vacillate quite rapidly between being very high at times, to little more than skimming the horizon at others – a very dramatic and noticeable phenomenon, especially at higher latitudes. This is because in a single month in a Major Standstill year the moon's orbit carries it well above and well below the ecliptic.

At the Minor Standstill year, nine years and a few months later, the winter full moon rises as far south of the midsummer sunrise position as it ever does while the midsummer full moon rises as far north of the midwinter sunrise position as it can. So the spread of the horizon between rising and setting positions is the narrowest that occurs.

There are further complications that affect our observation of the moon – perturbation, parallax and others – that we shall ignore here for the sake of preserving the sanity of those of us not astronomically-minded.

Archaeoastronomers have always assumed, and it seems rightly, that the ancient astronomer-priest(ess)s would have set solar orientations primarily to the rising or setting points at the eight key times of the ancient year (see above) and any lunar alignments to the standstill positions. Clearly, defining the lunar orientations at a spot would have required a much longer period of skywatching than those directed at the sun.

In 1901, Lockyer attempted to date Stonehenge by calculating back to when the first gleam of the midsummer rising sun would have been dead in line with the axis of the monument. Because of the limits to the accuracy with which this axis could be defined he could not arrive at an exact date, but he identified a period which after correction due to the use of inaccurate tables was roughly between 1600 BC and 2000 BC. The older date, we now see, is about right for the beginning of Phase III. Lockyer furthermore noted that this midsummer axis could effectively be extended as a landscape line many miles long linking Stonehenge with Sidbury Hill in one direction and Grovely Castle and Castle Ditches (all hilltops earthworked in the Iron Age) in the other. Of course, this smacks of geomancy, and was resisted by archaeologists at the time. Even today, an archaeologist like Christopher Chippindale, for instance, can warn that 'sites and structures which were of different dates should not be linked together, as Lockyer had done in dragging in Sidbury Hill.' On the other hand, prehistorian Aubrey Burl points out the more obvious possibility that 'the midsummer sun never rose farther north than the landmark of Sidbury Hill eight miles away nor the midwinter sun further south than the seven-mile distant Battery Hill. It would have been easy to set up a stone or post in line with these natural features.'[6]

Lockyer also suggested that a diagonal across the Station Stones rectangle gave certain cross-quarter day sunrises and sunsets. Lockyer went on to study other megalithic sites in Britain over the following years, particularly monuments in Cornwall and Wales. In 1906, he published *Stonehenge and other British Stone Monuments Astronomically Considered*, expanded in a second edition three years later in which astronomically-explained landscape lines between monuments were included. There is no doubt that Lockyer made errors and presented his material badly, and this gave ammunition to those who chose to reject the essence of his findings, but as John Michell states, Lockyer 'almost single-handed . . . developed the science of astro-archaeology.' Lockyer himself granted the German researcher Professor Nissen 'the credit of having first made the suggestion [in 1885] that ancient temples were oriented on an astronomical basis.'

There was a slow response to Lockyer's lead by competent researchers. One of the few to do so was Admiral Boyle Somerville, who was at times critical of Lockyer. In 1912, he produced a paper on his survey of Callanish, on the Isle of Lewis off Scotland's west coast, showing possible astronomical orientations. In France, Lieutenant Devoir made an astronomical study of the megalithic monuments of Brittany. In the 1920s Alfred Watkins had the help of Somerville in assessing the astronomical significance of some of his 'leys' or alignments of ancient sites (see Chapter 8). In Germany, in the 1930s, Wilhelm Teudt was working on very similar astronomically-oriented alignments of sites he called *Heilige Linien* or Holy Lines. But it was not until the 1960s that archaeoastronomy really began to come of age.

Some of the best archaeoastronomical work at Stonehenge was accomplished by a retired gas-board worker, C.A. Newham, early in the '60s. He directed the bulk of his attention to the Station Stones. As long ago as 1846, the Reverend E. Duke had noted that the alignment of 92 and 91 gave the summer solstice sunrise, and 94 to 93 indicated the setting midwinter sun. Newham confirmed these orientations and found more associated with the rectangle. Amongst these were an equinox orientation between 94 and stone hole C, Major Standstill directions indicated by 94 to 91 and 92 to 93. Some of the others required the holes most archaeologists consider to be natural to have been deliberate – still a moot point.

The Heel Stone stands to one side of the axis, and in megalithic times the sun would not have risen over it, as is popularly supposed, but to the left of it as viewed from the centre of the sarsen circle. But in 1979 a stone hole to the left of the Heel Stone was uncovered, and this is now catalogued as stone 97. This could have been a former setting of the Heel Stone itself, but it could be more likely that the scheme at Stonehenge was to have the midsummer run rising between the Heel Stone and its now lost companion. The two uprights would have framed the first gleam of the sun precisely, and the rising disk would then have grazed the tip of the Heel Stone. What the Heel Stone *does* mark by itself is the moon at various key times from different positions within the monument, including station position 94, as Newham was later to notice.

Apart from this astonishing display of astronomical significance, there is something else remarkable about the Station Stone rectangle. The French architect, G. Charrière, noted in 1961, as did Newham and Gerald Hawkins independently in 1963, that the astronomical alignments marked at Stonehenge cross at right angles and generate the rectangle because of the latitude at which Stonehenge is located. This regular figure could not be produced if Stonehenge was situated at any significant distance further north or south (the absolutely optimal position would have placed the monument in the English Channel!). If it was not located where it was, and if the ground level was different or the horizon altitude other than it is around the site, the astronomical lines at Stonehenge would make a distorted parallelogram. The implications of this are that the builders of Stonehenge had a knowledge of the global nature of the Earth, a significant piece of evidence as we shall note in the next chapter. This brings back echoes of the curious coincidences between Silbury Hill – only 20 miles (32 km) north of Stonehenge – and the Great Pyramid, noted in the previous chapter. Moreover, Gerald Hawkins recalls in *Beyond Stonehenge* (1973) that he was asked to design a Stonehenge-type monument for a recreational area being planned by the Tennessee Valley Authority. He found out that coincidentally it was only at the latitude of the TVA's site, 30 degrees north, that the astronomical directions apparently recorded at Stonehenge can form another regular figure (a hexagon). Hawkins omitted to mention the greater coincidence: the latitude 30 degrees north is also that of the Great Pyramid.

Newham felt that in its earliest stage Stonehenge 'was essentially a site for the investigation of lunar phenomena.' He felt that the post holes found in the entrance causeway (Figure 29) were the scars of lunar observations using marker poles which took place over a hundred-year period, created as the Stonehenge sky-watchers worked out the skyline position of the Major Standstill moonrise by methodically recording the swings of the moon on its 18.61-year cycles. He also noted that one of the 30 uprights of the outer sarsen circle was half the size of the others, and suggested that 29½ might have related to the days of a lunar month (literally 'moonth').

He published his Station Stone findings in *The Yorkshire Post* in March 1963. That he did not arrive at his conclusions earlier had been due to a typing error in his calculations in 1962. But even when his article did appear, no one took any notice. *Antiquity* turned down a paper from him, and a fire at his printers stopped Newham's self-published booklet from appearing in June 1963. Then events overtook him. In October 1963, American-based astronomer Gerald Hawkins published a paper in *Nature*, Lockyer's old journal, in which he described his work using a computer to assess the astronomical lines at Stonehenge. He proposed alignments not only for the earlier phases of Stonehenge but also for the Phase III sarsen structure. In this he suggested that the narrow gaps between the great trilithons allowed narrow viewing angles like gunsights to solar and lunar rise and set positions through the wider gaps between the uprights in the outer sarsen circle. Hawkins suggested that certain hollows in the trilithon uprights had actually been carved to allow for the slight sideways squint required for some of the sightlines. Nevertheless, despite the narrowness of the trilithon gaps, Hawkins' sarsen stones lines were still fairly wide, so pinpoint accuracy could not be claimed. Hawkins felt that scientific accuracy as we require it was not a priority of the Stonehenge designers, but rather that a more ceremonial usage of astronomical orientation was wanted.

In a second paper in 1964, Hawkins went further to suggest that the 56 Aubrey Holes had been a lunar eclipse calculator which may have employed a set of black and white marker stones. By using 56 positions (18.61 × 3 = 55.83) the stone-age computer could have been used for calculations covering many years. Later, the British

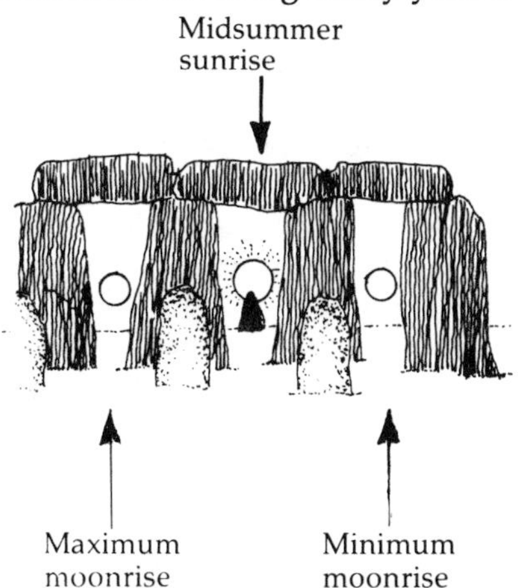


*Figure 30. Solar and lunar events at Stonehenge viewed through the sarsen 'windows', looking northeast along axis from centre of monument. (Smaller stones in foreground are bluestones)*

astronomer Fred Hoyle proposed a more sophisticated version of the hypothesised Aubrey Holes computer. Leading Stonehenge archaeologist R.J.C. Atkinson attacked Hawkins' ideas in an *Antiquity* article entitled 'Moonshine on Stonehenge', pointing out errors and questioning assumptions. Hawkins had used a faulty plan of Stonehenge, and later refined his earlier findings. His book, *Stonehenge Decoded,* written in collaboration with J.B. White in 1965, brought the whole matter of archaeoastronomy to the attention of a wide, general public. The idea of a modern computer being used to decode a Neolithic computer caught the popular imagination.

In 1984, Hawkins' Phase I Stonehenge alignments were subjected to statistical tests and showed that the early Stonehenge, at least, was designed 'to point to the sun and moon with odds in favour ranging from a thousand- to a billion-to-one depending on the assumptions made,' (*Archaeoastronomy* VIII, 1985).

But back in the '60s Atkinson remained sceptical of astronomical interpretations of megalithic sites generally. The man who changed his mind for him was Scotsman Alexander Thom, a retired professor of engineering at Oxford University. Thom had surveyed hundreds of British megalithic sites, publishing his findings piecemeal in scientific journals. Somewhat like Newham, no one really noticed. The impact of Thom's meticulous work only began with the publication of his *Megalithic Sites in Britain* (1967).[7] It was detailed, mathematical material, and because of this its powerful astronomical and other evidence took a while to sink in to the archaeological community and other interested parties. It was, said Atkinson, like a 'well constructed parcel-bomb.'

Thom had apparently found three main things: that groundplans of stone circles were carefully constructed geometric shapes where they were not true circles; a basic measurement unit of 2.72 feet, which Thom called the Megalithic Yard, had been employed, and many sites could have been used as backsights for astronomical observation, making use of artificial and natural foresights such as outlying standing stones, mountain peaks and notches. During the rest of the '60s and through the 1970s Thom went on to survey more sites – in Brittany as well as Britain – and subject his findings to careful statistical analysis.

His findings suggested that some megalithic astronomy could have been very accurate, more so than that needed for simple agricultural communities. A classic example of this kind of accuracy is shown at Ballochroy, situated at the northern end of the Kintyre peninsula, on the west coast of Scotland. It consists of three slab-like stones arranged in line. The orientation of the line southwestwards, Thom found, passed over a cairn site (of which only a large megalithic burial cist survives) and indicated the midwinter setting sun behind one end of Cara island a few miles out to sea. The distance between the backsight, formed by the stone alignment, and the foresight, the island, made the sightline more accurate. Thom was also interested in the directions indicated by the axis of the slabs themselves, which were set at approximate right angles to the midwinter sunset line. He found that the axis of the centre stone indicated the distinctive mountains known as the Paps on the island of Jura 19 miles (30 km) away. The centre stone accurately indicated the midsummer setting sun behind a peak.

Another accurate solar line, the midwinter setting sun, is apparently indicated at another Scottish site, Kintraw. Here, a possible viewing platform of pebbles was uncovered by archaeologist Euan MacKie,[8] though controversy over this has not been fully resolved.

Thom also identified sites that could have acted as backsights for lunar observation, too. Among these is the Ring of Brogar on Orkney Mainland, north of the Scottish coast. Thom found it to be the same size as each of the inner circles at Avebury (Chapter 3) many hundreds of miles away in southern England. There are four natural horizon foresights available from the Brogar site which allow lunar observations relating to major and minor standstill events. The sightlines involve the use of mounds and an outlying stone surrounding the great circle itself.

It took Thom many years, deliberately, to get round finally to Stonehenge. Here, too, he looked for longer, thus more accurate, sightlines than those provided by the stone alignments within the monument itself. Thom made a new, accurate survey. His azimuth for the Stonehenge axis provides for an indication of the midsummer rising sun at around 2100 BC when half the solar disc was above the horizon. For the lunar indications at Stonehenge, Thom concurred with Newham that the postholes at the entrance causeway were the remnants of a lunar extrapolation device, and he identified distant landmark features as foresights. He deduced that the Major Standstill southerly midsummer moonrise would occur behind Figsbury Ring, an Iron Age hillfort six and a half miles (10.5 km) southeast of Stonehenge, and would set behind Chain Hill to the southwest. Aubrey Burl comments:

> Thom suggested that at these places foresights had been constructed so that people might record and analyse the moon's movements from Stonehenge, but in this he was probably

> mistaken. What matters is that if Stonehenge observers had aligned posts on these positions and then marked the midway point between them they would have produced a line less than 1° from True South, a line, moreover, looking towards Rox Hill, once Rocks Hill, two and a quarter miles (3.6 km) away and a convenient landmark for 'catching' the moon on its path across the night sky.
>
> This must have been the first sightline established at Stonehenge . . .[9]

Burl further comments that the original axis of Phase I Stonehenge had actually been directed at the rising of the major standstill midwinter full moon, thus making the fundamental cosmological line at the site originally lunar, not solar. Later, when the axis was altered almost five degrees, a solar orientation was created: Burl sees this as possibly expressing a shift in cultural archetype from the feminine moon to the masculine sun.

Other lunar landmarks noted by Thom in the landscape around Stonehenge included Hanging Langford Camp (Minor Standstill southernmost moonset), Coneybury Barrow (Major Standstill southernmost moonrise) and Gibbet Knoll (northernmost Major Standstill moonset). 'Stonehenge was no longer an isolated monument,' wrote Michell, 'but the centre of a vast system of astronomically placed stations extending far across the Wessex landscape . . .'[10]

The kinds of alignments mentioned so far rely on the site being the point from where observations are made (the backsight), but in Brittany Thom found an example where this situation was apparently reversed. He felt that Le Grand Menhir Brisé (or Er Grah – 'the stone of the fairies'), a huge fallen and broken stone near Locmariaquer, 70 feet (21 m) long and weighing 340 tons, had acted when upright as a massive foresight for lunar observations from positions all around Quiberon Bay. Thom's theory has been attacked by statisticians complaining that there are so many sites around Quiberon Bay that backsights for Le Grand Menhir Brisé could occur on the appropriate sightlines by chance. This, however, is a problem that belongs to the modern mind rather than the Neolithic situation at Quiberon Bay. The criticism may be true but incorrect – there is a difference. It does not stop the Neolithic use of the great monolith having occurred as Thom had proposed. Also in Brittany, Thom provided the first meaningful explanation for the curious stone row complexes occurring in the Carnac-Ville area. He calculated that some of these might have been used as grids to sort out lunar declinations – probably the extrapolation of

*Plate 18. The great fallen and broken monolith of Er Grah, Brittany*

lunar observations made using Le Grand Menhir Brisé. He made a similar suggestion for the mysterious fanned lines of low stones to be found in northeast Scotland, such as the 'Hill O'Many Stanes' site (Mid Clythe). As Michell has pointed out, the ability to record and extrapolate the results of observations suggests 'the existence of a Neolithic school of mathematical philosophy.'

To Thom, the megalithic builders were brilliant engineers and astronomers, constructing sophisticated observatories with unsophisticated materials. There were intellects then, he was sure, the equivalent of our Einsteins today. He looked for, and found, precision. This may partially have been a function, as Chippindale comments, of Thom and his family co-workers being 'in the classic Scots tradition of physical science and engineering, that in the end has been leading thought astray.'[11] Certainly, all aspects of Thom's work – the geometry of site groundplans, the precision and ubiquity of the Megalithic Yard, the accuracy and authenticity of some of his astronomical alignments – have come in for criticism to one degree or another. The general archaeological consensus seems to be today that there *were* astronomical dimensions to megalithic sites, but that they tended to have been for ceremonial application or generalised calendrical value, rather than prehistoric scientific projects. Burl feels that the astronomical lines at

Stonehenge 'are not honed to the stilletto sharpness of a laser beam. They are as diffused as bars of sunlight through stained glass.'[12] This echoes Stukeley's comments on the design of the rings at Avebury: 'This is done with a sufficient, tho' not a mathematical exactness, where preciseness would have no effect.' Astronomer Douglas Heggie regards the megalithic astronomers as practising an empirical rather than a theoretical science, a science based on close observation. Like Burl, Heggie notes that a number of the lunar alignments seem associated with burial sites, with death and associated rituals, suggesting that the sites 'were not simply observatories in a narrow sense.'[13]

However, as we saw at Avebury in the previous chapter, there can be precision of a geomantic kind that does not happen to match the concept of exactitude that we are cognitively locked into today. The archaic perception of the land was undoubtedly more precise than the modern view. The poor vision we have of the landscape today is probably a partial cause of the cognitive inability of modern mainstream scholarship to perceive the startling worldwide evidence of geomantic activity in the past. There was also an ability to be precise even in our modern sense in the megalithic world, as sites like Ballochroy demonstrate, but it is almost certainly the case, as Burl and Heggie intimate, that it was pressed into the service not of an isolated discipline of science or engineering, but of a whole cosmological worldview.

Despite the criticisms and less valid nitpicking, Thom's work remains a tremendous achievement. If Lockyer was the father of archaeoastronomy, then Alexander Thom was the midwife.

Thus brought forth, archaeoastronomy has grown and travelled. Interest in native American astronomy began in the 1960s, but little sustained research had been conducted when the American astronomer Anthony Aveni began his studies at the ancient sites in Mesoamerica. In 1973, Aveni co-chaired a conference with architect Horst Hartung in Mexico City. Twenty-six researchers who had recently begun investigation into American archaeoastronomy presented papers. 'This small group formed the New World basis for the rapidly developing interdisciplinary study of archaeoastronomy,' astronomer Ray A. Williamson has declared.[14]

American archaeoastronomy developed a special dimension, ethnoastronomy, because unlike their European colleagues studying the astronomy of the megalith builders, the American researchers had the myths and traditional activities of living remnants of native cultures, and the historical records of the

Europeans who first encountered them, in addition to ruined sites. The historical records are only partially useful, however, because they reflect the problem the Indo-European cognitive framework had when it met the substantially different world-views of the peoples of the New World and elsewhere. 'The chronicler's own ethnocentric bias obstructed their attempts to obtain correct and complete information,' Williamson notes. For example, many of the early Europeans in Mesoamerica failed to note that the Inca calendar of 12 months was in fact different to their own, and was based on more exacting astronomical observation. The number of days in the Inca year was 328, equalling the number of *huacas* or sacred places intersected by 41 straight landscape lines called *ceques* that radiated out from the Temple of the Sun in Cuzco, the Inca capital. Each *huaca* represented a day of the year. This association between calendar and landscape, between astronomical motion and the land, between heaven and Earth, which Europeans find so difficult to perceive, may well have been similar to the geomantic sensibility of the prehistoric megalithic builders. But the Europeans came to the Americas across seas of forgetfulness, bringing another state of consciousness, history, with them – hence history in the Americas is now understood to have begun with the arrival of the Europeans.

Another example of the dangers of ethnocentricity is provided by the skylore of the Andean Indians. Because it is natural for the Western mind to make patterns, constellations, out of groups of stars, it is all too easy to assume that all cultures would look at the night sky in the same way. But American anthropologist Gary Urton found otherwise when he lived in an Indian village high in the Andes. To the Quechua-speaking villagers the Milky Way was the key to their cosmology, it being such a vivid feature of the Andean night, and their 'constellations' were the dark shapes in it (formed by interstellar dust blocking out the light of the stars)! Moreover, Urton believes that Inca Cuzco had its groundplan related to the angle of the Milky Way across the sky.[15]

As with prehistoric Europe, the knowledge of the tribe was passed on in oral tradition. The Zuni Indians of the American Southwest, for instance, encode some of their astronomical lore in a ceremony known as the Long Talk, or Sayatasha's Night Chant. The Zuni also have a concept of the four, cardinal directions, which are determined from solar or stellar observation common to principles of geomancy the world over. Their word for Earth contains the root word for four – a conceptual linking of heaven and Earth. In Zuni myth *K'yan asdebi*, the Water-Skate, showed the

> Stone markers extending from behind Campo Santo up to top of high hill west of town. From Campo Santo to top approximately 1½ km. Sun rises on lines PS and OS observed from stones O and P on March 19, 1940, two days before the equinox. Sun rises this day at six degs 31½ ms. Direction observed with simple adjustable compass. Observations of the sun are made at the stone today by zahorins (shamans) for planting and harvesting.[16]

(The use of horizon clocks and calendars was also part of the Old World's living astronomy. In Belgium and France, sun positions relative to horizon features were known as *points de jours,* and there are several known horizon clocks in the Alps. At a position near the village of Moos at the northeast edge of the Dolomites, for example, the sun in the hours bracketing noon passes over three peaks called Elfer, Zwölfer and Einser – thus incorporating the German for 11, 12, 1 – at the appropriate times.)

The probable ancestors of some of the present-day Pueblo peoples were what the much more recent Navajo call the Anasazi, 'the ancient ones', a lost culture that peaked about a thousand years ago. Its heartland was the San Juan Basin where the Four Corner states meet, and Chaco Canyon in northwest New Mexico is now thought to have been its ritual centre. The canyon has many ritual sites scattered along it, and is at the focus of a great network of straight tracks (see Chapter 8). There is evidence, too, of astronomical practice at Chaco.

At points along the canyon walls are Anasazi petroglyphs (rock peckings) and pictographs (rock paintings). Some of these are thought to indicate astronomical events and to mark the look out positions for sun priests. On a low knoll on the south side of the canyon floor is Casa Rinconada, a large ruined, kiva structure, 60 feet (18 m) in diameter and over 12 feet (3.5 m) deep. It was probably built in the eleventh century AD. Kivas are Pueblo buildings, usually circular, that are typically set into the ground and covered over, access being by ladder through an opening in the top. They were, and are, places of ritual. Casa Rinconada is set to the four cardinal directions, and in the northeastern wall is a distinctive opening or window through which the rising midsummer sun shines. Astronomer Michael Zeilik has expressed doubts (*Archaeoastronomy VII,* 1984) about the authenticity of the event, and it seems impossible now to be sure if the effect was deliberate or a chance occurrence. But it is suggestive, for there is a dramatic instance of astronomical practice at Chaco (see below), and across the canyon from Casa Rinconada is the largest prehistoric ruin in the United States – Pueblo Bonito. This was a great religious

*Plate 19. The window or aperture at Casa Rinconada which allows in the beams of the rising midsummer sun*

complex of rooms and kivas. Anthropologist J.E. Reyman has found that two corner windows in the surviving third floor rooms appear to align to winter solstice sunrise.[17] The complex also has a dividing wall that runs true north-south.

There are other Anasazi 'sun temples': at Hovenweep, Arizona, for instance, or Mesa Verde, Colorado.

Vestigial evidence survives suggesting astronomical activities at Cahokia, southern Illinois, the greatest complex of ancient Amerindian earthworks. Over a hundred mounds comprise the site of Cahokia, the largest of which is Monks Mound, which rivals Britain's Silbury Hill. Most of the mounds and plazas are rectangular and oriented to the cardinal directions. Archaeologist Warren L. Wittry has revealed post holes in the complex that seem to be part of a circle. There is a central pit too. Wittry feels that giant posts were placed in a ring, a 'Sun Circle', and that a sun priest watched astronomical events from the centre. Wittry reconstructed some posts and confirmed by direct observation from the circle's centre that one post indicates equinox sunrise over Monks Mound, and others mark the midsummer and midwinter sunrises.

Far to the south, in Mesoamerica, we have the archaeological remnants of a variety of ancient Amerindian cultures, some of

*Plate 19 (a). Pueblo Bonito – America's largest prehistoric ruin*

*Plate 19 (b). Part of the circle of wooden posts nicknamed 'Woodhenge' at the ancient Indian site of Cahokia, USA. Viewed from the central post, the equinoxial sun would rise from behind Monks Mound (the flat-topped mound in the distance), where the king or chief lived. The post marked in white, right of centre, denotes the exact alignment from the central post. The existing posts are a reconstruction*

which indicate astronomical practice. One of the oldest examples comes from the ruins of Alta Vista, built about AD 400 by the Chalchihuite culture, near present-day Zacatecas, Mexico. An observer at the 'Temple of the Sun' at Alta Vista sees the sun at the equinoxes rise over Picacho Peak, over nine miles (15 km) from the ruins. On Cerro El Chapin, a high plateau some six miles (10 km) to the south, there is a flat rock at the summit on which is pecked a double circle quartered by intersecting lines. Someone situated here will see the midsummer sun rise over Picacho Peak.

This pecked cross symbol is found elsewhere, notably 400 miles (650 km) south of Alta Vista at Teotihuacán, a great city of the first millennium AD, comprising an eight-square-mile area laid out in a grid pattern of temples, squares, houses and enclosures. The cross symbol is found on surrounding rock surfaces and in the floors of buildings. Aveni informs:

> Fifteen pecked cross markers are found in the valley of Teotihuacán, northeast of modern Mexico City. A pair of them are so situated that they could have been used to orient the rectangular grid plan of the ancient city by astronomical alignment, most probably with the setting point of the Pleiades star group.[18]

Even the river was diverted and channelled to fit in with the city grid.

Venus was a major player in the cosmology of the central American Indians. This seems well shown in the Caracol, a cylindrical tower on a two-tiered rectangular platform built around AD 1000 at Chichén Itzá, a Maya ceremonial centre with later Toltec influence, in Yucatán, Mexico. Parts of the upper segment of the original tower have crumbled away in such a fashion as to give a false impression of a domed structure much like a modern observatory. Aveni, Hartung and Sharon Gibbs found that the alignment of horizontal shafts that feed into a sealed chamber at the top of the tower 'nearly perfectly' indicate the extreme northerly and southerly setting points of Venus. (We know the Mayans, were very interested in Venus, as surviving pre-Columbian codices, painted on long strips of deerskin or bark paper, display Venus information.) Additionally, a diagonal of the slightly asymmetrical platform gives summer solstice sunrise in one direction and winter solstice sunset in the other.[19,20]

Another Maya site in Yucatán is Uxmal. It is a harmonious consortium of open plazas with elevated buildings and tall, massive pyramids. Construction began around AD 700 and continued for approximately three centuries. The precise geometric layout of

Uxmal is oriented nine degrees east of north, one of a family of axial alignments the purposes of which are unknown. Aveni has discovered several astronomical sightlines between Uxmal's buildings, giving the last gleam of midsummer sunset, the due west and south directions, and the setting point of Venus at its southerly extreme in AD 750. A line to a building nicknamed 'The Palace of the Governor' to a skyline mound three miles (5 km) away was noted by Horst Hartung to indicate the rising point of Venus at southerly extreme in AD 750. Aveni later showed that the mound was in fact part of the ruins of another site, Nohpat. American astronomer E.C. Krupp notes that 'some archaeologists have argued that some Maya sites were arranged to an overall geometric plan. The line between Uxmal and Nohpat may suggest that the Maya also incorporated cosmic phenomena into the interrelations of their ceremonial centres.'[21]

In South America the Incas were an advanced culture using astronomy, as we have noted above. Another example is at the famous high Andean city of Machu Picchu where one of the buildings, the Torreon, has windows that are oriented to the rising of the Pleiades and Collca (the tail of Scorpius). Both these star groupings have seasonal and directional significance to the Quechua-speaking Andean Indians. The 'Pleiades window' could also have accurately given the June solstice, using the effect of shadow and light on an altar stone. We will be returning to the Inca again, when discussing geomancy.

Throughout this chapter we have been primarily looking at sites as places of observation, whether or not such activity was for ceremonial or scientific purpose, but there is another way ancient peoples incorporated astronomical phenomena at their sacred places. They 'brought in' the light, the power of sun, moon and perhaps planets, into the sacred space. They used lightbeams and shadows for calendrical and ritual purposes, and, it would seem, for sheer spectacular, ceremonial effect – as the Castlerigg shadow path and Silbury double sunrise seem to demonstrate.

This aspect of ancient astronomical usage is clearly expressed in the shamanic caves of the Californian Chumash Indians. These people had an astronomer-astrologer priest, an *'alchuklash*, who sun watched and kept the calendar. At the winter solstice he took the hallucinogen *Datura* (jimson weed). He would retire to a cave shrine which allowed in narrow sunbeams, which sometimes interacted with wall paintings in these places (see Chapter 10). The effect of this on the shaman's altered state of consciousness must have been profound. It may have been that at the great ritual kiva of Casa Rinconada at Chaco, calendrically significant sunbeams entering the darkened interior were used in conjunction with psychoactive substances to produce profound spiritual experience. Because of its own attitudes, our culture has difficulty appreciating that to other peoples hallucinogens had the status of sacraments.

Other examples of sites subject to astronomical effects should include Long Meg and her Daughters, a large stone circle and an outlier (Long Meg) also in Cumbria in northwest England. At midwinter sunset, John Glover observed that the shadow of Long Meg is thrown across the vast circle, so that the tip of the shadow just touches the opposite side of the stone ring.[22] R.D.Y. Perrett later showed that at the equinoxes Long Meg's shadow provided true tangents to the circle. Shadow positions at Stonehenge have been calculated by astronomer Gerard Vaucouleurs. He found that at midwinter noon the shadow of the southernmost lintel of the sarsen circle would have fallen precisely on the centre of the monument. In addition, it seems probable that at midsummer the shadows of the lintels would fall on the bluestone circle within the sarsen ring.[23]

The stepped pyramid known as the Castillo at Chichén Itzá gives a remarkable display at sunset on the equinoxes: the jagged shadow of the stepped corner is thrown onto the balustrade of the

*Plate 20. The northwest quadrant of the Daughters stone circle, with the outlying pillar, Long Meg, in the distance*

*Plate 21. Fajada Butte, Chaco Canyon*

pyramid's northern staircase, so that it looks as if a serpent is wriggling down from the top of the pyramid. The illusion is completed by a stone serpent head at the bottom of the balustrade to which the shadow connects. Fajada Butte, at the southern entrance to Chaco Canyon, has a ledge near its top where three stone slabs are leaning. This grouping allows slits of sunlight to be thrown on the otherwise shaded rock wall behind them where two spiral carvings are located. Artist Anna Sofaer discovered that at midsummer noon a 'dagger' of sunlight cleaves down through the middle of the larger spiral, and at midwinter two sun daggers exactly frame the petroglyph. At the equinoxes, a slit of light precisely divides the large spiral's turns, while another pierces the centre of the smaller carving.

At Maes Howe, a chambered mound on Orkney Mainland dated to the third millennium BC, the midwinter setting sun sends its last rays like golden fire down the entrance passage to illuminate the dark inner sanctum. The line of the passage extended outwards across country encounters a tall standing stone called Barnhouse. This in turn stands in another alignment involving another monolith, the Watchstone, and the centre of the Ring of Brogar. Here is a clear example of astronomical orientations and landscape lines interrelating.

There may have been moon effects at some sites: Aubrey Burl

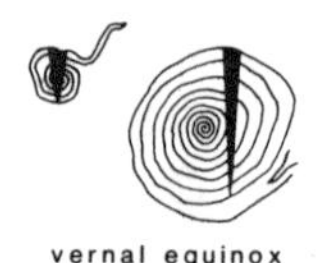

*Figure 32. The relationship of the 'sun daggers' to the petroglyphs on Fajada Butte at key times of the year (courtesy E.C. Krupp, Griffith Observatory)*

*Plate 22. Light from the setting midwinter sun entering the passage of Maes Howe, Orkney (courtesy Charles Tait)*

has suggested that recumbent stone circles in northeastern Scotland may have been roughly aligned to the moon.[24,25,26] A recumbent circle has a large, altar-like stone lying within the circumference of uprights, often with a perfectly horizontal upper surface. In some cases, it seems, a Major Standstill southerly moon might appear to roll across the top of recumbent stones at certain circles when viewed from inside the ring. At Gavrinis in Brittany, both sun and moon seem to have been involved. The entrance passage there accommodates one alignment to midwinter sunrise and another to Major Standstill southern moonrise. In the side of the passage is a quartz block, at the intersection of these lines. It is the only undecorated stone surface in the place, and Burl suggests that it 'may have been illuminated by the light of the rising sun and moon.'[27]

But perhaps the most magnificent examples of lightbeam and shadow effects are to be found at the giant Irish chambered mound of Newgrange and other Irish Neolithic sites. Newgrange is situated in a bend in the Boyne river some 30 miles (48 km) north of Dublin, along with its attendant great mounds Knowth and Dowth and a variety of lesser monuments. In earliest recorded myth it was the *Bru na Boinne,* the palace by the Boyne. The pre-Celtic Lords of Light dwelt there. Rumours began to circulate from

*Plate 23. The recumbent stone in the Midmar Kirk circle, Aberdeenshire. A fairly modern churchyard has been established around the monument*

*Plate 24. Looking out along the entrance passage at Gavrinis, Brittany*

at least the nineteenth century that on a special day sunlight entered what was then the tumbledown state of Newgrange. There were eyewitness claims from local people. In the 1909 edition of *Stonehenge,* Lockyer remarked that Newgrange was oriented to the winter solstice, and in *The Fairy Faith in Celtic Countries* (1912) the folklorist W.Y. Evans Wentz also commented that Newgrange was astronomically aligned. These tales and observations coalesced into a background murmur, a legend, by 1960. But Glyn Daniel dismissed it then as 'the jumble of nonsense and wishful thinking.' Archaeological excavations began at the site in the 1960s under the directorship of Michael J. O'Kelly. As far as archaeologists were concerned it was simply a big tomb. But O'Kelly found a curious rectangular opening, a 'roof box', above the entrance to the passage that led into the mound. This had been partially exposed as early as 1837. O'Kelly had a suspicion that the roof box might be connected with the tradition of the sun entering the mound, and at the winter solstice of 1969 he became the first archaeologist to witness the sunbeam enter Newgrange. Even when O'Kelly reported the event, there was stubborn resistance to it, with claims of 'chance effect' being bandied about.

All in all, the astronomy at Newgrange was dealt with shamefully by archaeology. The modern European mindset came face to face with an element from its own prehistory, and reacted like those people who cannot remember their dreams so swear they do not dream.

Early in 1980, Irish readers of *The Ley Hunter* wrote telling me of rumours of astronomical findings being made at Irish mounds by a man called Martin Brennan and his colleagues. As a result, a group of friends and I visited Brennan in Ireland in May 1980. In a whirlwind three days, Brennan introduced us to his colleagues, including his closest co-worker Jack Roberts, and whisked us around various megalithic sites including the cairns on the Loughcrew Hills and Newgrange itself. We drove, explored and talked night and day. We did not stop for sleep. A fantastic tale of discovery unravelled, a story now told in Brennan's two books.[28,29]

Brennan, a first generation American of Irish parents, has a visual arts background. Searching the world for spiritual meaning, he had arrived in Ireland in 1970. He was fascinated by the rich legacy of Neolithic rock art to be found around and in the Irish chambered mounds. No one understood it, and Brennan set about trying to decipher it, living in the Boyne valley much of the time. By 1976 he was working full time on the enigma, analysing and documenting the rock carvings. He visited Newgrange at a num-

*Plate 25. Martin Brennan measuring Kerbstone 52 at Newgrange. Note the broad vertical groove in the centre of the stone, which Brennan believes indicates the midwinter sunrise alignment*

ber of winter solstice periods. Eventually 'all the needles were pointing' to the carvings as being sundials and images of sun, moon and celestial motion. He was sure the sunbeams and the rock imagery somehow interacted. He also recalled how Lockyer had suggested sunbeams had penetrated deep into the Egyptian temples. He suspected that Irish chambered mounds, not just Newgrange, had been built to accept sunbeams at various key dates of the year, and that these would mark their passage over the interior rock carvings. In effect, the sunlight was the software operating the megalithic hardware. He and Jack had no option but to test the ideas directly in the field. They checked Cairn T, a chambered and carved cairn on top of one of the Loughcrew Hills 30 miles (48 km) inland from Newgrange. Over dawns approaching the spring equinox in 1980, they saw dazzling golden sunlight spear into the mound. The shape and angle of the entrance passage caused the sunlight to cast a fairly regular rectangular patch on the inner walls of the passage and chamber, sweeping across the images carved there:

> What impressed us most was the careful and delicate modelling of the light beams by the huge stones forming the passage and chamber and how the shape of the beam conformed to the patterns engraved on the stone. For the first time we were seeing the signs and symbols in the context in which the artist had meant them to be seen. Suddenly markings that had appeared to be random and haphazard became part of an intricately structured system that derived its meaning from the solar event we were witnessing.[30]

On the day of the equinox, the rectangle of sunlight reached its furthest point into the chamber, framing an eight-petalled carving on the rear stone. The sun framed its own symbol which was also that of the ancient eight-division solar year. On its journey into and out of the mound, the shape of sunlight crossed and framed a sequence of carvings.

Brennan's team of archaeoastronomical guerrillas went on to make more discoveries, with sunbeam (and some moonbeam) events being noted at a number of chambered mounds. Some exquisitely engineered Neolithic light shows were observed.

Newgrange is a huge mound. Its entrance passage is almost 70 feet (21 m) long and leads into a high, corbelled stone chamber which has three subsidiary cells. A number of the interior stone surfaces have carvings. There is a retaining wall on the outside of the mound, and either side of the entrance is faced in white quartz. Running around the perimeter of the mound are 97 kerbstones,

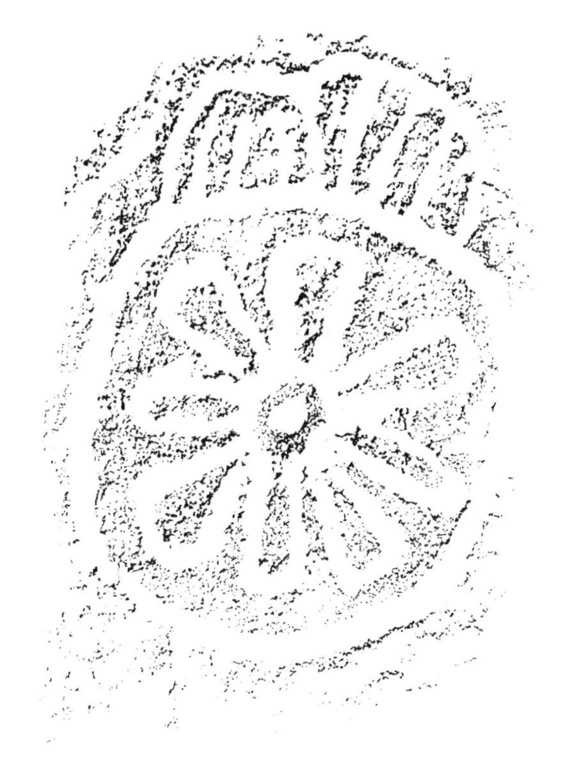

*Figure 33. The eight-rayed sun symbol carving in Cairn T (from rubbing)*

only three of which are fully carved. The entrance is visually (but not physically) blocked by a large entrance stone (Figure 34). This has a vertical groove, with left-hand spirals to the left, and right-hand spirals to the right. Encircling the entire mound is a ring of standing stones. The whole site is now dated to the early fourth millennium BC. It is one of the earliest surviving pieces of architecture, old before the pyramids of Egypt were built.

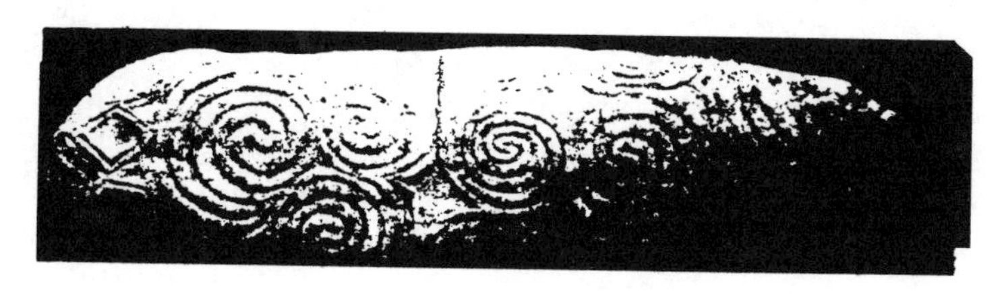

*Figure 34. The entrance stone at Newgrange*

Brennan suddenly realised that the vertical groove on the entrance stone was probably the Neolithic glyph indicating the midwinter lightbeam alignment (a point independently noted by Michell some years earlier). Brennan found that kerbstone 52, on the diametrically opposite side of the mound, thus on the alignment, also had an even more pronounced vertical mark as a major feature. It was as if a Rosetta Stone had been found, and the Irish rock carvings could start to be deciphered. While the rising midwinter sun is shining its beam into Newgrange, Brennan discovered, a standing stone in the surrounding circle is throwing a shadow which points like a finger on the vertical groove of the entrance stone. Another stone in the circle also casts a finger of shadow onto carvings on kerbstone 93 near the entrance. Light enters the passageway directly, but the roof box allows a finely sculpted lightbeam to reach deep into the back of the central chamber, lighting up the stones like living gold. This fine lightbeam strikes the base of the chamber's rear stone at the furthest point of its journey into the mound. Carvings in the passage interact with the lightbeam, and may encode information. Brennan feels that great stone bowls found in Newgrange were not for the remains of the dead as archaeologists suppose, but in fact contained water to act as reflective surfaces designed to interact with the sunbeam.

*Plate 26. Part of the ring of standing stones surrounding Newgrange*

*Figure 35. Sketch of the double spiral shape that American artist Charles Ross ended up with when he traced the passage of the sun throughout the year by photographing the trace of its burn mark on planks of wood*

The spirals on the Newgrange entrance stone (and elsewhere) almost certainly communicate the idea of solar motion, or, more accurately, the interaction of the relative positions of Earth and sun through a whole Earth orbit. The spiral is appropriate to represent this, as American artist Charles Ross discovered in the early 1970s. He set up a lens to focus the sun's rays in order to burn a track across a plank during the course of a day. He did this each day for a year. He noted that the curve of the path gradually changed. 'We took photos of the burns and placed them end to end following their curvature to see what a year's worth looked like,' he said. 'The sum of days generated a double spiral.'[31]

Newgrange receives the sunrise lightbeam on midwinter morning, and the nearby great mound of Dowth receives the sunset lightbeam that same day. The sun penetrates to the backstone of Dowth's chamber, its beam narrowed to focus on that stone. The brilliant light on this stone is reflected onto a stone carved with sun symbols in a side recess of the chamber. The stone seems angled to achieve this effect.

The third great mound in the bend in the Boyne is Knowth. It is the largest of its kind, covering an acre of ground. It has two passages, facing east and west, and is an equinoctial site. The entrance stones at both passage mouths have vertical grooves – the Neolithic glyph for alignment. Two upright stones outside the west entrance throw shadows on the entrance stone's vertical line and on the carvings on an adjacent kerbstone. The setting equinoctial sun sends a narrow beam deep into the western passage, longer than even the Newgrange sunbeam. Brennan considers it 'one of the great wonders of the Neolithic world.'

Brennan's work is one of the heroic endeavours of modern archaeoastronomy, though it has been largely shunned by archaeology in general. In 1989, an astronomer at the Dublin Institute for Advanced Studies with the synchronistic name of Tom Ray provided statistical proof that the midwinter ray of sunlight at Newgrange occurred by design and not by chance.[32] No mention was made of Brennan's work, at least not in the preliminary report I have seen. But, it is nice to know that the sunbeam is now officially approved. The spirits of Newgrange's Lords of Light can feel appeased, and know their living, working, message has bridged the ages.

It is interesting to note that Brennan, Glover, Sofaer (and myself for that matter) are visual artists. This is not accidental in my view. It took the kind of cognition operative in the visually-oriented mind for their sort of discoveries to have been made. It is unlikely that archaeologists, with the characteristics of the analytical mind-set that is usually found in archaeology, would have initiated the kind of observations of those in Ireland, Cumbria, Chaco Canyon or Silbury Hill (though now alerted they may go on to do so). Many kinds of description are needed.

In conclusion, then, it is unlikely that astronomy was used at ancient sites as a scientific enterprise in its own right, for science in that sense is a construct of the modern mind, as I have argued. But astronomy was undoubtedly practised, and, equally surely, it was an element of the spiritual worldview of the archaic societies involved. Indeed, the separation of 'scientific' and 'religious' is almost certainly erroneous in any case, as Heggie points out, '. . . this whole argument is misguided. It may be that the distinction between "scientific" and "mystic" is one which would have seemed perplexing to the megalith-builders, as it might have done to Kepler.'[33] Archaeoastronomy also makes it clear that certain kinds of sacred sites of antiquity have to be seen in association with the sky and the surrounding landscape. The word for that wholeness is geomancy.

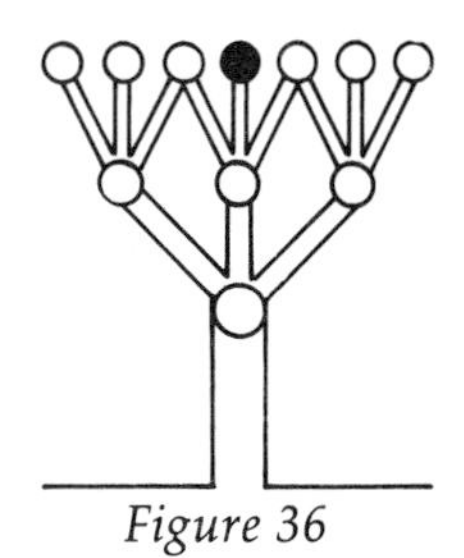
Figure 36

CHAPTER 5

# SACRED GEOMETRY

## Demonstration

Professor Thom found that the groundplan of Castlerigg formed a flattened circle that fell into his 'Type A' category. He marvelled that four of the seven solar or lunar declinations at the site 'are defined by the Type A geometry.'[1] This was especially remarkable in mountainous country, with its variable horizon heights. He felt that any engineer wishing to replicate the feat today would require 'a large group of surveyors working for an indefinite time fully equipped with modern instruments.'

Architect and geometer Keith Critchlow has studied Castlerigg's groundplan geometry and commented, 'The builders of Castlerigg found a site with a convenient horizon for measuring the exact sun-setting axis of midsummer day. This was the key axis . . .'[2] Working from what he knew about ancient principles of temple building, he suggested that another major astronomical line at Castlerigg, that of the most southerly moonrise, was used as a second foundation axis for the groundplan. Using these solar and lunar axes the circle builders generated interlocking circles and from them derived the rest of the groundplan geometry. The figure on page 128 shows these stages.

## Discussion

In the previous chapter we noted that during the foundation ceremony for an Egyptian temple a cord was used for aligning the astronomical axis. The cord's other function was to lay out the groundplan geometry of the temple. The cord used would have 12 knots forming 13 equal divisions. By this simple means a right angle could be arrived at, by arranging the cord into a triangle with four divisions on one side, three on another and five on the third and longest side (the hypoteneuse) opposite the right angle. This, of course, produces the famous 'Pythagorean' 3:4:5 right-angled

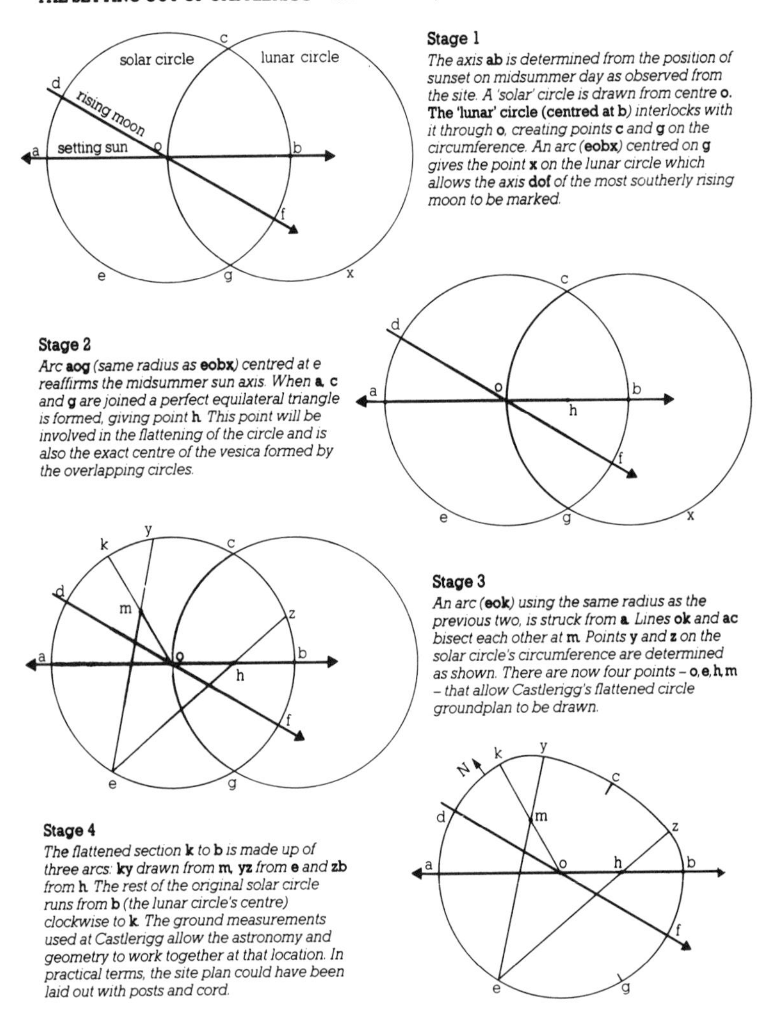


*Figure 37. (After Keith Critchlow. Courtesy Eddison Sadd Editions)*

triangle. Pythagoras was a sixth-century BC Greek, and the reason his name has become attached to this much older piece of geometrical knowledge is simply because the ancient Greeks absorbed much learning from the earlier Egyptian civilisation. As John Michell states, it was:

> the chief object of Pythagoras and his school to reconstitute and reinvigorate the ancient numerical code and the philosophy

> associated with it . . . it becomes evident from current research that the same numerical canon was once possessed by civilisations world-wide.[3]

The ability to lay out geometrical figures was important to the Egyptians not only for temple groundplans but also for re-establishing boundaries that were destroyed each year by the Nile flood. The literal meaning of geometry is thus 'Earth measurement' (geo-metry), which can come as a surprise to those who were bored by apparently abstract lines and theorems on the yellowing pages of school books.

Sacred or canonical geometry is not some obscure invention of the human mind, but an extrapolation by it of the implied patterns in nature that frame the entry of energy into our space-time dimension. The formation of matter ('dense energy') and the natural motions of the universe, from molecular vibration through the growth of organic forms to the spin and motion of planets, stars and galaxies, are all governed by geometrical configurations of force. One can dissect a plant or a planet and not find the Maker's blueprint anywhere in sight, of course: it is inherent. An example of this inherent nature was provided by Schwaller de Lubicz – the axis of a spinning sphere. We can think of the characteristics of the axis, measure its properties and location, yet it does not exist as an objective thing. A drawing of a figure of sacred geometry is thus like a still frame from a movie – a film called 'Creation'. A frozen moment in the endless process of becoming. A thought from the mind of God.

Because sacred geometry is the geometry of nature, it was obviously of importance to temple builders, who wished to encode into their structures the ratios of creation, to mirror the universe, to create a microcosm of the macrocosm; 'as above, so below.' In such a way, the temple, the sacred place, could become a doorway into the workings of nature in both the outer world of matter and the inner world of consciousness. An interface between human being and manifest nature. A point of integration. The gods could be expressed by number, and represented the forces at work in the universe, inner and outer.

This is not the place to offer a treatise on sacred geometry, but we can glimpse a few of its facets, and note its occurrence in a very brief selection of sites.

The nature of sacred geometry is such that only straightedge and compass are required to manifest it; it is to do with ratio and proportion, not quantitative measurement by number. Number is an expression of geometry, and is another mode of thinking about the ratios and proportions. We use words and numbers today, and they form the bases of our thinking processes, but the way we think of number is not the magical manner or arcane tradition. As Robert Lawlor puts it:

> Modern thought has difficult access to the concept of the archetypal because European languages require that verbs or action words be associated with nouns. We therefore have no linguistic forms with which to image a process or activity that has no material carrier.[4]

Let us take the prime, fundamental geometrical figures, the circle and square, and observe how other figures important in sacred geometry can be derived from them, and the importance of the interaction between them.

The circle is the image of wholeness. Its circumference has no beginning or end. The symbol of eternity. Drawing the circle is the first action of creating order out of chaos. The ratio between the diameter and the circumference of a circle is referred to by the Greek letter $\pi$, *pi*. So, for example, if we assign the value 1 to a circle's diameter, its circumference is 3.141593. The area of a circle is found by multiplying the square of the radius by $\pi$ or by multiplying the radius by half the circumference. A fractional expression of $\pi$ is $^{22}/_{7}$, which yields the marginally less exact value of 3.14287. We have here an immediate example of how the relationships in geometry, explicit and clear as visual statements, cannot be expressed in whole numbers. Typical of the modern mindset, the numerical attempts to categorise such ratios are referred to as 'irrational' numbers.

If the circle represents the heavens, then the square represents the Earth. It symbolises matter, created form. The relationship of the diagonal of a square to its side provides another 'irrational' number: the diagonal of a square with side 1 will have the value 1:4142, which is the square root of two ($\sqrt{2}$). When an arc is taken from this, allowing the square to be extended in one direction, a root two rectangle is formed. The diagonal of this in turn produces a root three rectangle, and so on for a series of 'root rectangles' (Figure 38). The square is essentially a 'root 1 rectangle'. Nigel Pennick comments that although:

> . . . the sides of these rectangles are not measurable in terms of number, the Greeks said that such lines were not really irrational because they were measurable in terms of the squares produced from them. Measurability in terms of square area instead of length was the great secret of ancient Greek sacred geometry. The famous theorem of Pythagoras, known to every schoolchild, is

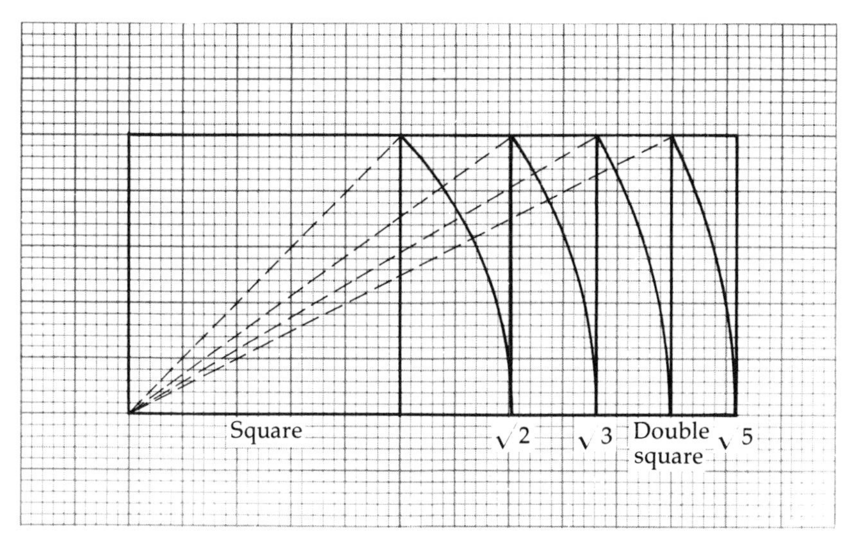


*Figure 38.*

understandable only in terms of square measure. For instance, the relationship between the end and side of a √5 rectangle is exactly one fifth of the area of a square constructed on its side. Such rectangles possess a property which enables them to be divided into many smaller shapes which are also measurable parts of the whole.

This brings us to another fundamental factor in the design of sacred architecture: proportion, and its Siamese twin, commensurability.[5]

The √4 rectangle is a double square. In Figure 38 we can see that the diagonal of this allows it to be extended to a √5 rectangle, which has a direct relationship with the Golden Section or Mean, one of the magic keys of sacred geometry. This relationship can be demonstrated as in Figure 39. The semi-diagonal OC of square ABCD is taken as the radius of an arc swung from O which allows AD to be extended to H, from which golden rectangle ABGH is formed. Rectangle DCGH also is in the golden proportion. If the radius OC is swung the other way, to E, rectangle EFGH is a √5 rectangle.

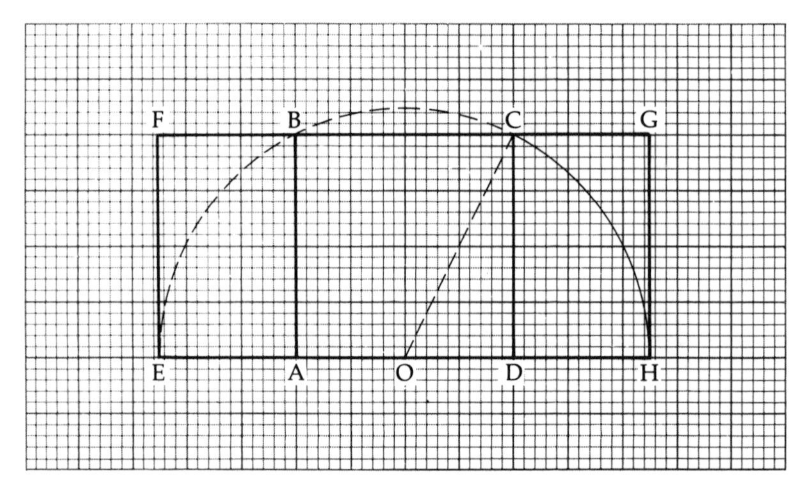


*Figure 39.*

The golden proportion in rectangle ABGH is expressed in the relationship of its length to its width. Numerically, this ratio is 1.618 and is referred to by the Greek letter ∅, *phi*. The Golden Section is shown on the line AH where it is cut at D. Phi is expressed by the ratio of DH to AD. Furthermore, DH is to AD what AD is to AH – that is, the shorter length is to the longer, as the longer is to the whole line. Proportionally, the ratio works out at about 8:13. It has been claimed that in tests where large groups of people have been asked to pleasingly divide a line at any point but its centre, most divided the line intuitively at or around the golden cut. Lawlor reminds us of Gregory Bateson's phrase 'the differences that make the difference':

> A ratio then constitutes a measure of a difference, a difference to which at least one of our sensory faculties can respond . . . a ratio . . . signals one of the most basic processes of intelligence in that it symbolizes a comparison between two things . . .[6]

A golden rectangle has the property that a square taken from it leaves a smaller golden rectangle, and this process can be repeated, theoretically, *ad infinitum* (Figure 40). A spiral can be produced from this, and is known as a logarithmic or growth spiral. It is the inherent pattern in many examples of growth (Figure 41). Other growth spirals can also be generated by golden triangles and root rectangles.

The $\sqrt{5}$ rectangle shows the relationship of the Golden Section to pentagonal geometry. Indeed, a pentagon can be produced from the geometry shown in Figure 39 which produced the golden and

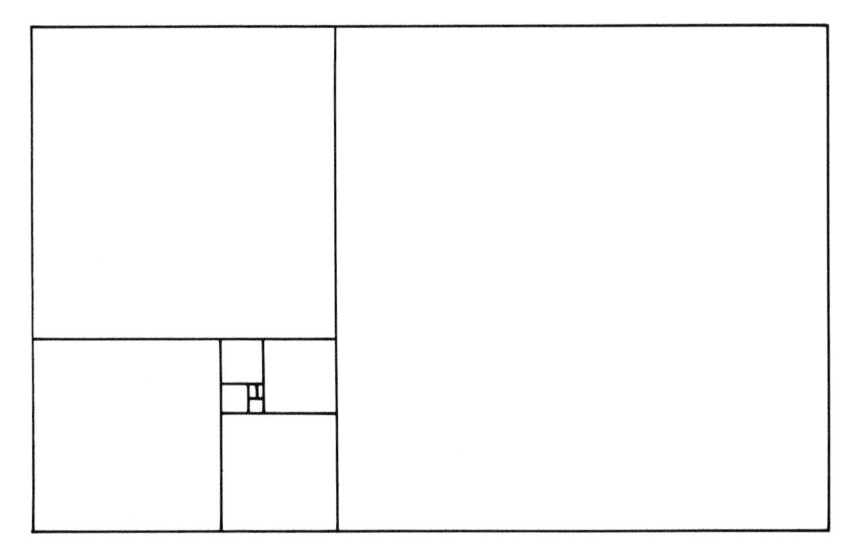

*Figure 40.*

$\sqrt{5}$ rectangles. In Figure 42, use A as centre with radius set at AH. Swing arc HJ. Keep compasses set and use D as centre producing arc EJ. Using A and D as centres with radius AB swing arcs to intersect EJ at K and HJ at L. Points A, K, J, L and D are equidistant. Connect with straight lines to produce a pentagon. It is of course easy from this to create a pentagram using just straight lines (Figure 43).

Pentagonal geometry is present in many aspects of nature. The human frame relates to the Golden Mean and pentagonal geometry (Figure 44), more humbly in a wayside flower (Plate 27), or in the structure of a snowflake. A temple based on Golden Mean and pentagonal geometry will therefore automatically integrate the human being with the cosmos. In this way we can see how sacred

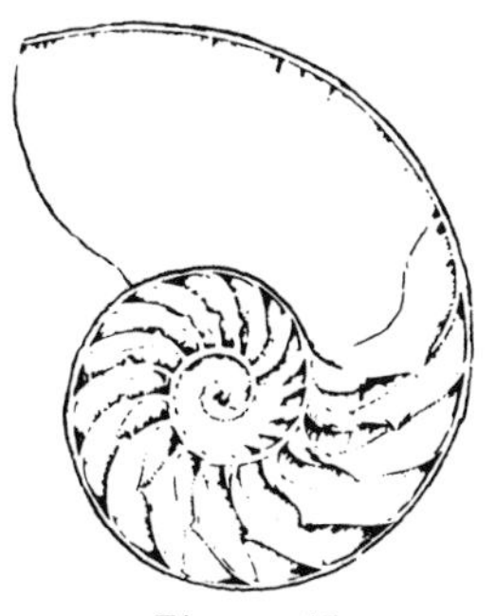

*Figure 41.*

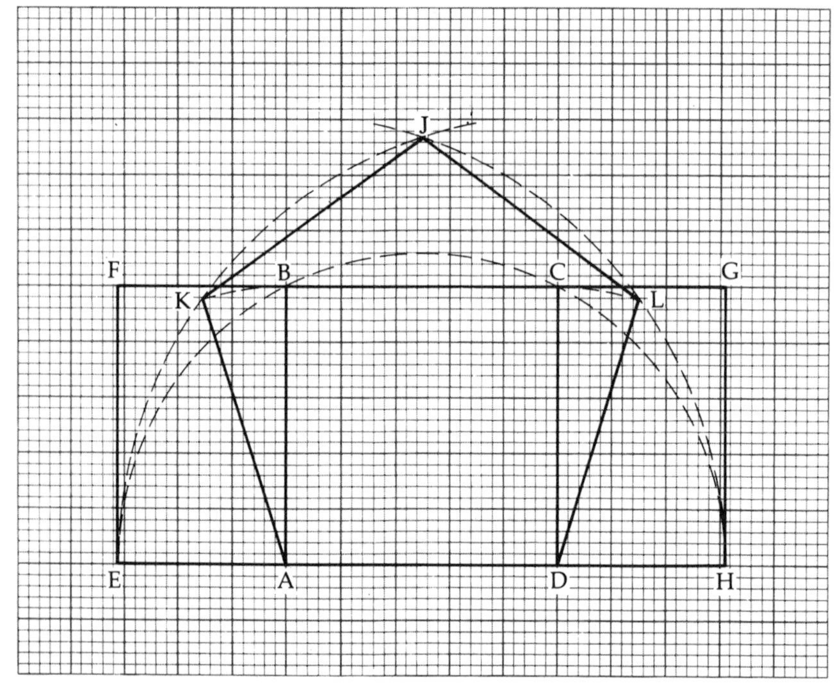


*Figure 42.*

geometry is a 'systems' methodology. The numerical analogue of the golden proportion is the Fibonacci Series, brought to European attention from Arabic sources by Fibonacci around the beginning of the thirteenth century AD. This series operates by each number being the sum of the two preceding ones, hence: 1,2,3,5,8,13,21,34,55, and so on. This relationship is likewise found expressed by nature in growth patterns and forms, the famous example being the distribution of seeds on the head of a sunflower.

Lawlor refers to 'the web of modulated relationships which surround the Golden Division', and we have touched on just some of them here.

A similar web of relationships derives from the circle in the form of the *vesica piscis* (vessel of the fish), produced by two equal, overlapping circles, the circumference of one passing through the centre of the other. Here we have the foundation figure of Castlerigg as divined by Critchlow (above). Michell considers the *vesica piscis* 'the matrix figure of sacred geometry'. Indeed, this 'mysterious figure' as William Stirling called it has esoteric associations with the womb, the vulva, and the Mother Goddess. (The

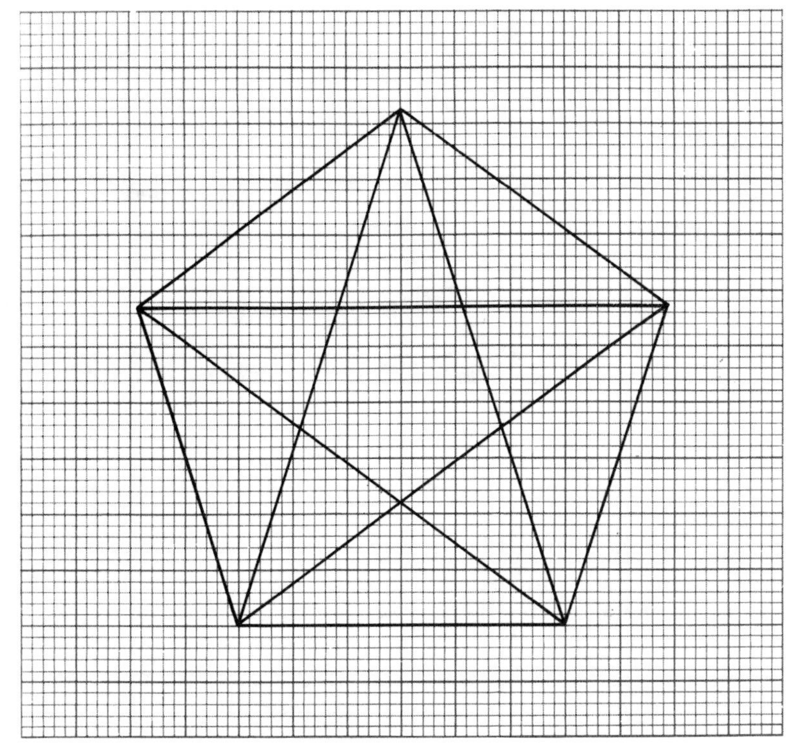

*Figure 43.*

*vesica* is likewise associated with the Blessed Virgin – the Christianised version of the Goddess.)

Figure 45 shows the vesica formed from the two circles. Its longer axis has a $\sqrt{3}$ relationship to the shorter one (1:1.732), so a square drawn on the longer axis would have three times the area of one drawn on the shorter. The rectangle containing the vesica is

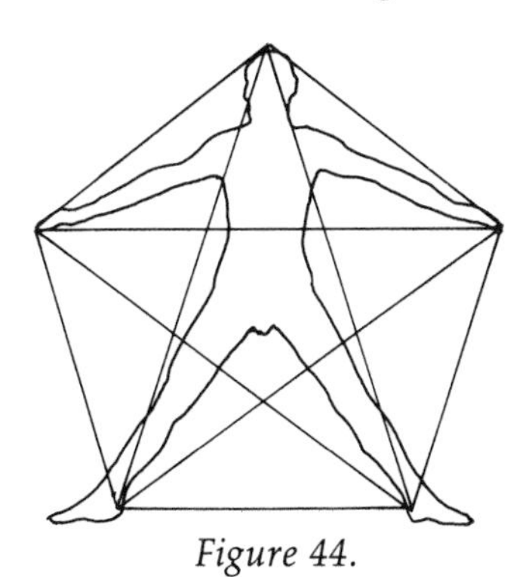

*Figure 44.*

*Plate 27.*

thus a $\sqrt{3}$ rectangle. The rhombus within the vesica is formed from two equilateral triangles sharing the common base of the shorter axis.

The *vesica piscis* is particularly relevant to Christian esotericism, and it became the symbol of the early Christians in the catacombs, later becoming an essential part of the sacred geometry in Christian architecture. It is fish-shaped, the esoteric name for Christ was Jesus the Fish, and the Christian era coincided with the Zodiacal Age of Pisces. Hence we can find the figure wrought in iron on the lid of Chalice Well at Glastonbury.

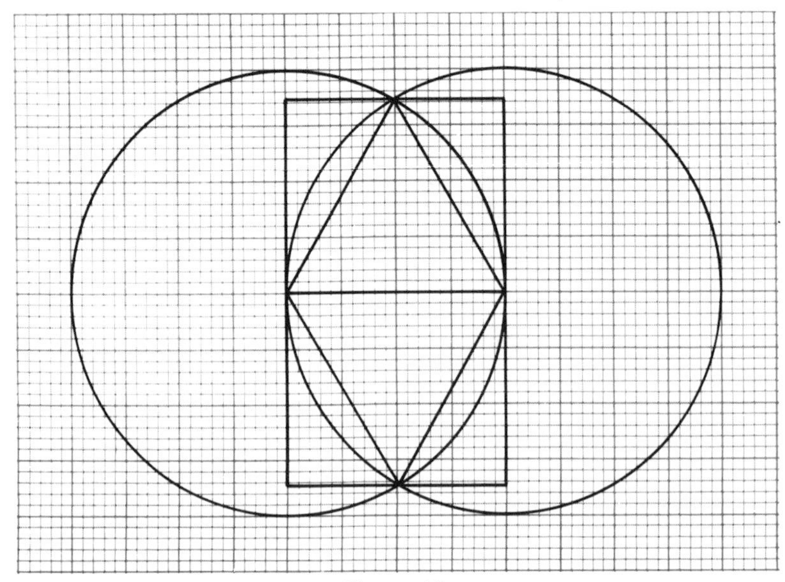

*Figure 45.*

*Plate 28. The wrought-iron* vesica piscis *on the lid of Chalice Well, Glastonbury*

The vesica generates the hexagon and six-fold geometry. In Figure 46, take A as centre for an arc with radius AD cutting the circle at E; repeat with C as centre cutting the circle at G. Connect points G, C, D, A, E, F to form the hexagon.

Probably the best known natural hexagonal structure is the honeycomb of the bee. In natural mechanics, it manifests in the boiling and mixing actions of liquids – in physics, hexagonal patterns forming in the diffusion of liquids were called 'Bénard cells'. Nigel Pennick notes that in his work as a marine biologist he found that the body of the marine algae *Pyramimonas virginica* was covered with hexagonal structures 'smaller than the wavelength of visible light'.[7]

By joining the alternate vertices (corners) of the hexagon, a 'Solomon's Seal' or hexagram can be formed. We can see that this glyph of equilateral triangles interpenetrating one another, adopted as its sacred symbol by Judaism, is in fact a precis of whole systems of sacred geometry and hidden natural structure. The triangles symbolise the fusion of opposites, of air and Earth, of the masculine and feminine principles of the universe (yang and yin in ancient Chinese philosophy). These are all examples of the way sacred geometry can communicate to esoteric scholars.

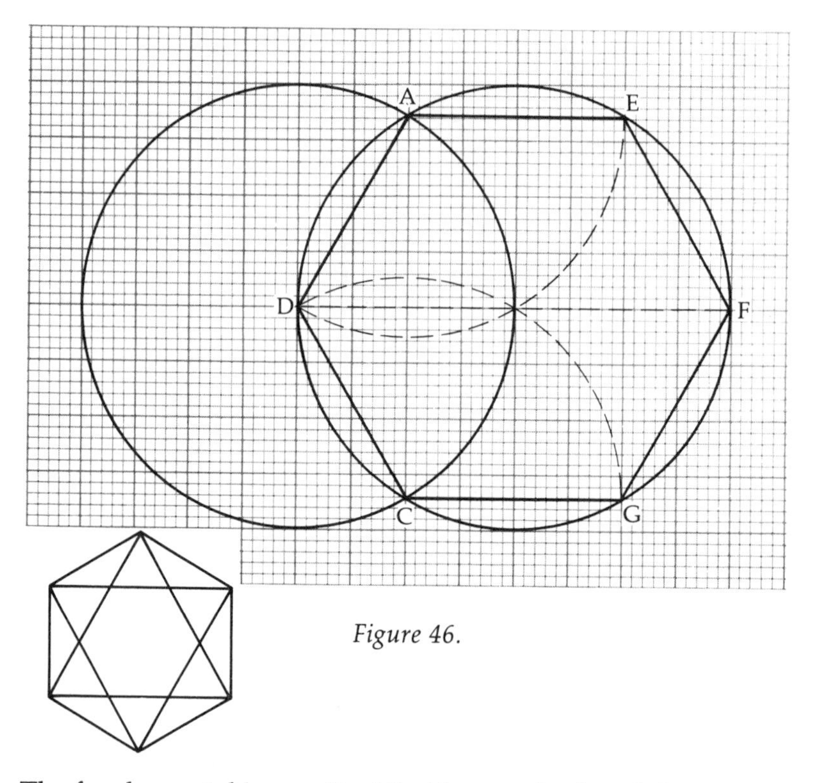


*Figure 46.*

The fundamental 'opposites' that have to be fused, however, are the circle and the square. This is achieved by a process called 'squaring the circle', one of the great acts of the ancient philosophers. In this, a square and a circle of either equal perimeter/circumference or equal area are combined in a single figure by compass and straightedge. There are a number of ways it can be achieved. One is shown by John Michell in *The Dimensions of Paradise*, using the 22/7 value for pi (Figure 47). A 3:4:5 triangle is produced initially, and a square is drawn on its shortest side. Another, reciprocal triangle is formed on the opposite side of the square. Based on the units employed in the original triangle, this gives a total base line of 11 units. A square is drawn on this line. A circle is struck from the centre of this larger square, with a radius extending to the centre of the smaller square. The circumference of the circle produced is equal to the perimeter of the square. 'This is the pattern,' says Michell, 'which lies at the foundation of every traditional scheme of sacred geometry.'[8] Another way in which the squared circle can be produced is by the elegant expedient of using two vesicas at right angles to one another (Figure 48).

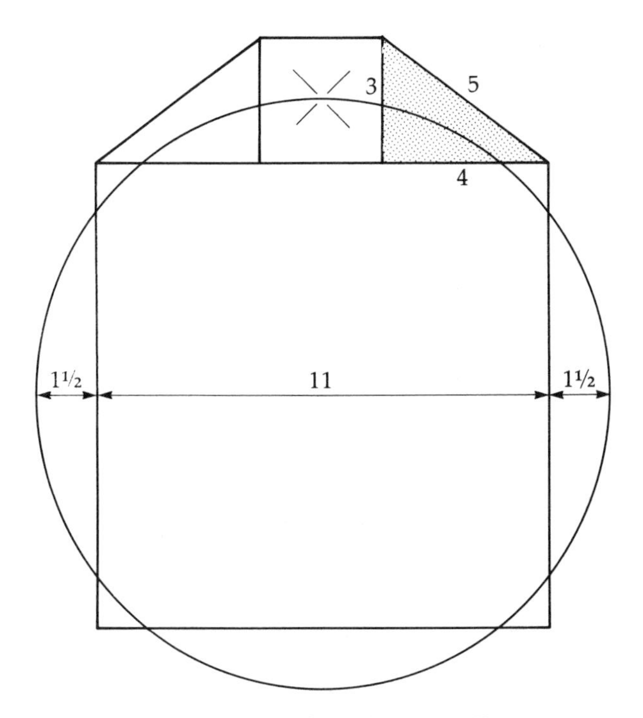


*Figure 47. (After John Michell)*

Architectural geometry can be 'frozen music', Goethe said, and this relates to how sacred measure and geometry is active in ways other than visual. Pythagoras discovered that stretched strings when plucked sound in harmony when their lengths are related to one another. The pitch of a string half the length of another will be an octave (diapason) higher, and various ratios produce different sound relationships. 'When this scheme was re-publicised in the sixteenth century,' Pennick observes, 'it formed the basis of the harmonic systems of Renaissance sacred architecture. Pythagoras' discovery was seen in terms of a divine revelation of the universal harmony . . . In order to achieve mastery of this universe, the Pythagoreans claimed, man had to discover the numbers hidden in all things. The revival of this doctrine 22 centuries later was responsible for the explosive development of science . . . The Pythagoreans held that numbers were independent units which possessed certain indivisible and eternal spatial dimensions.'[9] To Pythagoras numbers and their proportions underpinned the entire structure of the universe. A century or so later Plato developed these ideas and identified seven numbers which he stated were fundamental to the harmony of creation, and were especially

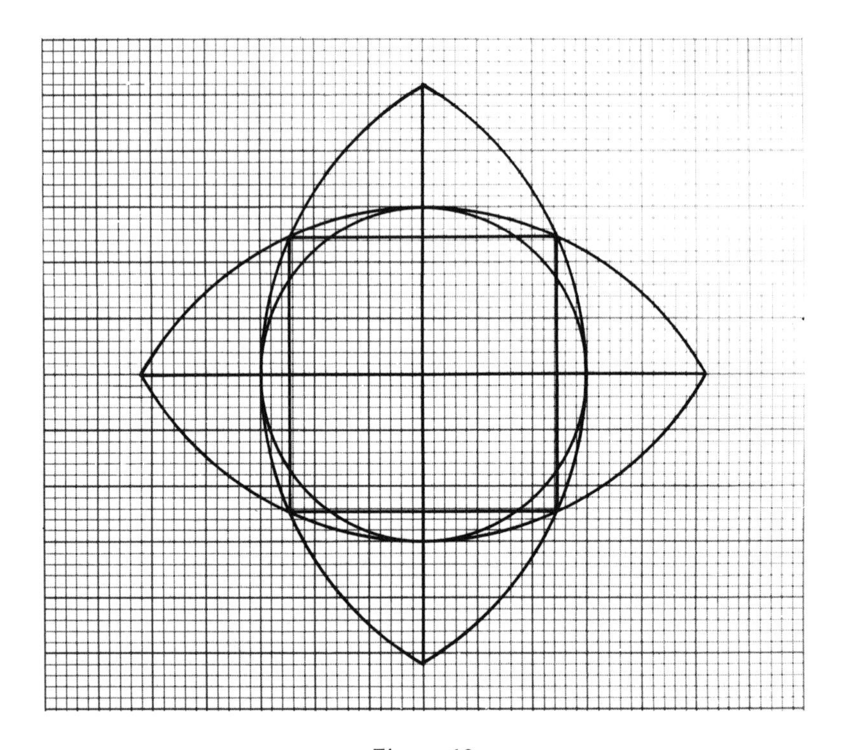

*Figure 48.*

suited for use in sacred architecture. Plato also identified the basic regular solids, which are thus known as the 'Platonic Solids' (Figure 50).

All this ancient Greek knowledge was, of course, simply the rediscovery or restatement of much earlier, arcane material. Critchlow, for instance, has noted that Platonic solids can be found enshrined in curious Neolithic stone balls that have been unearthed from time to time in Britain. They can be held in the hand.

*Figure 49.*

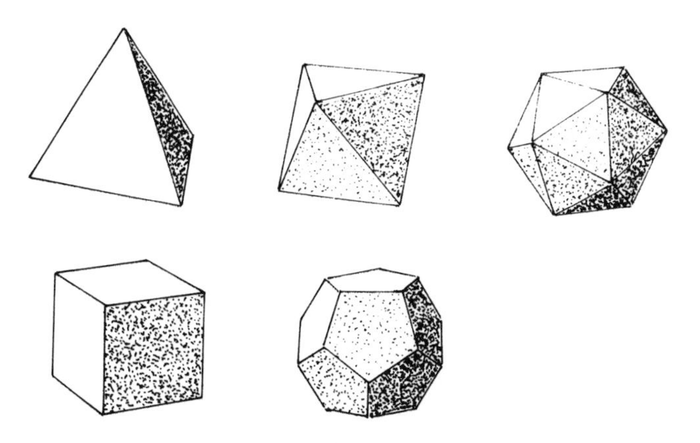

*Figure 50. The Platonic solids*

No one knows what they were used for, but as Critchlow pointed out in *Time Stands Still*, we do not have to know their function to observe that the detailed knowledge of three-dimensional geometry in Neolithic Britain is confirmed by their very existence.

This proof of geometrical skill only supports Thom's assertions that in addition to round stone circle groundplans, there were other schemes too: he identified ellipses, flattened circles he termed Types A and B, and egg shapes ('Types I and II'). These shapes were used, Thom believed, so that whole units of the Megalithic Yard (2.72 feet) could be incorporated into the dimensions of a stone ring – radius, circumference, and so on. In the case

*Figure 51. A Neolithic stone 'ball', displaying sophisticated knowledge of geometrical solids (Jay Swaine)*

of Castlerigg, Thom was sure that the combined astronomy and groundplan geometry had been arrived at for 'symbolic, mystical' reasons. The groundplan shapes put forward by Thom from his detailed surveys have been contested by some archaeologists who have argued that they are not the product of careful and skilled geometry but rather shapes produced by the efforts of people simply trying to form circles roughly 'by eye'. John Barnatt has shown that some similar patterns can be obtained by people being asked to set out a circle on the ground by guesswork. In these experiments buckets of sand were used. But buckets of sand are not heavy stones which require more deliberation in their placing, and it seems illogical that the geometric knowledge obviously present in Neolithic society as evidenced by the stone balls was not applied to sacred groundplans. The exactitude Thom sought may not always be present (or recoverable from a site's remains) but the intention can hardly be doubted.

We have already seen the vesica geometry at the heart of Castlerigg's groundplan, derived from astronomical orientations at the site. The vesica also occurs in the foundation of other sites, such as Long Meg and her Daughters, also in Cumbria, and stone rings all over the British Isles. It seems clear that the perennial nature of sacred geometry was available to the megalith builders.

A brief, whistle-stop tour of a handful of other sacred monuments through the ages will have to suffice here to illustrate some of the site aspects of sacred geometry.

Starting in Egypt we have the Old Kingdom's Great Pyramid, an obvious and mighty expression of geometry. It is a profoundly accurate structure, geodetically and thus astronomically oriented. The presence of *vesica piscis* geometry is expressed in its very form, and a fairly accurate profile or elevation can be drawn using vesica geometry (Figure 52). Two interlocking circles are drawn, forming the vesica. With centre A and radius AB, an arc XY is swung, with the procedure repeated with B as centre, thus forming a larger, enclosing vesica. Rhombus XBYA is drawn. The bottom of the smaller vesica, and points C and D where the circles are cut by the rhombus, fall on a straight line. This is produced to meet the outer vesica at E and F. Lines drawn from these points to the top of the inner vesica give a triangle which matches the Great Pyramid's elevation. If the drawing is done with care, base angles close to 55° 51′ will be formed automatically. These are the base angles of the Great Pyramid.

It was noted in the nineteenth century that these angles were the pi angle, and the Great Pyramid encodes both this and the Golden

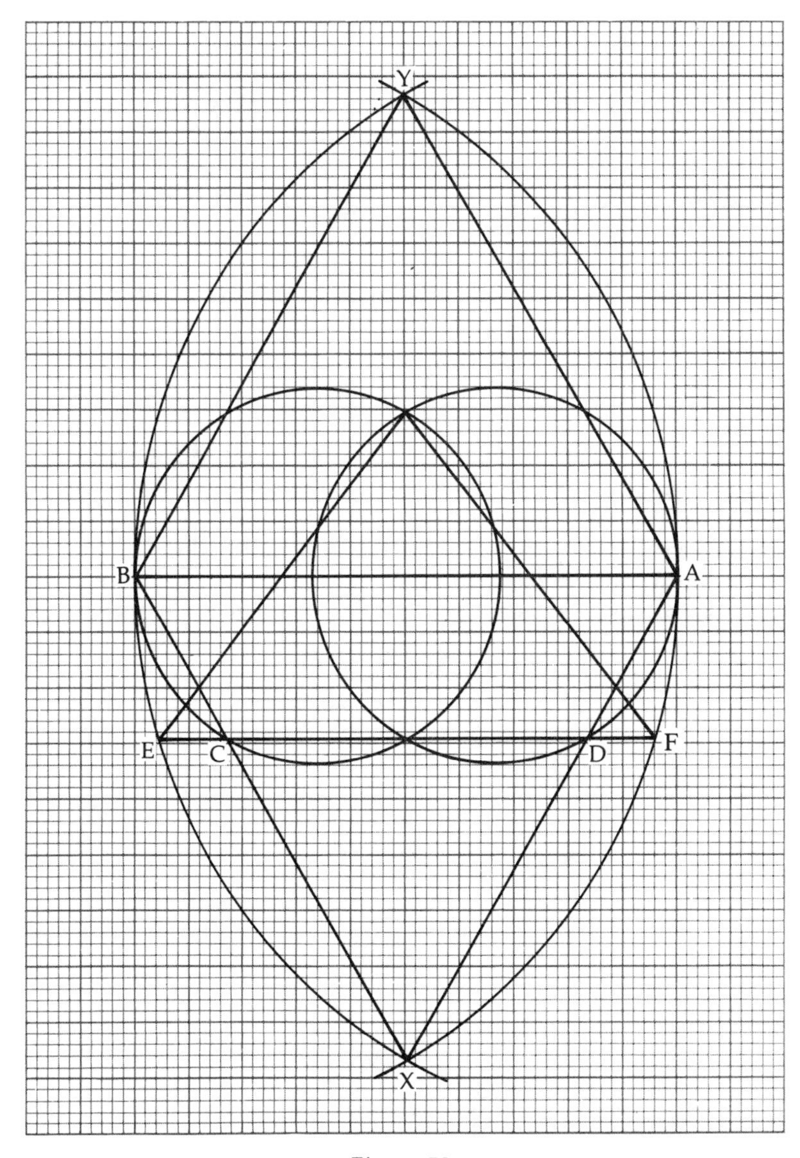


*Figure 52.*

Mean in its proportions. The apex of the pyramid is missing, which affects measurement, as does some of the damage caused to the structure over the ages. Michell argues convincingly that there was a pyramidion at the apex of the main structure, which was either graded with lines or made of separate units so the Golden Mean or pi geometry could be variously expressed.[10]

When Penrose measured the sixth-century–BC Parthenon, he found the front elevations to be determined by the Golden Mean and the sides by pi, thus there was a two-ratio scheme reminiscent of the situation at the Great Pyramid.

Karnak at ancient Thebes (Luxor) is a temple complex that evolved from at least the Middle Kingdom onwards. Egyptologist John Anthony West notes that a fallen 70-tone granite obelisk at the site will issue a ringing sound if the pyramidion of the stone is struck with the hand. West comments that this literally relates to Goethe's idea of 'frozen music'.[11] The nearby Temple of Luxor has some curious changes of axes, and seems to have been constructed originally on these. In his *Le Temple de l'homme,* Schwaller de Lubicz sees the Luxor Temple as a major key to the sacred geometry and religious cosmology of the ancient Egyptians. The additions to the temple over many centuries have all rigidly observed the axes, suggesting that the guiding principle of the place was handed down over generations. Schwaller de Lubicz put forward evidence to explain the changes of axial orientation as symbolising the human frame. Lawlor notes that the segments of the temple are also related to various Golden Mean proportions that are coincident with the phases of growth of the human body.

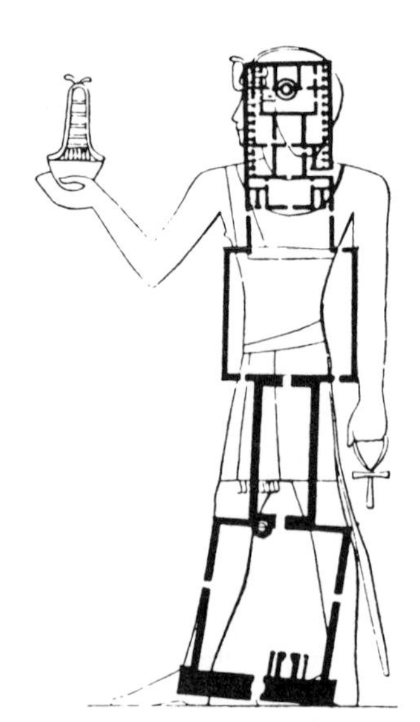

*Figure 53. Groundplan of a prehistoric megalithic temple on Malta depicting an outline of the Great Mother Goddess*

*Plate 29. The Temple of Luxor*

Figure 54 shows the same idea related to Hindu temple building, and Figure 55 shows it being applied to a church in a drawing by F. di Giorgio in the fifteenth century, who based his architectural ideas on those put down by Vitruvius, a Roman architect and engineer of the first century BC.

Vitruvius wrote a set of works on architecture which in effect provided the last summary of esoteric principles of the ancient world prior to the current era. They came to have a great influence on the artists and architect-philosophers of the Renaissance. The image of Vitruvian Man as it is called is certainly a fundamental element of ancient esoteric thought. Man is the microcosm of the universe, a part in which is reflected the whole, a concept not encountered in our day until the invention of the hologram. Vitruvius was careful to stress that the anthropomorphic proportional element in architectural structure should be reserved for

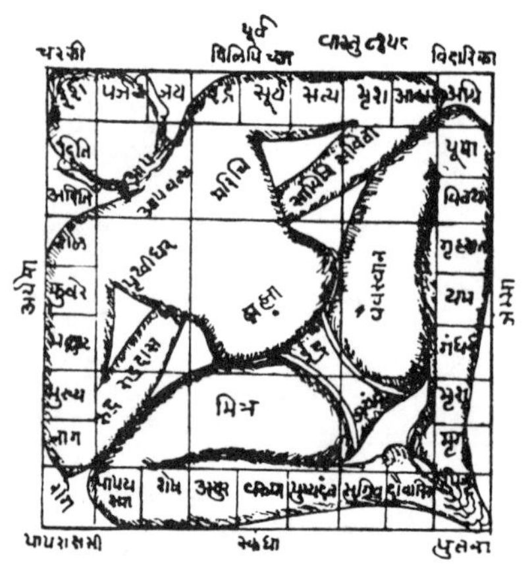

*Figure 54. Temple plan and the Cosmic Man (Purusha) in the Hindu* Vastapurushamandala *tradition of temple design*

temples, not secular buildings. Amongst the many aspects of ancient knowledge passed on by Vitruvius is the use of a gnomon (a shadow-throwing upright) in the setting out of the cardinal points astronomically produced from the sunrise and set shadows thrown by the gnomon. This practice was employed by primary peoples worldwide (Plate 30) and is described in the ancient Hindu text on temple foundation, the *Mansara Shilpa Shastra.*

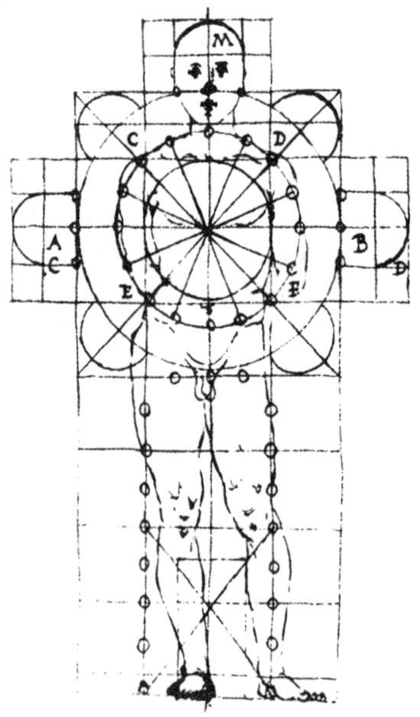

*Figure 55. (F. Di Giorgio)*

*Plate 30. Borneo Indians measuring the shadow thrown by a special gnomon*

While Vitruvius was rediscovered by the Renaissance world, today's esoteric scholars often overlook the fact that he had an earlier rediscovery. This is marked by the cathedral at Aachen (Aix-la-Chapelle), West Germany, built in the late eighth century by Charlemagne. This is often considered to be a copy of sixth-century S. Vitale, Ravenna, also built to canonical principles, but as art historian Jean Lassus correctly warned, 'one must look closer'.[12]

Charlemagne (AD 742–814) decided to make a permanent residence for himself at Aachen, which already held his father's court, and it became the centre of his empire. The place was known to the Romans as Aquis Granum, after a Celtic god. The Yorkshireman, Alcuin had developed a wide reputation for his esoteric knowledge, and Charlemagne invited him to Aachen, charging him with the responsibility of reviving the arts and sciences. There can be no doubt that Alcuin brought with him the remnants of ancient British secret knowledge, possibly passed down to the Druids, and kept alive as arcane tradition within the monasteries of the Dark Ages. As well as Germanic peoples, there were also many foreigners at Aachen – Jews, Arabs, Sicilian and Byzantine Greeks, Romans, and others, so many traditions rubbed shoulders. In Charlemagne's cosmopolitan court the ancient traditions were recharged. The writings of Vitruvius and those of Plinius (AD 24–

79) were translated. 'There were goldsmiths and builders,' Lassus has remarked, 'and all the different traditions had to merge together.'[13] In other words, Alcuin had to be a systems manager.

The cathedral of Aachen manifests aspects of this revivification of ancient wisdom. The selection of the site at sacred springs is not an accident, for Vitruvius advised that temples should be built at springs. Moreover, in the main entrance hall of the cathedral is a bronze effigy dating from the second century AD. The fabric of the cathedral is partly eighth century and partly fourteenth century. The oldest part is the Palace Chapel, which is octagonal, and it is here where the greatest interest lies. The plan of the octagon shows startling similarities with the proportions of the sarsen circle and trilithon horseshoe at Stonehenge (Figure 56). Furthermore, the cathedral and Stonehenge are on very nearly the same line of latitude, Stonehenge being 0.12° above the 51 degree parallel, and Aachen being 0.16° below. An alignment extending from the chapel in what would be the 'Heel Stone' direction, the midsummer sunrise axis, has been identified in plans to run through megalithic sites, ancient springs and churches. Moreover, it has recently been accidentally discovered that the octagonal chapel possesses remarkable astronomical properties, allowing entry of sunbeams. The light displays are stunning and complex and

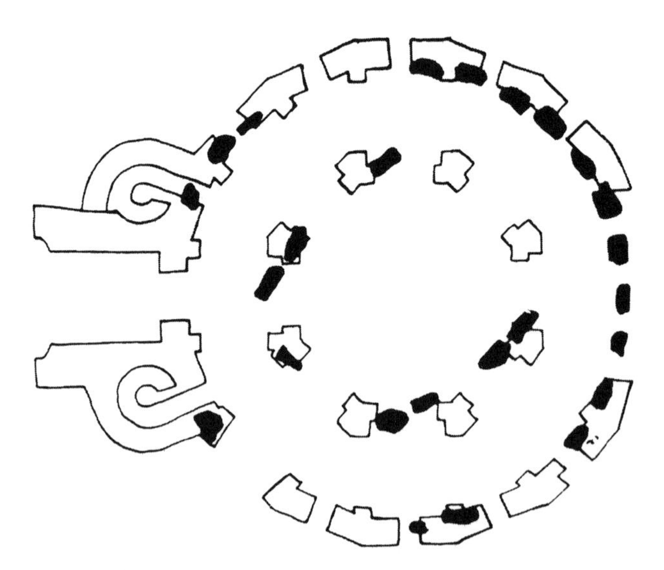

*Figure 56. Plan of the Carolingian Palace Chapel at Aachen Cathedral, superimposed by the groundplan of Stonehenge (in black) to same scale (after Hermann Weisweiler)*

cannot be described here, but one pattern of sunlight traces the Great Pyramid triangle, hinting again of that curious link between the latitudinal band of Avebury, Stonehenge, and, now, Aachen, with that of the Great Pyramid.

It is clear that Charlemagne's court provided a major doorway for the entry of ancient, esoteric knowledge into the occult (that is, secret) scholarship of historic Europe.

Another such 'doorway' was provided by the Crusades of the eleventh century, and, particularly, the Knights Templar who ostensibly were supposed to guard pilgrims on their way to Jerusalem. The Western Christians ('Franks') came in contact with Arabic traditions, and the secret wisdom teachings of the Middle East filtered back into Europe. The Knights Templar were certainly instrumental in this, and many believe them to have been an occult order whose job in Jerusalem was quite other than their exoteric role, being more concerned in finding out the secrets of the Temple of Solomon.

During the twelfth and thirteenth centuries, as the Middle Eastern traditions and survivals of ancient Greek knowledge were coming to the attention of Western scholars, Gothic architecture began its appearance. Little is known in written form of the Gothic system of proportion but Caeserino's commentary on his translation of Vitruvius (published in 1592) 'serves as a basis of fact from contemporary sources that the *vesica piscis* was the fundamental determining shape and proportion of the groundplan of Gothic cathedrals.'[14] That epitome of Gothic cathedrals, Chartres, was designed by an unknown master and built in a very short period of time, being begun in 1194 and virtually completed by 1220. The west spires had been built a little earlier. There had been churches on the site since at least the fourth century, and they all stood on a Neolithic mound. There is a well beneath the building, and a carving on the north door shows a Celtic well. The spot was a focus for pilgrimage from the earliest centuries of the Christian era, and who knows how long before that. There are also astronomical events clearly built into the fabric of the building, most notable being the summer solstice noon sunbeam which enters through a hole in a south window to strike a special slab marked with a metal plug. French writer Louis Charpentier has noted carvings representing the Ark of the Covenant (at the north door) along with the command 'you are to work through the Ark'. He questions the immediacy with which Gothic architecture appeared, particularly Chartres, and how it was concurrent with Romanesque, not deriving from it. How could it spring up so readily? There must have been a *school* from which the master builders emerged, Charpentier reasoned. The awesome logistics involved in the building of Gothic Chartres, and the curious fact that monarchs from all over Europe contributed to its costs, led him to ask: 'Was Chartres the "Golden Book" of the West in which sages wrote the message of their wisdom?'[15] The first Gothic buildings began to appear 11 years after the return of the original Knights Templar in 1128.

The ogive arch at Chartres is based on the pentagram; the choir is a double square, 'The ratio 2 to 1 is exactly that of the Egyptian and Greek temples,' Charpentier observed, 'likewise of Solomon's Temple as far as the Holy of Holies.' The diagonal of the double square yields $\sqrt{5}$ systems which relate to the Golden Mean and a whole train of further associations. Charpentier also argued that the structure might be associated with sonic frequencies related to Gregorian plain chant.

There are many other elements of sacred geometry inherent in the Gothic fabric of Chartres Cathedral, and other mysteries too, some of which we will touch on in a later chapter. It is obvious that with its siting, its astronomy, its water, its geometry, it embodies the continuation of perennial principles known from remote antiquity, by whatever channels that information survived.

Ruins of the twelfth century are now all that remain of Glastonbury Abbey, but the origins of the place are, again, much older. Legend has it that Joseph of Arimathea came to Glastonbury bearing the Grail, the cup of the Last Supper, along with twelve missionaries. They are said to have founded the first church in Christendom at Glastonbury. Whether or not this is literally true – if a myth, it still contains information discernable to the esoteric scholar, for myth is another systems language – there was certainly a most ancient church at Glastonbury. In the following centuries, churches were built to the east of it, but all was destroyed by fire in the twelfth century. A new abbey was then built, with St Mary's chapel at its western end. This chapel is said to be on the location of the original church, and its dimensions record those of the old church. We can see from Bligh Bond's plan[16] (Figure 57) that sacred geometry informed those dimensions. There is the vesica, the root-three rectangle and the hexagon.

The Renaissance period was catalysed by 'the works of Plato and the Neoplatonists newly revealed to the West through Greek manuscripts brought to Florence from Byzantium.'[17] One of the very influential works to come via Byzantium was the *Corpus Hermeticum* by Hermes Trismegistus, a supposed Egyptian sage from around the time of Moses. The survival of ancient wisdom

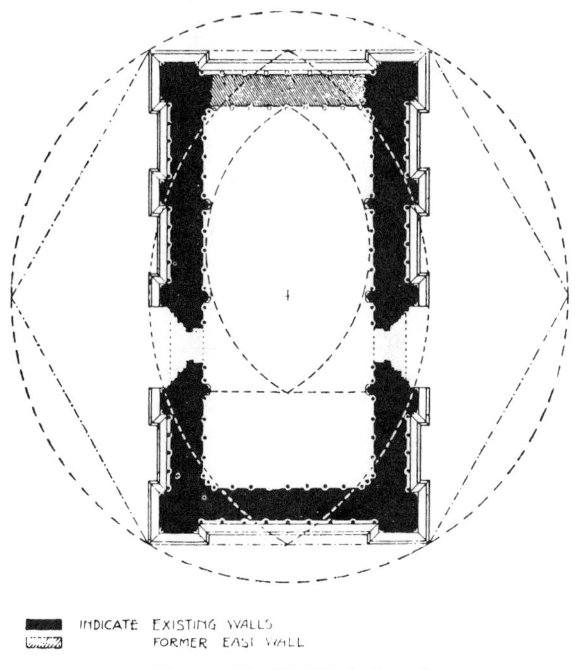


*Figure 57. (F. Bligh Bond)*

through the Greek writings, the works of Vitruvius, and the Hermetic and Cabalistic traditions proved a heady brew that permeated Western art, philosophy (especially in the form of alchemy) and architecture. Ultimately, of course, the worries of the Church about the arcane goings-on in its midst, the rise of secularism and the emergence of a strain of analytical thought estranged from a holistic, metaphysical context, conflicted with the occult philosophy. A kind of watershed was crossed in the seventeenth century, and science as secular, rationalist logic gained dominance. Also, the traditional masonic lodges, formerly comprised of working, practical masons, gave way to 'speculative masons'.[18]

The first offspring of sacred geometry is sacred measure, and is thus a related way in which knowledge can be transmitted by ancient sites. The classic repositories of ancient sacred measure are the Great Pyramid and Stonehenge. Of the Pyramid Michell says:

> As the dimensions of the Great Pyramid are multiplied by the ratios of the ancient number canon they expand to frame the

dimensions of this earth, and it is possible that they could have been taken further to represent the dimensions of the grand orb (the circle described by the Earth's path around the sun), planetary intervals and the measurements of time. Going the other way, into the microcosm, these same Pyramid measures contract proportionally through a series of pyramidions at the apex, shrinking from miles to inches, to mere specks and finally into the world of the atom.[19]

The plethora of measures evident in the structure of the Giza Pyramid is beyond the brief of this book to present and evaluate, but excellent works exist for the interested reader to delve further.[8] While some fantasies that have been built on the measures of the Pyramid are excessive, amounting to pyramidiocy, the basic metrological and geodetic factors of the monument are undoubtedly valid. One example of geodetic information that can be read into the monument is the fact that it represents the Earth's northern hemisphere at a scale of 1:43200 (a tenth of the sun's radius), the apex being equivalent to the north pole and the perimeter of the base the distance round the equator.

John Michell has made a detailed study of the measures of Stonehenge.[21,22] With exhaustive scholarship, he has shown that the lintel ring of Stonehenge encodes geodetic information, such as the Earth's polar radius and meridian circumference, as well as all the principle units of measure in the ancient world. The lintel ring was honed to remarkable precision, using only stone tools. Each lintel curves slightly so that the whole formed a complete, carefully levelled ring of stone supported 14 feet (4 m) in the air by 30 uprights. The lintels are secured in place atop the pillars by means of mortice and tenon connection. The ring was clearly a precision instrument.

Michell finds the basic sacred or canonical numbers incorporated in sites like Stonehenge and the Great Pyramid to occur in the dimensions of the New Jerusalem given in St John's Revelations. St John's visionary celestial city is thus a microcosm of the Earth, derived from the archetypal proportional system that was the corpus of geodetic and other knowledge amongst the ancients. The information is distributed through time and encoded in many modes, from sacred buildings to sacred texts. The canon transcends geography and chronology, and is thus *perennial,* a word we have encountered in earlier pages.

According to Michell, the canon is framed by the number 12 and its powers.

Canonical geometry, measure and number are part of the information that can be accessed at ancient places; it is a form of communication that can speak from age to age. It is timeless. It can mirror the world, the universe and the human psyche. It is the ultimate systems language.

*Figure 58. A vision of Stonehenge restored, showing the complete lintel ring*

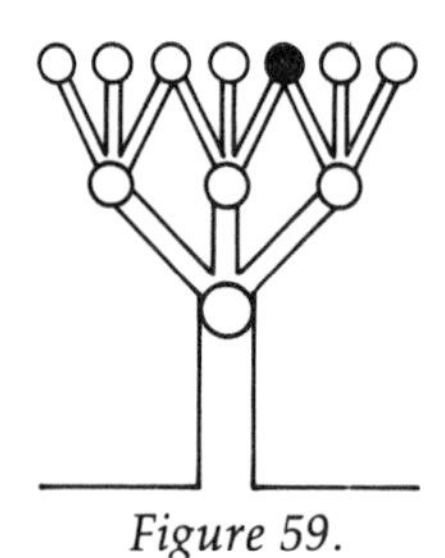

*Figure 59.*

CHAPTER 6

# FOLKLORE

## Demonstration

Little seems to have been recorded in written form about legends associated with Castlerigg. However, a Mrs Linton in the 1860s reported that the stones of the site were 'like so many enchanted creatures sitting in mute perpetual council, and which the saying is that no one can count twice alike.' This identifies one major theme in folklore attached to megalithic sites, that the stones are *uncountable*. It seems another motif is also being alluded to in Linton's account, that of *pertrifaction* – the turning of people into stone.

*Plate 31.*

## Discussion

The language of myth, legend and lore is a less formal type of systems communication than sacred geometry, using word pictures, metaphor and motif to get its message across. The story-telling matrix of folklore is a way for knowledge to be passed down generations, the story tellers themselves usually unaware of any hidden content in the tales they pass on. Legend and lore are time capsules of information.

Myth is the high form of the art, and tells us much about the workings of the human psyche. Myth, like sacred geometry and measure, is perennial, and relates to our inner lives now just as much as it ever did; it is only that we have lost touch as a culture with the patterns of consciousness that mythological motifs represent. The heroic tales of Greek myth, the legends of King Arthur and the Grail, the creation myths of indigenous peoples – this genre of high myth relates to the dreamtime of the mind, those areas of consciousness, like the sites themselves, behind and beyond the small compass of contemporary waking awareness.

Legend and lore are 'low church' by comparison, but nevertheless can still contain information. They have been passed down through numberless evenings around rural hearths. Many examples have found their way into written form, but most only in recent centuries, concurrent with the appearance of antiquarianism. Outside of a specific locality where we might have access to surviving local oral tradition, we cannot know what was never put into writing, nor how old the origins of a legend might be. Folklorists tend to date a folktale from its first appearance in writing – that is literally its only documented date, after all – but some themes certainly originated before that time.

Folklorist Jeremy Harte has said, 'Archaeology began with folklore, and developed from popular traditions into an academic discipline. It is easy to forget that sites like Maiden Castle, Knowlton, or the Nine Stones were not "discovered" by the antiquarians of the sixteenth and seventeenth centuries: they were shown to them by a peasantry who had long been familiar with the sites . . . to regard the legends of prehistoric and Roman monuments as merely curiosities or popular fancies is to discard a potential source of evidence . . .'[1]

As our concern here is with understanding ancient sacred sites, only those folk themes that have become specifically attached to prehistoric monuments are considered. This site-specific aspect of folklore tells us of long-term human response to the monuments.

Unknown generations of people would inevitably observe the Old Places in all seasons and weather conditions; by day and by night. Any qualities they had, even if not understood, and even if occurring only occasionally, would become recorded in the local stories or superstitions passed down from parents to children. While rulers and religions came and went, the rural population remained fairly permanent; they became the land's memory – in Britain, at least, until the Industrial Revolution and the demographic changes that created.

British site-related folklore is a useful body of data to select because the British Isles happen to have relatively good documentation of that kind. It is possible to pick out perhaps a dozen primary motifs that could possibly be of considerable antiquity.

One of the most common themes is that the old stones can heal. Water splashed on the stones of Stonehenge was supposed to acquire healing properties. Sickly children passed through the holed stone called Men-an-Tol were thought likely to be cured. This Cornish stone was also used as an oracle, and divination or prophesy is another folk theme.

Both prophesy and healing were strongly associated with holy wells. Many of these sacred water sites were venerated in at least late prehistoric times, the process simply becoming Christianised later. At Bath, for instance, the hot springs were venerated from the early Neolithic period, then became a Celtic cult centre, then Roman baths where healing and divination took place, and, finally, a spa in recent times where people 'took the waters' for health reasons. A degenerate version of well divination is the 'wishing well' – the 'three coins in a fountain' syndrome. A British example is the Silver (or St Augustine's) Well at Cerne Abbas in Dorset. Nowadays people just throw a coin into the water, but the old tradition was that to ask the future there one had to find a laurel leaf to use as a cup and drink the water while facing the nearby church. This sounds like the Christianisation of a pagan practice of some antiquity.

Many megaliths are said in lore to move of their own accord. The Enstone near Oxford is typical in that it goes for a midnight drink at a nearby stream. On the other hand, like numerous other megaliths, it either cannot be moved by human agency or will return of its own accord if it is displaced. Some stones are petrified people. The stones of the Merry Maidens circle in Cornwall were dancers who, spinning ever faster as the musicians accelerated their playing, collapsed with exhaustion and became stone. The musicians, too, were petrified – a few fields away stands a pair of

*Plate 32. The Roman Great Bath at Bath, Avon*

stones called the Pipers and not too far away is another monolith known as the Blind Fiddler. The stone circles at Stanton Drew near Bath are said to have been a wedding party petrified for allowing their merrymaking to go on into the sabbath. Remarkably, virtually the same folktale is attached to the Kaur stone circle in Senegambia, West Africa.[2] The Rollright Stones near Oxford are said to be a king and his men turned to stone by a witch. The stones of the Rollright circle are also said to be uncountable – this motif was associated with at least 11 stone circles or other megalithic structures in Britain, according to folklorist Leslie Grinsell.[3]

Some legends tell that bad luck will befall desecrators of the old stones and mounds, or that a storm will erupt if they are so disturbed.

*Plate 33. The Merry Maidens stone circle, Cornwall*

Fairies are said to dwell in certain prehistoric mounds or stone circles, and anyone partaking of fairy food or drink will become enchanted at those sites, reminiscent of modern 'abductee' UFO stories. The fairies were actually seen as *lights* in many cases, rather than little figures. Nowhere was this confusion stronger than in Ireland. The prehistoric earthwork of Crillaun near Castlebar, County Mayo, is considered a 'fairy fort'. Irish writer Dermot Mac Manus noted that 'in the neighbourhood it has always been known to be a busy centre of fairy activity. From time to time the fort has been seen ablaze with little winking lights. They are said to move from one fort to another sometimes, though this is rare.'[4] Mac Manus interviewed local people who claimed to have actually witnessed the lights. Lights only were seen – the fairy designation was purely a cultural reflex. Similarly, in Cornwall in the nineteenth century, tin miners returning from work claimed to have seen 'lights burning and fairies dancing on and around' the Carn Gluze barrow. We have the term 'fairy lights' today, and this probably reveals the whole matter.

Old stones were undoubtedly associated with fertility and fecundity. Marriages were consummated at some, others were appealed to for good crops or rain, and stones from Ireland to Ethiopia were shaped into phalli, or carved into Mother Goddess effigies.

Buried treasure is another strong motif in the lore of prehistoric sites. Willy Howe, a huge neolithic mound in Humberside, was said to contain a chest of gold. The story goes that people dug into the mound and attached a chain and horses to it, but the harder the animals pulled, the deeper the chest sank into the barrow. An almost identical tale is attached to another prehistoric barrow, Mutlow Hill in Essex, the treasure there being a golden coach. At the Welsh Dyffryn Ardudwy stone chambers, treasure concealed there will only be disclosed 'when the end of a rainbow rests on the middle of the stone'. A great many other sites around the country are said to conceal treasure. In some cases, dragons and tunnel motifs are associated with hidden treasure.

Lights also figure in treasure lore. In some countries, curious lights that appear periodically at the same locations are said to mark buried treasure. In Cornwall, the Iron Age earthworks on Trencrom Hill are supposed to harbour giants' treasure. It is said that a tin miner a hundred or so years ago saw lights on the hill and climbed up to find a long passage, along which was unguarded gold. This may be related to the tradition prevalent amongst medieval mines of copper, tin and other metals that light phe-

*Plate 34. The Wasu stone circle, Sengambia, one of many such sites in this region of West Africa. A legend attached to this circle states that a light can sometimes be seen shining amidst the stones at night, but disappears when one approaches (courtesy Kay Honkanen)*

nomena emerging from the ground indicated the presence of good veins of ore (see Chapter 11).

In Senegambia, once again – where there are over 800 stone circles, nearly as many as in the British Isles – a genie holding a bag would materialise out of a stone in one of the Sanguli stone circles. If anyone tried to take the bag, it and the genie would simply dissolve back into one of the stones. One local man was said to have gone insane when he experienced this.

It is to be expected that some folktales would involve accounts of spectres at ancient places. A particularly interesting story involves the apparition of a gigantic golden figure seen at the Welsh barrow of Bryn-yr-Ellyllon (the Hill of Goblins), near Mold. It seems possible that this old story pre-dated the finding of a gold cape and other golden artefacts along with a male skeleton in the mound when it was cleared in 1833 (or 1831, dates vary). If this is in fact the case, then it would seem that relatively specific memories can be encapsulated in lore down a great many generations. Conversely, it could mean that people did see a phantom as the story describes. This is what seems to have happened to a respectable historian, R.C.C. Clay, in the winter of 1927–8. Driving past a group of Bronze Age round barrows on Bottlebush Down in Dorset, he suddenly saw a horseman, apparently a Bronze Age warrior, who paced his car and made threatening gestures before vanishing. Bottlebush Down, which also has an enigmatic Neolithic earthwork called a cursus crossing it, has yielded other ghostly incidents.[5]

Lights, once more, have been associated in folk tradition with spirits and ghosts at prehistoric features. Several independent witnesses told antiquarian G. Wilson in the 1880s that they saw, on repeated occasions, a light move from the Scottish Torhouskie Cairn to a stone on top of a water conduit. The stone supposedly had been taken from the cairn, so the light was 'claiming its own'.

Certain numbers recur in legends. Grinsell has noted that 'customs still (or recently) practised at most prehistoric sites usually involve the numbers three, seven or nine.' J. Harland and T. Wilkinson in *Lancashire Folklore* (1882) noted the presence of 'sacred and mystic' numbers in various dragon legends:

> In the case of the Dragon of Wantley (Wharncliffe) there are *seven* heads mentioned, and twice *seven* eyes; the monster itself ate up *three* children, the fight lasted *two* days and *one* night, and he turned twice *three* times round when he received his fatal wound. The Lambton Worm had *nine* holes on each side of his mouth, he encircled Worm Hill *three* times, he drank the milk of

> *nine* cows; the reckless heir of Lambton returned a true knight at the end of *seven* years, and for *nine* generations the sybil's curse remained on his house . . .

In his book on Northumbrian dragonlore,[6] Paul Screeton also comments on the repeated emphasis on the number nine in the Lambton Worm tale (where the dragon or 'worm' is finally killed by the knight, John Lambton, who wears armour bristling with sharp edges so the creature lacerates itself when it tries to crush him to death). He notes the same number in other dragon legends and also that in Chinese dragon lore heaven had nine regions, each ruled over by a dragon. In addition, the Chinese dragon also had nine similarities to other beasts.

Numerous prehistoric sites are associated with procedures involving certain numbers. Those being healed at Men-an-tol, for instance, had to be passed three or nine times through its hole, and dragged around the stone the same number of times. Another example is at Kit's Coty dolmen in Kent, where, if a person places an object on the capstone at the full of the moon and circumambulates the monument three times, the object will disappear.

Some sites are said to have underground passages linking them with some other site or feature. In the central English county of Leicestershire, the Humber Stone (now just a stump) was said to

*Figure 60. Sir John Lambton in mortal combat with the Lambton Worm*

have a tunnel connecting it with the former St John's Stone in Abbey fields, Leicester, about three miles (5 km) away. There is no physical tunnel. Another mythical tunnel is said to link the Neolithic Coldrum Barrow in Kent with the nearby church of Ss. Peter and Paul at Trottiscliffe (Trosley). Folklore has it that two brothers discovered the entrance to the tunnel at the Coldrum site, and one went inside playing his pipe while the other attempted to trace the course of the tunnel by walking along on the surface listening to the faint music coming from below. But suddenly the pipe-playing stopped, and the subterranean brother was never seen again.

There are of course other aspects of folklore attached to prehistoric sites (Grinsell identifies almost 30). The idea that megaliths and mounds were placed by giants is a common theme, applied to sites in Africa as well as Europe, but probably tells us more about the ignorance of the peasantry regarding who the builders were. Giants have always haunted the human subconscious. There is a legend attached to Stonehenge, though, that might be the ivory amongst the bone: according to this story the bluestones of Stonehenge came from Ireland by means of Merlin's magical art, and they got to Ireland by being brought from Africa by giants in remotest antiquity. There may be a very deep memory enshrined here. The giant theme was Christianised at some point and the giants became the Devil, but the tales remained the same. This tells us more about religious attitudes in history than about the sites. Similar points apply to the legendary claim attached to several prehistoric sites that they were erected miraculously overnight, often by the agency of the Devil. (Variations on this theme are commonly associated with the foundation of old churches, especially those in out-of-the-way places. In these instances it probably relates to the building of the church on a former pagan site.) The magical property of ceremonial monuments is the likely reason why Arthurian names and themes have become attached to many of them. This is probably an artefact of medieval Romanticism. Many of the other motifs, such as the use of the sites for assembly, plays on the meaning of names, associations with historical personages, and so on, seem likewise to reflect sociological conditions and attitudes of the peasantry and their times rather than information about the sites themselves. But the main themes outlined in the previous paragraphs may conceivably contain hints of site information if they can be deciphered.

The tales stating that stones can move in a variety of ways, that they are petrified people, cannot be counted, impart fertility, suggest an underlying sense that the stones have something *animate* about them. This is endorsed by other, widespread, traditions claiming stones can grow. The stones are alive, have energy, in some way. Healing traditions also attest to the belief in certain stones having qualities about them that can beneficially affect the human organism. Modern medicine now accepts that low-level electromagnetic therapy can help healing in certain medical conditions – especially bone disorders. We will see later that at least some megaliths do possess magnetic and other energetic properties. The fertilising capacity of some stones was probably closely linked to the healing theme.

The meteorological powers of some sites in both fertility and desecration legends are interesting, and may hark back to perceived geophysical peculiarities of certain *locations* intermixed with notions of curses, which undoubtedly were implanted at some remote point to help preserve old sacred places.

Lore and names hinting at the use of sites for divination, as oracles, may possibly be memory-relics relating to the production of altered states of consciousness at these places: an aspect that will be explored further.

We can be pretty sure that the secret tunnel motif is a folk recognition of the relationships of sites one to another in the landscape – their sacred geographic (or geomantic) and orientational characteristics. The tunnel theme is sometimes linked with the treasure motif which may in general be a symbol for secret, forgotten aspects of these places which were clearly so important in antiquity. In the tunnel folktales mentioned above, the Humber Stone, St John's Stone 'tunnel' was recognised as long ago as 1911 by local historian Alice Dryden as probably referring to a midsummer sunrise line between the two stones. At Coldrum, the mound-church 'tunnel' is on an alignment that continues on to incorporate other old churches and an ancient river crossing. Trosley church has megaliths embedded in its Saxon foundations. This seems to bear out the contention of Alfred Watkins that the tunnel motif indicated the existence of an alignment of sites – a 'ley line'. This is further supported by a Navajo legend which claims that the mysterious straight tracks left by the lost Anasazi culture around Chaco Canyon in New Mexico were 'not really roads' but 'tunnels' along which the Anasazi could travel with invisibility. The human mind can come up with surprisingly similar images for similar matters even in unconnected cultures.

Another folkloric factor about some sites that needs to be taken into account is the *names* they were given. Quite a selection of these emphasise the numerological aspect. Another name for the Merry Maidens stone circle is *Dawns Men*, Cornish for The Dancing Stones. Perhaps this recalls what the site was used for. There are numerous site names that are associated with numbers. Nine can be found in stone circle names, there being several examples of Nine Maidens and Nine Stones, even though there may be more megaliths present at the sites. This is true of barrow groupings too – the Priddy Nine Barrows clustering on the Mendips in north Somerset near Glastonbury number more than nine. Other 'Nine Barrows' names occur elsewhere. Why nine? We can only guess, but our guesses can arrive at telling possibilities. Nine is 'the all-powerful 3 × 3, it is the Triple Triad; completion . . . beginning and end; the whole . . . the Earthly Paradise,' J.C. Cooper tells us.[7] All very appropriate associations for stone circles.

Others link with geometry and geodesy: 'Nine is also the number of the circumference, hence its division into 90 degrees and into 360 for the entire circumference.' In Celtic tradition nine represented the central point and the eight directions (the spatial corollary of the eightfold division of the year). The Celtic Triple Goddesses are three times three. There are nine Celtic maidens, and nine white stones represent the nine virgins attendant on the goddess Bridgit. The Beltane fire was attended by 81 men, nine at a time. Nine had an important role in the cosmologies of the ancient Egyptians and Greeks as well as in Scandinavian-Teutonic mythology. *Seven* on the other hand – and there are several 'Seven Barrows' groups, again irrespective of the actual number of prehistoric mounds involved – is also associated with completeness, totality, and is the number of the Great Mother. Astronomically, the number can be associated with the stars of the Plough or Big Dipper and the Pleiades.

A telling possibility regarding the name of a site was well spotted by country walking author Laurence Main (personal communication). One of his Welsh walking routes took in the remote stone circle of Lled Croen yr ych, near Llanbrynmair.[8] The name means 'Width of the Ox's Hide'. Main recalled that there is a story in the ancient bardic texts known as the *Mabinogion* called 'The Dream of Rhonabwy'. In this, Rhonabwy encounters a 'black old hall' which is almost derelict inside, except for a dais on which is stretched a yellow ox skin. Rhonabwy sleeps on this and has a visionary experience.[9] Main wisely wonders if the ox-hide connection hints at shamanic practices at the Lled Croen yr ych circle.

One matter that is never identified in its own right in folklore is the presence of *lights* at sites. We have seen lights being a part of three of the above themes – fairies, spirits and treasure – and may be entirely responsible for the fairy theme. There is the possibility here of the underlying observations by generations of local people of unusual phenomena at megalithic and earthworked monuments.

Folklore is complex and eclectic, gathering its images and rationale from many sources. The surface of folklore is regularly repolished and embellished, long after the possible meanings of the fundamental motifs have been forgotten. But it is these legendary cores that are the important components of folklore, and if one sums up those aspects of the themes itemised above, the general sense is that the old stones and other places have been regarded as foci of *power*, of unusual phenomena and particular effects, and that the usage of such places was for magico-religious activity.

Nor is folklore dead. In his award-winning study of Dorset folklore *Cuckoo Pounds and Singing Barrows* (1986), Jeremy Harte found that oral traditions of the 1980s represented 'the largest single body of evidence' in his inventory of sites. 'New folklore is continuously being generated and collected,' he discovered. But:

> . . . the need for oral tradition to find a place in literate society has led to several changes from earlier patterns of folklore. Legends have disappeared, and no new stories about giants or the Devil seem to be current – evidently the existing combination of orthodox and alternative theories has satisfied the need for origin stories . . . The other response to the challenge of the written word has been a new emphasis on the primacy of personal experience. Most of the material collected in the 1980s was testimony at first or second hand to supernatural experiences, so that evidently this kind of response to ancient sites has taken over from the legendary, story-telling approach.[10]

Cases dealing with light phenomena in Harte's Dorset folklore inventory exemplify both kinds of change he refers to, but also challenge his thesis that personal experience has overtaken the legendary approach. An informant told Harte in 1984 that along with a companion she had seen an orange glow around the top of a mound at Bincombe from which flames were darting. Harte himself notes that this is identical with the Norse tradition of spirit lights at their burial cairns, about which his informant knew nothing. This immediately suggests that the old legends of lights were themselves the result of direct experience, but because of the longer passages of time involved the accounts became handed down and may not have related to the personal experience of the storyteller so became a matter of belief rather than direct observation. (Interestingly, there is another mound at Bincombe which has been considered from at least the nineteenth century as being a 'music barrow'. By placing one's ear to the top of the mound a 'fairy melody' could sometimes be heard. Ignoring the inevitable fairy allusion, the story might well have derived from locals actually hearing a sound phenomenon at the site. These accounts of light and sound in a small locality suggest geophysical factors.)

At the great earthworked hill of Maiden Castle, just south of Dorchester, lights have been reported from time to time. These were known as 'fairy lights' in the old tradition, and were still being referred to by that label in the early 1980s. However, at another prehistoric earthworked hill in the county, Eggardon, there was an incident in 1974 when a man saw a bluish ball of light emerge from the hill coincident with his car's electrical system cutting out. By 1983, this was in the local oral folklore and the light was identified as a UFO.

What this seems to show is that some motifs of folklore do come from phenomena directly experienced at sites. In the case of traditional lore, this was associated with the acceptable images of the day, fairies and dragons, and became embellished down the years. Again, place names can be significant here. In Longdendale Valley in the Pennines near Glossop, there is a hill called Shining Clough. In the 1970s, there were two cases of multiple witnesses seeing the hillside actually glow with an eerie light. In addition, the hilltop and ridges around it have been regularly affected by the appearance of inexplicable balls of light for years. There are many instances in the Pennines of places named after 'boggarts' (local for spirit; elemental being) where light phenomena have been seen in recent times, most of them associated with geological faulting. Much of this material has been researched by Project Pennine, whose findings are summarised in *Earth Lights Revelation.*[11]

Whether or not this sort of information about sites comes from prehistory or more recent centuries is open to question. It hardly matters: what the lore is encoding in either case are long-term local observations at sites. Harte feels that 'no one would now claim, with the Victorian anthropologists, that the traditions of the rural working class preserve real memories from prehistory.' While this is undoubtedly largely true, I feel it is too sweeping. I suspect the numerology involved in the lore of sites *is* a relic from at least Celtic times, and the hints of ritual also. Grinsell observes that customs relating to the sun and its movements, such as the deasil (with the sun, or clockwise) and widdershins (against the sun) circumambulation of certain healing stones, for instance, could be a memory of Bronze Age sun worship. The desecration 'curses' also must spring from some pagan matrix, although this could be in historical times as paganism never quite died out in certain rural areas. I also feel the themes suggesting an animistic quality to the stones are exceedingly ancient, though this master theme is very fugitive, being spread through other motifs. The healing and divinatory properties of water and stones certainly go back to Iron Age times, and thence very likely to earlier phases of prehistory. The phallic and goddess stones show without doubt that fertility and fecundity were associated with megaliths from the very beginning.

Leslie Grinsell comments:

> A curious aspect of much folklore is that the present local inhabitants maintain that it was 'what the old people believe, or used to believe', and to some extent *this has always been the case.*[12] (My emphasis.)

The lore of ancient sites is thus analogous to the images in a corridor of mirrors – the original subject may be way back along a series of reflections with the image quality decaying all the time. But it is undoubtedly a revealing facet of ancient sacred monuments and so has to be included in the systems approach to understanding such places.

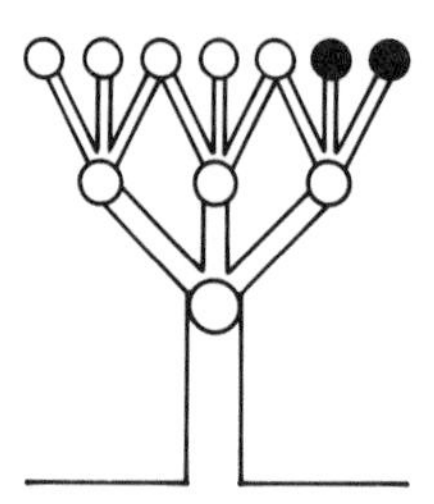
Figure 61.

# CHAPTER 7
# SENSING AND MONITORING AT SITES

## Demonstration

Theosophist Geoffrey Hodson visited Castlerigg in 1922. He was a psychometrist, a person who can receive information or impressions from an object or place by psychic means.With his inner vision he found incidents to be 'vividly impressed' upon Castlerigg. 'Standing out vividly, against the background of many strange scenes which pass before the inner eye, is the impression made upon the place by the powerful personality of one man,' he wrote. This man was tall, with long dark hair and beard, clothed in a single white garment that reached to his feet. Hodson saw him standing within the ring of stones, backed by a group of other priests in similar garb. Hodson's mental snapshots showed an ancient ceremony within the ring of stones in which energy was summoned from the sky and which 'materialised so as to be visible to physical sight.' A 'very powerful magnetic insulation' existed around Castlerigg, providing as much occult seclusion 'as would a complete and solid temple.' The downflow of energy from above appeared to Hodson's inner eye as 'a veritable pillar of living power . . . fiery mother-of-pearl, opalescent and tinged with an inner colouring of rose.' He felt it penetrated deep into the ground within the circle. Hodson glimpsed people onlooking from outside the circle, and banners with symbols draped over some of the stones.

In 1978 physical monitoring work was conducted at Castlerigg on behalf of the Dragon Project (see below). Electronic 'listening' for high frequency sound (ultrasound) took place, and on the third dawn of the study the detector picked up apparent signals around a stone on the eastern side of the ring. A resistivity meter was also employed to study by means of variable electrical charge passed through the ground any signs of prehistoric earth disturbance at the site. The instrument went haywire every time it passed between stones, and eventually ceased functioning altogether. (An-

*Plate 35.*

other energy finding at the site is mentioned in the opening of Chapter 11.) On this same session, the use of the pendulum gave dowsing responses that suggested the recognised northern entrance to the circle was for human use, but that another gap in the stones was for the entry of spirits.

## Discussion

For many years, but especially since the 1960s, there has been a rumour of strange and mysterious forces manifesting at sacred sites of antiquity. Folklore, as we have seen, is the traditional source of such a rumour. When I took over editorship of *The Ley Hunter* magazine[1], in 1976, I invited papers on the subject. Items of interest were submitted, but it was clear that people were operating on anecdotal experience (usually second hand) or a pet theory basis. So in late 1977 I suggested a meeting at a designated London pub to discuss the matter. A wide range of people attended – Earth Mysteries aficionados, electronics engineers, physicists, chemists and others. It was finally agreed that a research effort should be mounted and that it should adopt a two-pronged approach, one dealing with the monitoring of any physical energies and the other focusing on direct human sensing at ancient monuments. It was hoped, perhaps naively, that in due course correlations between the two modes might present themselves. Californian researcher John Steele took on coordination of the direct sensing, 'psychic archaeology' approach, and did so until 1986, and inorganic chemist Don Robins had oversight of the physical monitoring, and this was effective until about 1982. I agreed to overall directorship. At a suggestion of Steele's we called the effort 'The Dragon Project', after one of the old Chinese symbols for a force or *ch'i* within the ground *(telluric current)*. Through the good offices of dowser Tom Graves, the project was allowed to use the Rollright stone circle near Oxford as its main fieldbase.

So, there are two approaches to site energies, human and instrumental. Let us consider the direct sensing methods first.

'Being and Seeing' and folklore both relate to primary human response to sites. In addition, most people have experienced being at places where they have 'felt' something – a haunting quality, a feeling of joy, or perhaps of dread and terror. Some places feel 'right'; others less so. This is primary response.

Another, often marginalised, aspect of human response to sacred monuments is the aesthetic reflex. Down the years paintings (by Constable and Turner just as examples) and poetry (Wordsworth, for instance) have been inspired that reflect something of the elemental and mysterious qualities present at these places. In modern art, there has been the advent of 'Land Art' in which visual artists work on a landscape scale, responding virtually geomantically to the lay of the land. Names spring to mind such as Richard Long, famous for his 'lines' in remote landscapes, produced in many ways from simple walking to rows of stones; Michael Heizer and his great ditches, depressions and bulks of granite; Walter de Maria and his desert lines and lightning rods; Robert Smithson and his famous 'Spiral Jetty' in Utah's Great Salt Lake; Robert Morris, Richard Fleischner, James Pierce and Herbert Bayer whose respective earthworks evoke, variously, henge monuments, turf labyrinths and effigy or burial mounds. The work of artists like Nancy Holt, James Turrell and Charles Ross (Chapter 4) are astronomical on a scale that matches the great monuments of antiquity.[2,3]

Many other artists, on a smaller scale, and less mainstream have also responded directly to sites. In the late 1970s, a group of artists produced an 'Earth Mysteries' exhibition, partially funded by the British Arts Council, which travelled the British Isles, bringing out record crowds at a number of galleries and venues. Here were many media – prints, paintings, drawings, assemblage, sculpture, electronics, photography – all exploring the forms, atmospheres, geometry and time of old sacred places.[4] These and many more artists and poets in Europe and America now make ancient monuments a focus of their art as a fully conscious geomantic act. Sites and artists are now in dialogue. It is essential that the artistic mind as well as the analytical and scientific modes of consciousness are so engaged. And this can have surprising spin-offs: we have already seen how the artist's eye can identify hitherto unnoticed aspects of sites.

But what are usually thought of as the main modes of primary sensing by humans in connection with sites are psychic and dowsing responses. Psychic work at sites seems to have been first documented by Frederick Bligh Bond. He was appointed director of excavations at ruined Glastonbury Abbey, charged with determining the full extent of the site. Bond began to work with John Bartlett, who was able to write down 'spirit messages' with one hand while his attention was otherwise engaged (automatic writing). In the course of many sittings between 1907 and 1912, Bond and Bartlett amassed information in Low Latin, Middle English and modern English purporting to come from long dead monks associated with Glastonbury. Architectural details of the site were revealed in this manner which were apparently confirmed by Bond's excavations. In a 1918 book,[5] Bond unwisely revealed the

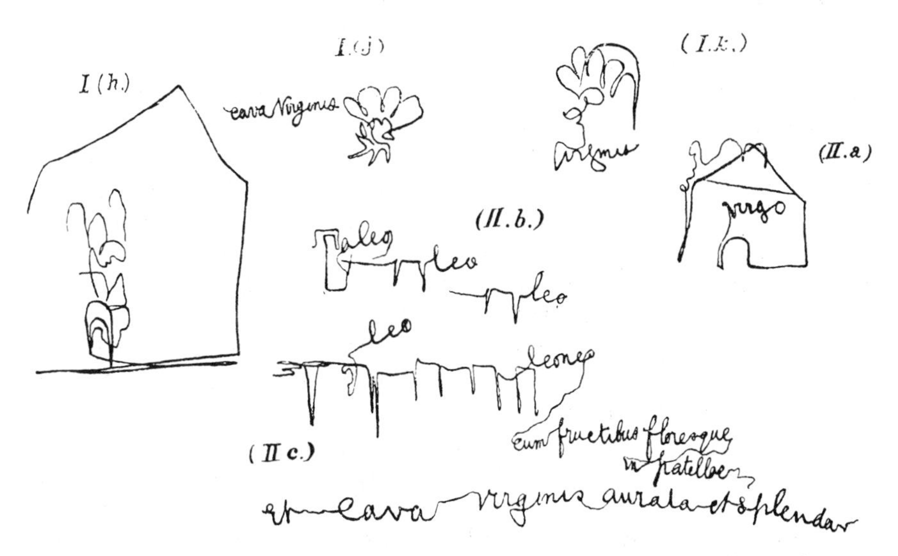


*Figure 62. Automatic writing and drawing relating to Bligh Bond's excavations at Glastonbury Abbey through the mediumship of John Bartlett*

source of his excavational guidance with dire consequences for his career. Bond himself kept an open mind as to whether the communications came from the Dead or from some form of 'greater memory' belonging to the human race as a whole, a concept foreshadowing C.G. Jung's Collective Unconscious and Sheldrake's species memory fields – all of which owe much to the long-held occult idea of the Akashic Records, a kind of astral-plane library.

In subsequent decades it was fashionable in Britain for psychometrists to be asked their impressions of prehistoric monuments. Even the respected archaeoastronomer, Boyle Somerville, used the Irish sensitive, Geraldine Cummins, on occasion at megalithic sites in Ireland. At The Three Fingers, she 'saw' Elders who had been able to 'draw power from these stones' and pass into trance. At the Drumbeg stone circle, she contacted an entity which said that a powerful midwinter ceremony used to be conducted there. 'Earth-power' was drawn from the ground and used for a low, elemental form of magic. Originally, there had been a period of 'pure worship' at the stones, connected with the sun.[6]

Another well-known psychic of the Thirties and Forties, Iris Campbell, did work at sites in tandem with John Foster Forbes, an antiquarian with occult tastes and Scottish 'second sight'. In books and on radio he argued that the megaliths had been placed by survivors from Atlantis and they were used for an elemental magic. The quartz rocks often found at megalithic sites were used to attract telluric currents and direct influences from the stars at certain times of year. Forbes correctly predicted that some old stone sites on the western seaboard of northwest Europe would be found to be older than those of the Mediterranean. Campbell found the Long Meg and Her Daughters circle to be a 'receiving station' tuned to 'other stations' throughout the land. The stones 'picked up the earth vibrations' and were used for the transmission of messages by pressing the palms of the hands on the stone. Campbell claimed that Mayborough Henge near Penrith had been 'an experimental area . . . where the magnetism was induced from the four points of the compass.' It had been used for enhancing the etheric centres in human beings.[7]

In more recent times, clairvoyance ('remote viewing') has been used specifically for archaeological purposes by some American researchers. In 1971, Geoffrey Goodman had two strong dreams in which he saw a place apparently in southwestern USA where he uncovered archaeological evidence for previously unsuspected early human presence on the continent. This led him to contact a remarkably accurate psychic, Aron Abrahamsen, who received information variously by means of clairvoyance, tapping a universal record and apparent discarnate spirits. Goodman eventually located the very spot he had seen in his dreams near Flagstaff, Arizona. Over a period of years there, making use of psychic information supplied by Abrahamsen, Goodman did indeed unearth evidence that seemed to push the normally accepted dates for Amerindian presence on the continent much further back in time.[8] In the late 1970s a research outfit called The Mobius Group made use of profoundly accurate remote viewing by an American sensitive to identify and carry out archaeological digs at hitherto undiscovered sites in Egypt. Both Goodman and Mobius had independent observers overlooking their work.

Less exacting material was published in 1979 by American explorer David D. Zink.[9] He described visits to a range of prehistoric sites worldwide where he used the impressions of a few psychics to supplement his own responses. According to this psychic synthesis, Callanish was built around 4400 BC, but the energies produced there 'created vortices of strength which disoriented many.' Callanish was linked with the Pleiades. Hagar Qim and other temples on Malta 'served one purpose . . . communion with extra-terrestrial beings who were expected from legends.' The Great Pyramid was built by the survivors of Atlantis to ensure an exact astronomical fix so any earth changes could be noted. It was also 'an energy collector and beacon,' and its stones could trigger out-of-the-body experiences. At Tiahuanaco one sensitive gave thoughtful readings on features at the site, some of which were later apparently archaeologically confirmed. Another psychic was more concerned about the 'guardians of secrets . . . from Mars.' The Easter Island statues were symbolic of awaiting 'a return to the stars.' At the curious lithic complex of Mystery Hill in New Hampshire, USA, the psychic was more concerned about 'warriors of South American origin' and struggles with Semitic peoples.

Dragon Project attempts to work with sensitives in the 1980s proved problematical. Dependably accurate psychics are hard to find – there are as many variations in their quality as in any other line of human activity. Steele and Robins conducted a double-blind test using Mesolithic and Neolithic artefacts with a couple of psychics who were keen to work on the project. The results were *worse* than chance. Other psychics felt their sensitivities were too great to work at the Rollright Stones, and complained of headaches and sinister feelings. Some baulked at the idea of getting to the site in the early hours of the morning when most Dragon Project work started at the site. Sensitives, we found, were sensitive in all sorts of ways! Nevertheless, some psychics were most helpful, and sessions were conducted. Healer John Gordon, for instance, went into trance at Rollright and saw entities within the ring of stones. He was able to describe these beings in detail. They told him that they possessed great knowledge, but would cease to exist if they left the circle of stones. In the late 1980s, we had an American sensitive at Welsh and Scottish sites. An academic, she had suddenly developed 'second sight' only a few years previously, and had taken steps early on to ensure that the field effects she could see around people and objects were objective by carefully cross-checking with other psychics. We were able to tape her real-

*Plate 36. Part of the Mystery Hill lithic complex, North Salem, New Hampshire, USA*

*Plate 37. Healer John Gordon (left) going into trance during a Dragon Project session at the Rollright circle, Oxfordshire, while coordinator John Steele looks on*

time observations of field interactions between standing stones and human beings. The detailed results of these and numerous other sessions with psychics remain on the unpublished files of the Dragon Project (a trust since 1988), so that any similar work in the future will not be compromised. If the time arrives when we feel we have enough psychically-obtained information from independent sessions that cross-references can be made to establish a degree of objectivity, then that will be the time to publish.

Decades ago, when working on my degree dissertation dealing with the paranormal, I had a number of sittings with psychometrists. What I typically found was that for most of a session the sensitive would bluff her way through, waffling on about dead Uncle George (I never had an Uncle George), but, every so often, authentic information that she could not have known about through normal channels would dart out like a fish from behind a rock. This is the way I tend to see much psychic work at sites. Sensitives need a 'stream of consciousness' to carry the occasional flotsam of real information, and that patter is likely to be chock-full of their own beliefs and prejudices. It is important on the one hand not to throw the baby out with the bathwater, and on the other not to swallow everything that a psychic comes out with. That is why the cross-referencing of independent sessions at specific sites is an important methodology.

The other major plank of primary response at sites is dowsing (water witching or divining). The reason it is major is mainly because it is nowadays very popular, but popularity does not necessarily bear a direct relationship with inherent importance. The traditional reasons for dowsing were the finding of water or minerals, and there is simply no doubt that some dowsers can perform such work with skill and accuracy. Good dowsers can also find lost or buried objects, and they have been employed at archaeological digs.[10] Some dowsers can date artefacts too – Stonehenge was correctly dated by dowser T.C. Lethbridge before the recalibration of radiocarbon dating. The work conducted most often at sites these days, however, tends to be concerned with 'earth energies'. A swift, potted history of dowsing is required so the current situation can be better evaluated, which is necessary because energy dowsing more than anything else tends to be the public face of Earth Mysteries, causing reactions ranging from cultish adherence to outright rejection. It biases understanding and communication quite out of proportion with its actual value.

Some form of dowsing has probably been known to humanity since ancient times but there is no coherent record. There is some evidence that a third-millennium-BC Chinese emperor had special knowledge relating to underground water and minerals, and a bas relief shows him with possibly a dowsing instrument.[11,12] There are references to the use of 'wonder rods' in the ancient literature but it is thought that the divinatory purposes they were used for may not have been dowsing.[13]

*Figure 63. Dowsing for metals in the 1600s*

*Figure 64. A German miner of yesteryear using a forked twig for dowsing*

One of the first clear, historical accounts of dowsing appeared in a German book on mining called *De Re Metallica* by Georgius Agricola in 1556. Agricola distanced himself from the practice, however, and expressed scepticism as did, surprisingly, the Swiss alchemist Paracelsus. Nevertheless, something made the Germans into the best miners and mineralogists of their day and they were much courted by Elizabethan Britain where some emigrated, bringing with them – or reintroducing – the secrets of the dowsing rod, or the *virgula divina* as it was called. In 1626, Baroness de Beausoleil and her husband, who were both mineralogists, were commissioned to conduct a mineralogical survey of France. They used dowsing for part of this process, though it was frowned upon. Notwithstanding the disapproval of the Church, dowsing flourished in France.

The earliest historical references relate almost exclusively to dowsing for minerals. One of the first mentions of water dowsing was given by John Aubrey (Chapter 2) in the latter part of the seventeenth century. He reported that in Wiltshire 'water may be found by a divining rod made of willowe . . .'

The Dauphine region of France produced many dowsers, but none more famous than Jacques Aymar. He could dowse for water and minerals but came into national prominence in France when he used his ability successfully to assist police with a murder inquiry. This aroused intellectual interest in dowsing. Aymar carried out experiments with the Abbé de Vallemont who wrote an important dowsing treatise called *Occult Physics* in 1693.

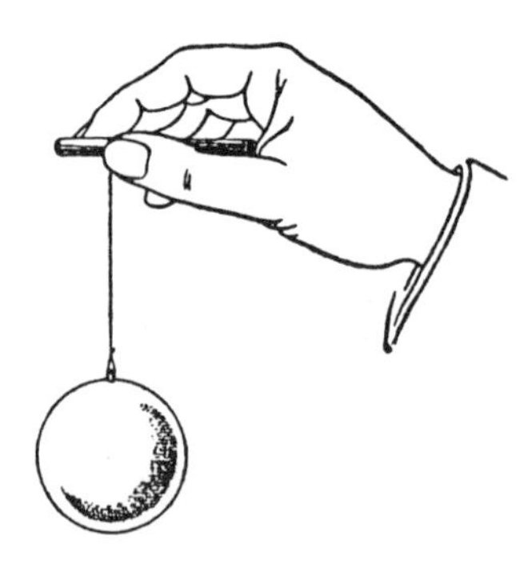

*Figure 65. A dowsing pendulum (after Henry de France)*

A famous French dowser of the following century was Barthelemy Bleton, who was subjected to various tests by the court physician, Pierre Thouvenel. These two joined forces and carried out numerous surveys which included the discovery of the mineral waters near Contrexeville in the Vosges mountains. In the eighteenth and nineteenth centuries, the use of dowsing for water overtook its usage in mining.

In the nineteenth century, the dowsing pendulum made its appearance. Up until this time dowsing had been associated with the 'rod'. This was traditionally a forked hazel twig, but in practice a whole host of implements of various designs were used – even German sausages! Although pendular devices were used in the classical world for divinatory practices, probably the direct ancestor of the dowsing pendulum was the spiritualists's 'ring and disk' method of obtaining 'yes' or 'no' to questions directed at discarnate entities. The significance of the pendulum to dowsing increased largely due to the activities of the German physicist, Johann Ritter. He heard of dowsing experiments in Italy and went there in 1806. He was impressed by Francesco Campetti, a gifted dowser, who was working with a scientist called Cannella. Another scientist, Carlo Amoretti, also showed Ritter the use of the pendulum. Ritter's later investigations convinced him that different parts of the human body had polarities, as the pendulum responded similarly when over the poles of magnets. Ritter's work intrigued and influenced Antione Gerboin, a professor at the faculty of medicine at Strasbourg.

Early in the twentieth century, Henri Mager arranged a series of tests with dowsers to see if they could find lost mines under Paris. The dowsers did this with notable success and the experiment aroused considerable public interest. After the First World War much dowsing research took place in France. A pioneer in the use of the pendulum for medical work was Mermet. In the 1930s, French dowsers claimed that standing stones were positioned over the crossing of subterranean streams. This was noted in England before the Second World War by dowser and archaeologist Reginal A. Smith. This line of dowsing research was picked up by Guy Underwood after the war and he proceeded to develop a complex theory which involved underground streams beneath megalithic sites and early churches, 'aquastats', 'track lines' and much else besides. He called this the 'geodedic system' and felt that 'water divining was part of prehistoric religions'. Underwood's findings were published as papers in the journal of the British Society of Dowsers (BSD) during his lifetime and posthumously as a book, *The Pattern of the Past*[14]. Most people, including dowsers, now feel Underwood went too far with his theory, dogmatically making the most extraordinary claims. Nevertheless, the essence of his work confirmed the findings of earlier dowsers that underground water had seemingly been an integral factor in the siting of megalithic structures.

The first society of dowsers was formed in 1920 in Germany, and France was next with the *Association des Amis de la Radiesthesia* in 1930. The BSD was formed in 1933 and the American Society of Dowers in 1960.

In 1976, after a long period without there being any fresh dowsing literature in England, Tom Graves wrote an excellent and graphic manual on dowsing.[15] In preparing for this, Graves had carried out a series of dowsing experiments in 1973 at the Rollright circle. His team found seven concentric circles of dowsable 'charge' within the stone ring, disclosed by the crossing of angle rods (metal dowsing rods bent into right angles and held by the shorter length). Graves learned from Welsh dowser Bill Lewis that standing stones have a dowsable helix of force around them, which can be affected by many variables such as weather and lunar phase. Certain points of force ('nodes') on stones could have specific effects on a dowser if he or she touched them. Graves also discovered overground dowsable lines in addition to underground water reactions. These connected the stones at Rollright and some went off into the surrounding landscape. Graves wondered if these could be 'the non-physical reality' behind Alfred Watkins' leys (cross-country site alignments).

He was not the first to suggest this: Arthur Lawton in 1939 had proposed that there were linear links between sites that could be dowsed, and in 1936 the occultist Dion Fortune had written a fictional work[16] which talked of 'lines of force' between prehistoric sites. All this came up after Watkins' death in 1935, however, and was not promoted by the man himself. German dowsers between the world wars found dowsable grids – Hartmann and Curry each had their own system.

In the emerging new wave of occult interest in the 'Swinging Britain' of the '60s, the findings of the German and French dowsers, UFOs, ancient Chinese geomancy and goodness knows what got lumped in with the alignment of sites. Leys as lines of energy became a new doctrine that became automatically assumed. By 1974, American dowsers were writing about 'ley lines' only as energy lines, and most Americans first got to hear about leys in that context. In 1978, Tom Graves developed John Michell's analogy of terrestrial energy lines being like acupuncture meridians on the human body in his *Needles of Stone*.[17] Tom Graves lived just round the corner from me in north London at that time, and I remember us discussing the last part of the book and swapping notes. *Needles of Stone* is an ideas book, not a research treatise as such, but it is now assumed by latter-day energy dowsers that it is all definite fact.

The matter of 'energy dowsing' has been further compounded and obscured by the rise of the New Age movement, in that some people floating in this milieu picked up on fragments of dowsing and Earth Mysteries material, always without any full, historical awareness of the literature or research that has (or has not) gone on, and built fanciful superstructures on what little they knew. This in turn has been taken as some kind of gospel by newcomers, and so the ideas of 'earth energies' (never defined) continue being built upon like a house of cards.

In the 1980s we had many dowsers take part on the Dragon Project. We had professionals and amateurs; those who did not believe in leys and said they could not be dowsed and those who found energy lines everywhere. We had dowsers seek water, minerals, chronology of sites, energies. Some sessions were highly controlled with cross-referenced groundplans and questions, others were more relaxed. We used the Mind Mirror, a sophisticated EEG device that showed the beta, alpha, theta and delta rhythms[18,19] sweeping across a dowser's brain as he or she worked on site. Bill Lewis in particular showed the tell-tale, 'search mode' theta and delta brain rhythms, which cannot be consciously manipulated, when he was dowsing at Rollright. We also saw him interacting with energy nodes on stones, causing measurable electrical changes in them.

The nature of dowsing has been a matter of debate over the

*Plate 38. Bill Lewis dowsing at the Kingstone, Rollright, while his brain rhythms are monitored on the Mind Mirror EEG device by Dr Faruq Abdullah*

centuries. The seventeenth-century scholar, Athanasius Kircher, was amongst the first to try to understand how dowsing worked. His studies led him to the conclusion that the dowsing instrument was not responding to mysterious radiations from the substances being dowsed – the common belief of the day – but to the muscular responses of the dowser. This opinion was also shared by the Jesuit Bernard Casius and echoed in the same century by German metallurgist Balthazer Rossler, who wrote that dowsing works because of 'the nature of man'. But while this work showed that the dowsing instrument itself was simply an amplifier of muscular movements it did not come any closer to explaining what stimuli were causing those reflexes.

With the growing awareness of electricity in the eighteenth century came a strand of opinion equating electrical energy with dowsing response. Thouvenel (above) thought that the water dowser was responding to subterranean electrical phenomena created by flowing underground water. Indeed, Amoretti, who had taught Ritter much about pendulums, was studying certain phenomena which were to become identified with electricity. Ralph Whitlock has summed it up:

> The research which resulted in the discovery and harnessing of electricity was . . . closely associated with the investigation of the dowsing pendulum. Subsequently throughout the nineteenth century continued research into dowsing phenomena was linked with that which resulted in the discovery of X-rays in 1895 and radioactivity in 1903. Each of these discoveries were, somewhat optimistically, hailed by contemporary dowsers as explanations of dowsing, and very probably there is a connection between them.[20]

In the 1930s two German researchers, Joseph Wüst and Joseph Wimmer carried out years of dowsing experiments and decided that it operated by means of an unknown force they called 'W-radiation' (the 'W' was for *Wunschelrute,* German for divining rod). In the 1940s some of their experiments were repeated by the meticulous Dutch scientist, Solco Tromp, who was able to confirm a number of them. However, Tromp felt that Wüst and Wimmer were wrong in attempting to ascribe the results of their experiments to an unknown radiation rather than to field effects. Another investigator, De Vita, found with the aid of electroscopes that the atmosphere above underground streams contained greater ionization than above normal ground and could be affected by season, weather conditions and position of the sun. At about the same time, G. Von Pohl and P. Dobler attempted to photograph 'earth rays' over dowsing zones using the Russell effect technique (see Chapter 11). Just before the Second World War, J. Cecil Maby, a British researcher, successfully repeated De Vita's experiments while investigating a variety of physical and physiological effects to see if a relationship with dowsing could be uncovered. He concluded that one of the stimuli appeared to be Hertzian rays resulting from the action of cosmic radiation.[21] After the war, Tromp carried out experiments and was able to demonstrate that small electrostatic charges applied secretly to dowsers could cause specific dowsing responses, and effective results were caused by magnetism as well.[22]

This was confirmed by the later research of Yves Rocard in France, and Z. Harvalik in the USA. Rocard, a physicist, also felt that dowsers were responding to changes in the magnetic gradient above ground caused by electrical currents from moving subterranean water, reminiscent of Thouvenel's ideas long before. Rocard tested this by getting dowsers to walk though wooden frameworks supporting electrical wiring (thus creating an electromagnetic field) and by passing an electrically-active coil over their bodies. Harvalik began his experiments in the late 1960s and over a number of years tested many people by asking them to dowse over ground through which he had arranged for varying current intensities to be randomly switched on and off. He found that the vast majority of his subjects were able to detect a current strength of 20 milliamperes while a few were able to detect a current as low as half a milliampere. He found subjects who could detect magnetic field changes as slight as $10^{-9}$ gauss (a unit of measure for the Earth's magnetic field) which can be occasioned by all manner of stimuli. Harvalik found that his most sensitive subject, the late German master dowser Wilhelm de Boer, could reliably respond to a magnetic field change of $10^{-12}$ gauss. He found he could block off the German's sensitivity by placing aluminium shielding around his head and kidney areas. Harvalik concluded that the magnetic sensors in the human body were located either in the pituitary or pineal gland in the head and the adrenal gland in the body. (Scientists have subsequently confirmed that the pineal gland is indeed sensitive to the geomagnetic field.)

There is clearly some extra-sensory-perception element in dowsing, however. In fact, the term 'dowsing' may cover a whole band of loosely-related and poorly understood human sensitivities. Site dowsing almost certainly has a major element in it of physiological response to physical energies of various kinds, but map and photograph dowsing would seem to be more akin to remote viewing. To this ESP aspect is added the possibility that dowsing can detect thoughtforms. This was indicated many years ago when a French engineer called Voillaume asked a subject to concentrate on an object in the room while he dowsed around that person's head. Voillaume was able to dowse an invisible straight line connecting the subject's head with the object and was thus able to determine accurately what the person was concentrating on. In the 1970s, John Steele, working with dowsers and the Mind Mirror, noted the ability of people to dowse thoughtforms ('virtual objects' as Steele termed them). A group of people would jointly imagine an 'object' somewhere in the room while the dowser was secluded outside. The dowser then came in and attempted to dowse the virtual object. The dowser's brain rhythms would change when the virtual object was walked over by the dowser, whether or not there was a muscular response sufficient to move the dowsing implement (personal communication). In another test carried out by The Dragon Project at the Rollright circle, investigators mentally laid out a line that random visitors to the site were invited to dowse. Most of them had a dowsing response when passing across the line. Subsequent experiments have similarly tended to confirm this phenomenon. It also appears that even when a virtual object has stopped being actively imagined by participants in an experiment, there is still some sort of dowsable trace detectable in the environment. The nature and longevity of such apparent traces are quite unknown at this stage.

Inevitably, we come back to contemporary energy dowsing. Its popularity stems mainly from the fact that swinging a pair of angle rods around, simply made from wire coathangers, or to wobble a pendulum, also easily made or purchased, is something seemingly as easy as taking snapshots (with the same mixed quality of results!). It has become a pastime for many people visiting ancient sites. But it can also allow a sense of 'research'. It is only when one edits a magazine like *The Ley Hunter* that it is really seen how many people can spend years of their time developing pet notions of 'energy systems' and 'grids' of the most intricate nature. A surprising number of such 'discoveries' cross the editorial desk, sent by folk convinced they have made the find of the century. They invariably present their work in obsessive depth and as beautifully presented as a debutante.

So what is energy dowsing exactly? What energies are being dowsed? How rigorous is the work involved with it?

Significantly, any attempt to bring a little rigour and accountability into energy dowsing is often met with hostility or incomprehension. Energy dowsing is held by some to be 'spiritual' and above the need for any form of accountability. It is thus a belief system. For example, a church with international links has been formed in Britain, its gospel being dowsed from energy script left on the land by ancient masters. 'Ley lines' are used to beam light and love to unsuspecting folk in various institutions who are clearly less enlightened than the energy cultists themselves. While the reader may dismiss all this as ludicrous fantasy, the problem is that material promoting this belief system gets included in the journals of important organisations like British and American dowsing associations, and 'alternative' groups involved with studying ancient sites in America and elsewhere. Because many orthodox archaeologists and scientists have an arrogant tendency indiscriminately to dismiss or ridicule alternative material, there is a natural unwillingness to apply rigour to viewpoints that seem heroically opposed to the myopia of the Establishment.

However well-meaning, such uncritical acceptance is fraught with dangers. The ability to discriminate is crucial, but is dependent on information which too often is not readily available to a general audience because of the marginalised 'alternative' situation modern geomantic awareness occupies. There are no research standards, there are no specialist libraries, there is no university-based continuity. Anyone can write and claim what they like, and many do.

In actuality, of course, dowsing as an activity is no more spiritual than riding a bicycle: spirituality is in the person. The bulk of the ideas promoted by what could be termed New Age dowsing are the inventions of the late twentieth-century Western mind, and there is literally a world of difference between invented mysteries and those which are perceived in nature. The real mysteries of Earth are rich, diverse and full of aspects that the human mind cannot invent. Mystery is a process, and our humanity is enhanced by contemplating those examples the universe places before our attention. Compared to this rich matrix of mystery, the New Age 'energy' ideas are conceptually bankrupt. Nature cannot be replaced by human invention.

As it stands, energy dowsing is currently neither an activity like yoga or meditation that can create enhanced states of consciousness by its own virtue, nor is it yet a tool that can be collectively used in the environment the way water dowsing can. So one must decide whether it is to be a belief system or a research capability. Fortunately, not all energy dowsers are superficial or pseudo-spiritual. Far from it. Many want to employ accountable research. But how? After many years' involvement with Earth Mysteries work, I have a few observations and suggestions to offer.

The first thing has to be the identification of the energy dowsing stimulus. Dowsing by a skilled practitioner can certainly work well for water, minerals and finding objects. Ultimately, these by their nature are testable reactions. A water-dowser's client will drill where the dowser says underground water is located. One cannot get more reductionist than that. For energy dowsing to be useful as an approach to ancient sites, it has to reach these standards. Cornish water dowser Donovan Wilkins has told me that he thinks the reactions of many eager energy dowsers are likely to be caused by water, inexperience in water divining leading interpretations astray.

But once a dowsing reaction has been established that is not due to water, then the next thing is to confirm or eliminate other measurable, environmental energies. We have already referred to research that shows how sensitive human beings can be to ambient energies. There is much other scientific research that clearly shows human and animal ability to detect minute energy effects.[23,24] A dowser could be picking up a natural magnetic anomaly, some ionisation effect, radon or gamma radiation from the ground or surrounding stones, or some electromagnetic field from a nearby artificial device. Natural infra-red and ultra-violet frequencies abound. A water or metal dowser can either focus on the material being divined, or carry a sample (called a 'witness') to aid in that process. An energy dowser simplistically concentrating on 'energy' is open to almost everything – even the daylight is energy! *By definition, a dowser cannot have a mental image of an unknown energy*. A process of elimination is therefore vital in order to find out if the reaction is due to one of these forces, or something unknown. An example of how important this can be is indicated by physical monitoring at the Long Meg site in Cumbria. Two or three of the granite megaliths there have small areas on them that emit constant gamma radiation, recordable by geiger counter (Chapter 11). Anyone standing near them getting an energy dowsing reaction could easily think they were picking up some exotic 'energy line'.

If, after such eliminative work, the dowser seems to be picking up a non-physical force, then there is one more hurdle. If it does turn out that *thoughtforms* are dowsable, then it needs to be ascertained that the form being divined is not being unconsciously transmitted by the dowser involved, or by a companion, or even the thought impressions of a previous energy dowser at the site! Thoughtform dowsing, if confirmed, would be a fabulously important discovery. It would open up whole new studies on the nature of consciousness, and have an enormous number of applications. But this refers to the *process itself*, not the specific thought patterns detected. Such patterns would have no inherent value, being merely the constructs of modern pet theories lodged in the environment, in the way that an image on the TV screen is transient and not the TV set itself.

There is also a sensitive issue to be addressed; dowsing tools on the whole are very easy to manipulate unconsciously to get a desired response (I have done it myself!). It is easy to be seduced by expectation as geomantic researcher and writer Nigel Pennick observed at a site that he happened to witness being dowsed at different times by German and British energy dowsers. The Germans found their grids and nets, but the British found merely wavy lines! (Personal communication.) Years of involvement have convinced me that, alas, most energy dowsers, however sincere, are in effect dowsing the insides of their own heads, so to speak.

So for all these reasons, when an exotic force seems to have been dowsed, double-blind testing is essential. Not to 'prove' anything, but simply to identify the objectivity of the dowsing stimulus, and additionally, the level of dowsing competence (not all dowsers are equal in ability). Incredibly, although the popular literature waxes on about ley lines and energy, a *double-blind* check of an energy line across country by dowsers seems never to have been conducted and published. The reader may be shocked at that, but it is true. All is currently a symphony of assumptions, sweeping claims and uncritical acceptance.

If the sort of measures outlined here were to be taken as protocol by energy dowsers, we could eventually end up with dowsers of known abilities in specific areas of physical energies; we could have a grading of reliability established; we might be able to confirm the objective existence of thoughtforms in the environment, and, even, we might establish the actuality of exotic and unknown energy patterns in the landscape. Let us hope that energy dowsing can soon mature.

Regarding physically measurable energies, the Dragon Project hardly knew where to start when it launched its monitoring programme. There were few precedents for such work at sites, and money and resources were in short supply. We could not conduct wide-ranging research so a method was adopted based on using anecdotal information. Human response and observation at sites was thus the basis for the instrumental approach too.

Some years before the Dragon Project, physicists invited by a dowser to a standing stone in Wales had detected magnetic anomalies,[25] so we knew that was one area we would need to investigate. But magnetometers are expensive to buy or even hire, and it was some years before we were able to buy our own. Another anecdote came from a zoologist shortly before the start of the project. He informed me that a colleague had picked up anomalous ultrasonic signals from an ancient site at dawn one day (he had been using an ultrasonic receiver for detecting bat behaviour overnight). So our first fieldwork (1978) involved the use of a 'bat detector' standard ultrasound receiver deployed at the Rollright Stones initially, and subsequently at many more sites. Other detectors were brought in at later stages. In the early days of the project, Keith Critichlow told me he had noted a geophysicist's geiger counter going haywire near a Welsh stone circle he happened to be surveying (a few days after a remarkable geophysical event centred on the area). So we very early on started monitoring background radiation at a whole variety of sites with a range of equipment. Although our equipment was primitive and slow, we

*Plate 39. Using an ultrasound receiver of the 'bat detector' type during a Dragon Project session at Rollright*

built up quite a knowledge of background levels of radiation in certain regions and were able to notice anomalies fairly readily.

Another anecdote involved the most widespread type of human response reported at sites – the reception of an 'electric shock' from a stone. It has never happened to me, but I have spoken to people of all ages and social groups at many different locations to whom it has happened; some of them I know and respect, and have no doubts at all that standing stones can somehow store electricity which can be discharged at times by someone touching them. So electrical and electrostatic monitoring was included on our schedule.

Other methods were added as we went along: infra-red photography and monitoring, Kirlian camera work, scanning for unusual radio signals – anything, in fact, where some lead suggested a possible avenue of enquiry and where we had the means to follow it to some extent.

Some of the work occupied a no-man's-land between physical and paranormal monitoring. For instance, we studied Electronic Voice Phenomena (EVP) at megalithic sites for a while. In this, it is claimed that paranormal voices can be found lodged in the background hiss of a tape, or in the 'white noise' of radio static.[26] Even in radio-screened laboratories these odd voices have been re-

*Plate 40. Monitoring local levels of radioactivity at the Moel-ty-Uchaf circle, Wales, during Dragon Project work*

corded. They have a peculiar, rapid rhythm, can be in any language or apparent gibberish.

For a decade the part-time, sporadic physical monitoring of the Dragon Project took place as and when it could, at a variety of prehistoric sites, primarily in Britain but also to a very limited degree in France, the USA and Egypt. The results of some of this work are given along with other findings in Chapter 11, and greater details are given in *Places of Power*.[27] The project is now the Dragon Project Trust,[28] and some of its plans for the 1990s are indicated in the final chapter of the present work. For now, it is sufficient for us to note that human direct sensing through sensory and possibly extra-sensory channels, and remote 'sensing' by means of instrumentation, are further important aspects of a systems understanding of ancient sacred sites.

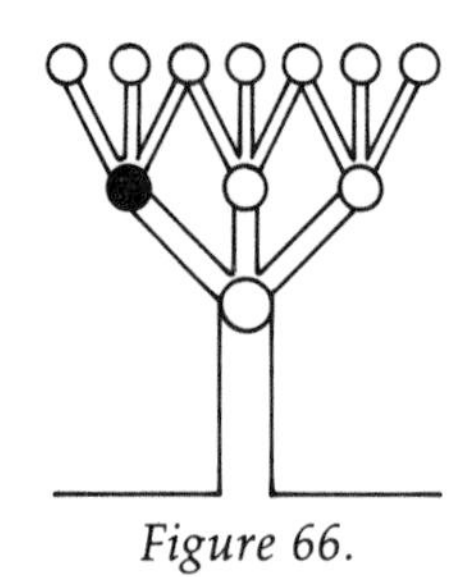

*Figure 66.*

# CHAPTER 8
# GEOMANCY

## Demonstration

After John Glover had discovered his 'shadow path' at Castlerigg, archaeologist John Barnatt and helpers surveyed its line. Something remarkable was discovered. Viewed from the circle, the midsummer sun seems to set behind a hill known as Latrigg: it was found that the angle from the top of Latrigg to the base of the shadow-throwing stone in the circle was continued in the slope of the ground beyond the site. Figure 67 gives a schematic representation of this, with the vertical scale exaggerated. This slope enhances the length of the shadow which, without the intervention of a modern conifer plantation, could have reached up to two miles beyond the circle. The questions this finding raises are enormous. Did the circle's builders really manage to locate a place where they could not only manage to mesh skyline heights, astronomy and geometry, but find a slope at the right angle for the midsummer shadow as well? Or did they *landscape engineer* the ground to the southwest?

Glover explored the extended axis of the shadow path in both directions into the surrounding countryside. He found that to the southwest the extended line would pass through a skyline notch visible from the circle and through an ancient holy well. To the northwest, the line passes through a magnetic anomaly spot, and bypasses a seventh-century-AD chapel. The line also incorporates key hilltops along its length. Such an alignment of ancient sites and important topographical features was called a 'ley' by Alfred Watkins.

The Castlerigg line, therefore, incorporates astronomy, topography and the siting and orientation of ancient monuments. This is typical of the synthesis of factors we refer to as 'geomancy' today.

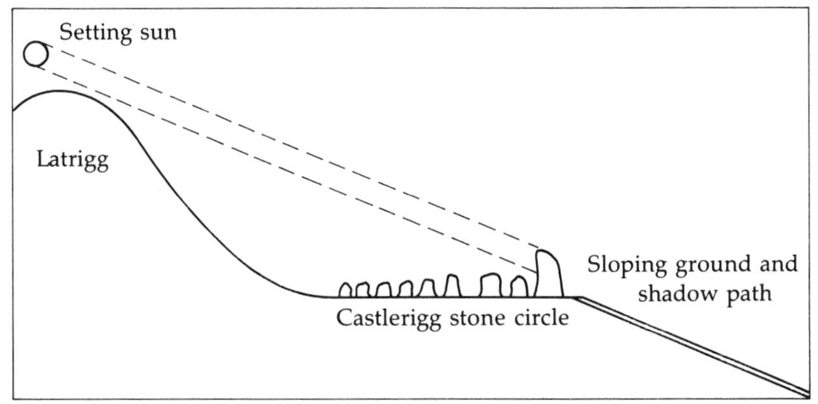


*Figure 67. (Courtesy Eddison Sadd Editions)*

## Discussion

We now descend to the second level of the Earth Mysteries Tree, which deals with the more integrated aspects of ancient sites. Each of the designated areas at this level represents a synthesis of some of the proposed 'front line' approaches described in the previous chapters. In the case of geomancy, elements of archaeology, being and seeing and ancient astronomy are brought together. In fact, other areas, such as sacred geometry, could justifiably be included as well.

*Plate 41. Surveying the shadow path*

It has already been suggested that geomancy could be defined as 'sacred geography'. Ideally, it is a celebration of time and space, linking sky and land in a unified whole that harmonises human beings, their temples and tombs, their secular buildings and the local topography. The word geomancy means 'earth divination' (geo-mancy), which was a fortune-telling procedure involving the casting of soil on the ground and reading the patterns produced – much like tea leaf reading. More sophisticated versions also existed. But the term was given a topographical meaning by the Victorian missionaries who encountered the Feng Shui system of sacred geography in China (see below).

The Castlerigg shadow path is a fine example of a geomantic feature, and in the case of Silbury Hill (Chapter 3) we see the monument as being the *very embodiment* of the geomancy of the Avebury landscape.

The basics of geomancy are simple enough. As Nigel Pennick puts it:

> The way we view the world is determined by the structure of our bodies, our physical existence in space and time. Our bodies have a fourfold form: in front, behind, left and right. Wherever we are, we perceive the world in terms of our body's position and our bodily directions. Traditional perceptions of the earth speak of the five directions – north, east, south, west, and *here*, the definition of human space. Our bodily structure defines the four directions and *here*, but also we have orientation, that is, a front and a back. It is this orientation that gives us our perspective on the world and our perception of space and time.[1]

We have seen that horizon calendars and clocks were used in the past. These only worked from a given point – *here*, which, geomantically applied, extended from a personal point of reference to one for the whole community. The four bodily directions were similarly transmuted into the cardinal directions, determined by astronomical observation. The directions were space, the astronomy time; the two essential co-ordinates of our existence. The Four Directions were reciprocally expressed in time as the four major divisions of the solar year – the solstices and equinoxes. The eightfold year incorporates the cross-quarter days, and these were marked in traditional cultures with great festivals and fairs. In many traditions the Four Directions were subdivided into an eightfold pattern too – in the old Norse tradition the day had eight time-directions, sometimes marked on the skyline, and each had certain numinous qualities.[2] It is possible that some of the stone top-skyline coincidences referred to earlier might relate to such horizon divisions. Certainly, the eight-petalled carving in Cairn T (Chapter 4) suggests that the eight divisions of the solar year were important as early as Neolithic Britain.

Orientation is understood to mean the easterly direction, deriving from a Latin verb meaning to rise – hence rising of the sun, east. Temples could be oriented to many astronomical events, though, not merely to the east. In Christianity, it has been traditional to orient a church to sunrise on the day of the saint to which it is dedicated (not always carried out in practice).

Terrestrial features, too, can sometimes be the focus of orientation. Mosques are oriented towards Mecca and synagogues towards Jerusalem. In other, more local, religions it may have been towards a sacred mountain on the skyline. Landscape architect Vincent Scully observed that Minoan palaces on Crete were oriented to symbolic landscape elements, including a twin-peaked or cleft hill.[3]

The *here* aspect in geomancy is dealt with by the concept of the *omphalos,* the navel or centre. The navel in the human being records the point of origin and sustenance, and so it is symbolically at the foundation point of a building or city. It is usually marked by a stone but sometimes by a pit or stake. The classic example of an omphalos is at Delphi, the oracle temple of Apollo (and formerly of Gaia, the Earth) in Greece. Here a rounded and elaborately carved omphalos stone, replaces an earlier, simpler and possibly meteoric rock, marked 'the navel of the world'. In legend the place was where two eagles sent by Zeus to find the centre of the world crossed their flightpaths, a mythic mnemonic for the Four Directions. At Mecca, Islam's most holy shrine, the

*Figure 68. Vincent Scully noted that Minoan palaces were oriented to distinctive cleft-peaked hills (after Vincent Scully)*

Ka'aba, contains a stone, also possibly meteoric. From this point paths radiate out in the eight directions. Israel 'is situated in the centre of the world, and Jerusalem in the centre of the land of Israel, and the Temple in the centre of Jerusalem, and the Holy of Holies in the centre of the Temple, and the foundation-stone on which the world was founded is situated in front of the ark.'[4] The navel stone of Jerusalem was known as the 'Compass of our Lord'. Every temple or holy place in the ancient world would have its centre, omphalos, navel. The idea lingers on in our own 'foundation stone' tradition. Procopius has left us an account of the foundation of a church in sixth-century Byzantium:

> Two lines were joined in the form of a cross joining one another in the middle, the upright one pointing to the rising and setting sun, and the other cross line towards the north and south wind . . . at the crossing of the two straight lines, that is, about the middle point of them, there is a place set apart, which may not be entered except by the priests, and which is consequently termed the sanctuary . . .[5]

The Romans, who took much of their learning in these matters from the Etruscans, would have an omphalos at the centre of their towns or camps. The layout of the streets would start from the crossing of north-south *(cardo)* and east-west *(decumanus)* roads. They called the crossing place the *cardo,* from which we derive the term cardinal points. In British market towns such points are often referred to as 'the cross', or 'high cross', and are often Christianised by a cross.

So the geomantic *here,* the navel or omphalos, represented a fixed point in time and space. The act of founding the central, navel point of a building or town was a geomantic act of great power.

The Zuni myth of *K'yan asdebi,* Water Skate, is a perfect expression of the omphalos, the Zuni's Centre. He showed the first Zuni the Four Directions by spreading his long legs, and his heart and navel marked 'the midmost place of the earth-mother' (Chapter 4). The marriage of time and space was well represented in the tradition of the Natchez Indians of Louisiana, where the chief, the Great Sun, would come to the doorway of his dwelling, built on a mound, and face the rising sun. He would howl three times, then blow tobacco smoke to the sun and the other three directions.[6]

But there are other elements in geomancy apart from the exoteric aspects of astronomy and orientation. The heavens could be reflected on the landscape not only astronomically, but also *astrologically,* certain areas having particular properties at appropriate

*Figure 69. The High Cross, Bristol (after Robert Ricart, 1478)*

times. And the omphalos was not just a survey reference point, it was also the cosmic axis, the channel between the worlds of spirits and humans. In animistic traditions, a special or sacred place was seen as having a spirit literally inhabiting it. This has developed into the analogous 'spirit of place' or *genius loci,* by which is meant the character of a place, its feeling or numinosity.

Archaic geomancy was, therefore, a mix of astronomy, topography and the *spirit landscape*. Geomancy is thus the geography of consciousness.

What remnants of archaic geomantic practices survive? In some cases, the record of whole systems remain, such as Vintana in Madagascar, the Hindu Vastuvidya, and the Chinese Feng shui.

We also have a fragmentary record of others, in documentation, in the traditions of declining ethnic groups, and in the silent evidence of prehistoric sites of vanished cultures.

The aboriginal peoples of Australia and Papua New Guinea display an inherent, subtle form of geomancy. The French anthropologist, Lucien Lévy-Bruhl, commented that 'observers of the Australian Aborigines have remarked on their highly developed sense of location.'[7] He quoted an early settler who remarked that he was often struck 'with the exact position each tribe takes in the general encampment, precisely in the position from each other their country lies according to the compass (of which they have a perfect notion).' Lévy-Bruhl referred to a '"local relationship", or *participation*, between a limited area of country and the creatures, human and other, which live in it.'

Raymond Firth, another anthropologist, similarly commented:

> Aboriginal beliefs or ritual practices tend always to be localised, to centre in the lands of their forebears, the particular trees, stones and waterholes of which are the abiding places of the spiritual being or supernatural forces . . .[8]

*Plate 42. Australian Aborigine at the totemic boulder of Jarapiri Bomba (courtesy Charles P. Mountford)*

The Marind-anim of Papua New Guinea likewise had a 'physiognomy of the landscape' which revealed the lineaments of myth, Lévy-Bruhl noted. As he put it: 'Legend is captured in the very outlines of the landscape.' So not only calendar time but *dreamtime* was linked to the landscape. We can never understand archaic geomancy until we become aware of that dimension.

The aborigines travelled along specific routes that had first been trod by the Dreamtime beings. Each sacred spot along the way would have its own ritual, song, imagery (rock or body painting) and sacred object.[9] The landscape was simultaneously topography and myth. Aborigines had no concept of a defined block of land; their words for land related to lines and 'ways through'.

A far more cerebrally-organised system of geomancy developed in ancient China – Feng shui, which means 'wind and water'. One of the Victorian missionaries who first encountered it was Ernest J. Eitel. He wrote that the Feng shui geomants:

> see a golden chain of spiritual life running through every form of existence and binding together, as one living body, everything that subsists in heaven above or on earth below.[10]

Feng shui as it has come down to us was practised from at least early medieval times, and there is evidence, indeed, that its principles were being used up to three thousand years ago in China. No dwelling or tomb would be built without a Feng shui geomant *(hsien-sheng)* studying the site and making necessary adjustment to the flow of energies there. As Eitel explained:

> . . . there are in the earth's crust two different, shall I say magnetic, currents, the one male, the other female; the one positive, the other negative . . . The one is allegorically called the azure dragon, the other the white tiger . . . This therefore is the first business of the geomancer on looking out for a propitious site, to find a true dragon, and its complement the white tiger, both being discernable by certain elevations of the ground . . . there must be there also a tranquil harmony of all the heavenly and terrestrial elements which influence that particular spot, and which is to be determined by observing the compass and its indication of the numerical proportions, and by examining the direction of the water courses.

The Feng shui compass, or *luopan*, is comprised of a central magnetic compass needle surrounded by numerous circuits of symbols representing a range of conditions and aspects which had to be balanced together in the optimum case of site divination. The planetary significance of the shape of hills and mountains were

*Figure 70. A Feng shui geomant studies his compass on site*

taken into account, the layout of the country being perceived in astrological terms amongst others. The dragon and tiger symbols represented, respectively, the *yang* and *yin* forces within the earth, discernable by topography. These masculine and feminine principles occur throughout all creation in ancient Chinese cosmology as in many others.

Two schools of Feng shui developed over the centuries: one concerned with the actual lay of the land, the other with correspondences between philosophical and astrological principles. But in both cases, the key matter was the state of *ch'i* at a site. *Ch'i* was considered to be a kind of universal essence or force that sustains all things, and operates at different scales. Acupuncture was the system developed to study and influence *ch'i* for human health; at the landscape level the system was Feng shui. There are various *ch'i* in the heavens and earth, and an optimum balance of these was desired at a site. In mountainous terrain, *ch'i* would rush vigorously; in flat, monotonous country it would become sluggish. Feng shui not only catalogued these characteristics, it also attempted to influence or control *ch'i*. So actual landscape engineering might take place. Altering the slope of a hillside, for example, or modifying water courses, planting trees, scooping hollows out of the ground, or installing fountains or ponds (water carried *ch'i* and could be used to attract or contain it in an area). Straight features – roads, water courses, ridges, avenues of trees, lines of posts, and so on – were 'secret arrows' along which *ch'i* would rush. A straight line pointing at a dwelling, for example, would bring harmful influences, and poltergeists.

Feng shui has officially been discounted in mainland China, but it blossoms still in places like Hong Kong, Singapore and Taiwan. The Feng shui we now see is a hotch-potch of authentic esoteric matter, common sense based on a close observation of the natural world, and rules and superstitions that have arisen for various reasons that have more to do with the sociology of medieval China than principles of geomancy.

In Europe, one of the last archaic geomantic systems we know of, and that fragmentary, came via the Romans, who in turn derived it from the Etruscans. This lost civilisation inhabited Tuscany and western Italy in the first millennium BC. Their writing has never been deciphered, so all we know of them is what can be gleaned from their tombs and artefacts and Greek or Roman writings. They used Greek letters and their writing, which was non-Indo-European, can be transliterated, but hardly any can be translated. No one knows where the Etruscans came from, but there was a strong Oriental influence in their culture. They traded widely and were materially advanced. They finally succumbed to Rome in the third century BC. They nevertheless had a profound influence on the Romans, and the Etruscan diviners or *haruspices* were always respected by them. These diviners could foretell the future by a variety of techniques, the most famous being by observing the flight of birds. They were also geomants. Plutarch described the Etruscan formation of the omphalos:

> A circular trench was dug . . . and in this were deposited first fruits of all things . . . and, finally, every man brought a small portion of the soil of his native land and these were cast in among the first fruits and mingled with them. They call this trench, as they do the heavens, by the name of *mundus.* Then taking this as a centre, they marked out the city in a circle round it.

Leonard Cottrell observed that the trench or pit:

> . . . at the centre of each Etruscan city, led directly to the underworld. It was covered by a great stone, called by the Romans 'the stone of souls', which was lifted up only on the days on which the dead were allowed to ascend among the living, or at the time when the first fruits were deposited underneath it as a harvest offering to the gods. The two main streets of the town crossed at this spot, dividing the area within the walls into quarters. This gridiron plan of the streets had a specific religious meaning; it reflected very closely the Etruscan view of the universe.
>
> The Etruscans believed that the heavens above them were divided into quarters, each of which had an occult significance . . . Diviners further divided the heavens into sixteenths and assigned a meaning to each portion . . .[11]

The diviners had a 'fundamental doctrine of orientation'. The word *templum,* which gives us our 'temple', was originally a term from the vocabulary of Etruscan divination for a particular area of

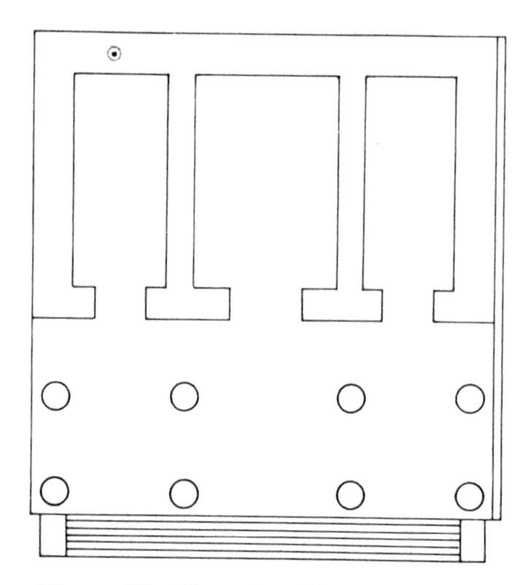

*Figure 71. Plan of an Etruscan temple*

sky where the diviner collected and interpreted omens, during which process he faced south. 'By an extension of this concept,' Raymond Bloch wrote, 'the temple designates the place on earth devoted to the gods, the sanctuary which, in Etruria, usually faces south and represents as it were the projection on the ground of a sacred zone of sky.'[12]

In Etruria, therefore, surveying was part of a sacred system, whereas the Romans used it primarily for secular purposes. We think of the straight Roman roads, for instance, used for martial and cultural conquest. But even the Romans would place shrines at intervals along their straight ways – the spirits of nature were never far away.

In all three of these examples of ancient geomancy, we can note that lines figure in some way or other. In the cases of the Chinese and Etrurian/Roman systems, at least, *straight lines.* The straight landscape line is one of the greatest mysteries of the archaic landscape and we find examples of it throughout the ancient world. Without understanding its import, we will never fathom the former view of the land, the body of Earth, and therefore possibly overlook some basic reality. The straight line relates to the *spirit landscape,* and only by studying it from many aspects, where we find remnants of it, can we perhaps glimpse some long-forgotten truth.

Although there were numerous other alignment researchers, it is to Alfred Watkins of Hereford that we owe the modern awareness of the ancient landscape line. In 1921 Watkins noted on a map that prehistoric sites – mounds, standing stones, cairns – in his Welsh Border district fell into alignments stretching for miles across country. He was 66 at the time, and was a well-respected businessman, local public figure, inventor and photographer. He knew his home ground intimately – 'every field, stick and stone in it'[13] – and it was probably this that allowed him to detect the subtle linear traces within it. Watkins was convinced he had uncovered the remnants of a system of traders' old straight tracks initially sighted across country in the Neolithic period. He conjectured that these old straight paths were maintained with modifications by following cultures until they fell into obscurity early in the historic era. For a few years Watkins referred to the lines as 'leys', for various etymological reasons, but he dropped this term in the years immediately prior to his death in 1935, preferring the simpler 'archaic' or 'old straight' track.

In addition to prehistoric sites, Watkins kept encountering distinctive boulders during fieldwork along alignments. He called these 'mark stones', and contended that they had been set in place by the stone-age surveyors of the lines. He also found hilltops involved in the alignments. These were frequently found to con-

*Plate 43. Alfred Watkins, discoverer of leys, sets up his camera on one of his alignments (courtesy Major Tyler)*

tain prehistoric summit earthworks with many of them being the beacon hills of Elizabethan times. Watkins felt this was only to be expected, because the beacon warning system, like the old straight track, required clear lines of sight. He called such hilltops 'initial points' which were used like the sights on a rifle barrel to set the course of a ley.

Watkins frequently encountered ancient crosses or old (pre-Reformation) churches on his lines. At first glance, this seems difficult to explain on alignments supposedly set down in prehistory, but Watkins correctly pointed out that sites can evolve, and that it was the policy of the early Christian missionaries to re-use pagan sites where appropriate. There is documentary evidence for this policy, and numerous examples exist in Europe and South America of churches occupying prehistoric sites. Site evolution was similarly used to explain the occurrence of medieval castles on leys, as they occupied (for obvious military reasons) key vantage points in the local topography. Watkins supplied a long list of castles where pre-medieval remains had been unearthed. The experienced old countryman noted other clues on his lines, features such as tree clumps, old river fords, holy wells and skyline notches.

The original old straight tracks had long since disappeared, Watkins realised, but certain lengths had been preserved by the courses of ancient roads. Aligned sections of ancient track in open country were a sure sign, Watkins insisted, and he photographed numerous examples of medieval (or earlier) hollow roads aligning to notches on the horizon. He was sure that Roman roads, too, preserved the line of earlier British tracks.

In the years between the ley discovery and his death, Watkins committed himself to mapwork and tramping the course of his alignments, using his skills as a photographer to record sections along them. He published a number of books on the subject, but *The Old Straight Track*[14] was his main work. The Straight Track Postal Portfolio Club was formed in response to his theory, and soon there were bands of 'ley hunters' around the country carrying out field and map research. With World War Two, the club virtually folded and was officially disbanded in 1948. Apart from a handful of individuals, the subject of ancient alignments lapsed into obscurity until the 1960s, when it enjoyed a new and greater lease of life, with all kinds of exotic additions being made to the theory during the 'psychedelic decade', as we noted in the previous chapter.

Sir Norman Lockyer, the 'father of archaeoastronomy' noted site alignments that involved Stonehenge, particulary remarking on the famous line that runs south from the henge monument through Old Sarum, Salisbury Cathedral and Clearbury Ring. This had, in fact, been recorded by an earlier researcher, Colonel Johnston, director of the British Ordnance Survey in the 1890s, and was independently rediscovered by Alfred Watkins in the 1920s. It is said of this line that it assisted in improving the accuracy of the Ordnance Survey.

Alignment research was conducted elsewhere than in Britain, too. Particularly relevant were the *Heilige Linien* (Holy Lines) of Wilhelm Teudt, a German researcher contemporary with Watkins. But it was Watkins' ley theory which provided the major catalyst for the whole subject of lines in the landscape.

Since the '60s, actual landscape work, true alignment study, has continued in addition to 'energy line' ideas, and it is this aspect which concerns us here.

Archaeologists initially responded to Watkins' ideas with utter scorn, and until very recently few professional archaeologists in Britain would deign to discuss the subject. With the gradual passing of the 'old guard' of British archaeology, though there is still doubt on the part of the orthodoxy, the matter is not so clear cut as it once appeared. As we have noted, one bone of contention

*Plate 44. Looking south from Old Sarum along the line of the ley originating at Stonehenge. Salisbury Cathedral is in the middle distance (the alignment cuts through the east end of the cathedral) and Clearbury Ring is the wooded knoll on the horizon*

*Plate 45. The Boscawen-un-circle, Cornwall, was found by John Michell to have a very precise alignment of standing stones running from it*

has been the occurrence of historic features on supposed prehistoric alignments. Nowadays, ley hunters can point to many examples of site evolution. If this still does not convince critics, then the modern ley hunter can indicate numerous cases of lines marked purely by prehistoric sites of the same period. There are henge (circular bank and ditch enclosures of the Neolithic period) and standing stone sites in Yorkshire that fit that requirement, and in 1974 John Michell published his study *The Old Stones of Land's End*[15] in which he extended astronomical alignments noted by Lockyer at the beginning of the century and found the continuance of the lines to be marked by standing stones. This study still causes argument and debate between statisticians and ley hunters.

Work by researchers such as Nigel Pennick, Brian Larkman and others, has shown that some urban alignments of ancient churches may be evidence of deliberate linear planning in medieval times: geomantic traditions seem to have survived or have been revived. A dramatic example involved the Old Sarum line referred to above. In 1979, Ian Thomson and I published a slightly modified version of the alignment,[16] which extended it beyond Clearbury ring to Frankenbury Camp. In 1989, Nigel Pennick published research[17] showing that this line, which passes through Salisbury

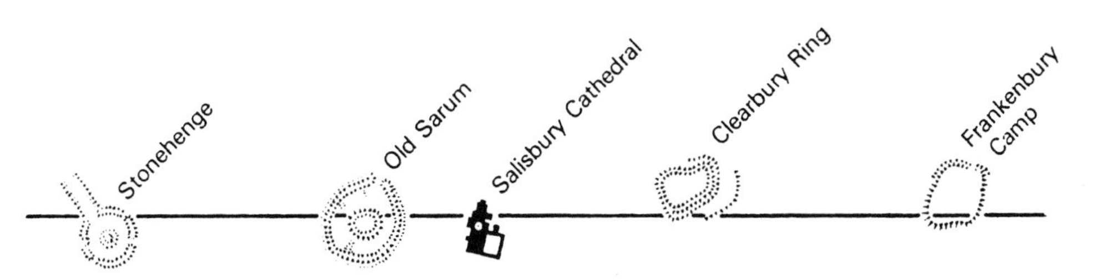


*Figure 72. The alignment from Stonehenge south through Old Sarum; Devereux-Thomson version (Ian Thomson)*

Cathedral, fitted *precisely* with the angular arrangement of Salisbury's street grid, laid out in the thirteenth century. It is beyond belief that this could be accidental. There has been much criticism of the Old Sarum line in the past, with sceptics complaining that a medieval site like the cathedral could not have been part of a prehistoric scheme, and, moreover, that Stonehenge is much older than the Iron Age earthworks at Old Sarum, Clearbury and Frankenbury. There can be no doubt now that the surveyors who laid out Salisbury were aware of the cathedral's position on this (largely visible) alignment, which they literally built into the city groundplan. Further, legend states that the site of the cathedral was found by bowshot or as the result of a vision (both versions mnemonics for divination – a 'bowshot' was almost certainly a measure), and it stands on an important Anglo Saxon geodetic spot known as a *trifinium*. As to the difference between Neolithic Stonehenge and the Iron Age earthworks, the matter is obvious: the hillforts are first and foremost *hills* – landmarks – quite probably holy hills of the Neolithic period. Relatively little excavation has been undertaken on Iron Age hill earthworks, but there are known cases where earlier, even Neolithic, remains have been found. Finally, John Michell has found that specific measures were used between the points on the Stonehenge to Clearbury length of the line.[18]

Other criticisms of ley theory have not proved valid or seriously problematical. The one area of contention that is still the subject of debate is statistical – whether lines of sites are the result of chance or design. Statistical arguments and evidence pro and con have been made, and the matter remains unresolved. Repeated patterns of alignments have been found, though, which suggest deliberation. In the chalklands of southern England, for instance, there are hills which have human or animal figures engraved on them, their white chalk shining out against the green grass. Three of these figures, at Wilmington, Cerne Abbas and Uffington, are certainly

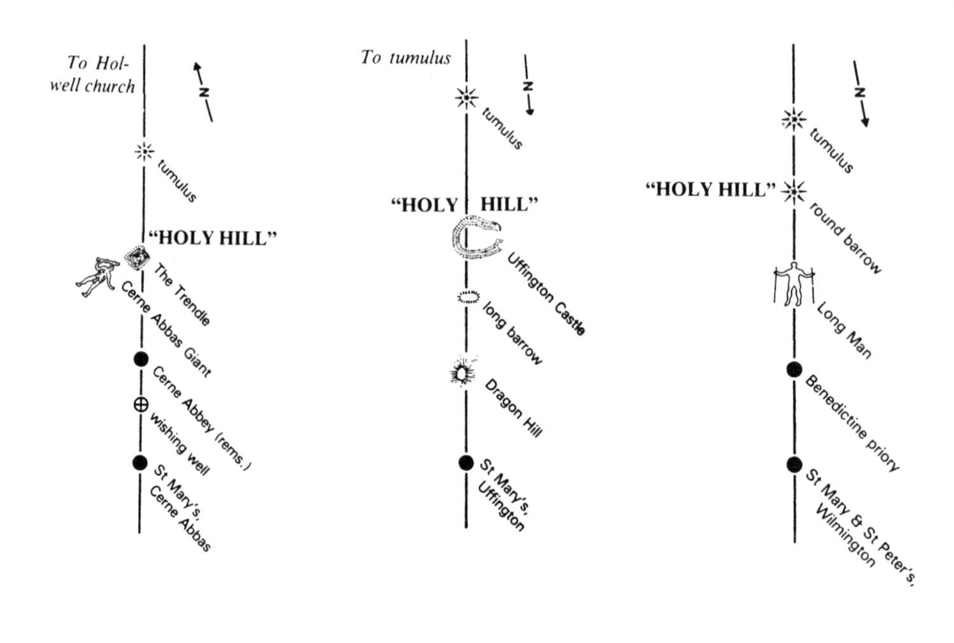


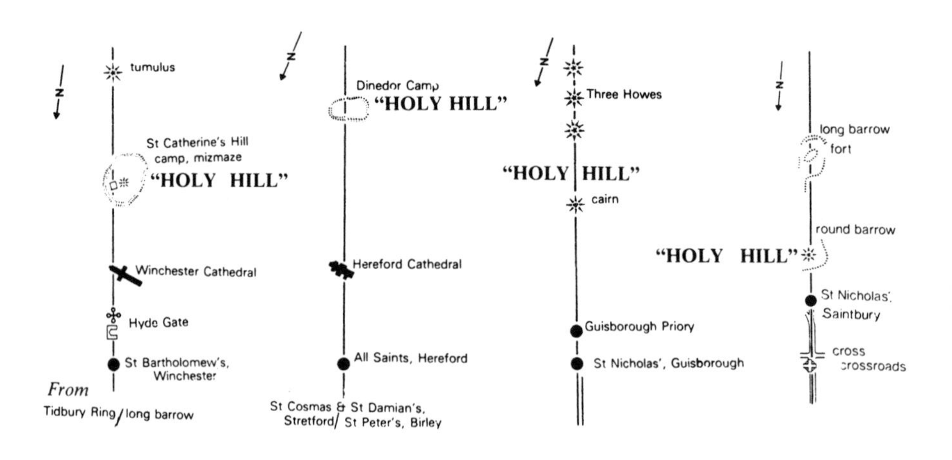


*Figure 73. Alignments through British 'holy hills'*

very ancient, probably prehistoric, and all have prehistoric earthworks on the summits of their hills. Figure 73 shows the great similarity in the components and orientation of the alignments that have been found to pass through them. Very similar lines have been found at a number of other prehistoric hills. Churches beneath the hillsides probably mark pagan shrine sites. The pattern of shrine-to-holy-hill alignment line is found in Germany, Bolivia (see below) and elsewhere.

But the arguments about the 'reality' of leys are purely academic. Prehistoric Britons *did* range out linear earthwork features in the landscape, and aligned them on their ceremonial monuments. In 1723, William Stukeley was the first to notice one of these earth lines, the nearly two-mile-long feature near Stonehenge. He thought it was a Romano-British racecourse, and so called it by the Latin *cursus*. Although these sites are in fact about 4000 years old, and a complete mystery, the name has stuck.

Cursuses are avenues of ditches and banks, with square or rounded ends (where these survive). They range in length from a few hundred metres to kilometres. Some cursuses are perfectly straight, others are straight in sections, simply changing axis at certain points, while others have straight sections linked by curvilinear elements.

By 1934, six cursuses were known, but with the advent of aerial archaeology over 50 have now been identified. Most of them are

Figure 74. William Stukeley's drawing of the Stonehenge Cursus

not visible at ground level, and reveal themselves only as crop markings from the air. Limited archaeological investigation has been applied to them, and where it has, little has been uncovered. Archaeologists feel confident that they tend to be related to the earlier long barrows in some way (the Stonehenge Cursus aligned to a long barrow, for instance) and that some of the cursus termini mimic long barrows. What they show the alignment researcher is that in Neolithic Britain people could and did range out lines over long distances, and that they had concepts involving linear relationships between certain sites.

Cursuses have less obvious alignment properties too. In 1947, an archaeologist noted that the line or axis of the Stonehenge Cursus could be extended to the east through the Cuckoo Stone and on to the centre of Woodhenge, another Neolithic site in the ritual landscape surrounding Stonehenge. This forms an alignment two-and-a-half miles (4 km) in total length, and is in every way a ley. I have further noted that the course of the alignment can be extended about three miles further east, beyond Woodhenge, to pass over Beacon Hill, visible on the skyline from Stonehenge. This is a classic Watkins 'initial point'. In further research,[19] I have studied about half of the known cursuses, and found that the axes of 64 per cent of them could be extended into the countryside beyond one of their ends and pass through another ancient site within about three miles or less. At Rudston, Humberside, archaeologist D.P. Dymond noted that a cursus there aligns to the Rudston monolith, the tallest megalith in Britain, standing at over 25 feet (7.5 m). But the line also passes through the Norman church: if the stone had been destroyed or removed, as many have over the centuries, then the alignment would only be to the church. At Fornham All Saints, Suffolk, a cursus passes directly beneath the village. The cursus is in three straight segments

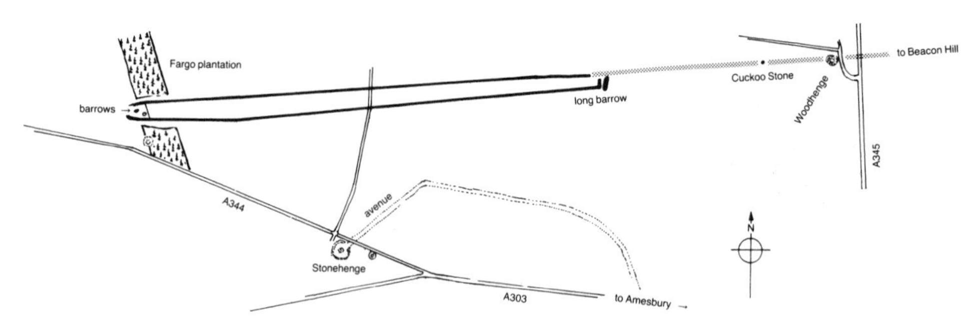


*Figure 75. Stonehenge cursus and alignment*

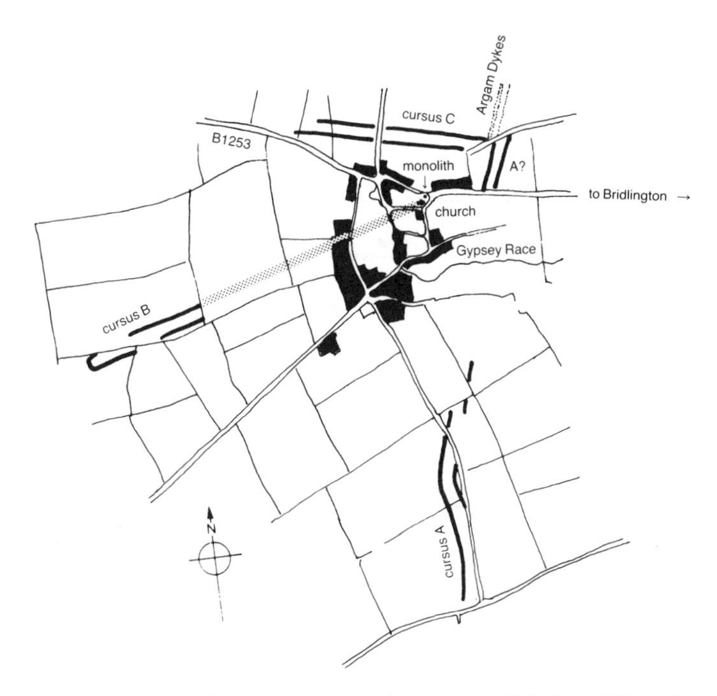


*Figure 76. Orientation of cursus B to Rudston monolith (modified after D.P. Dymond)*

*Plate 46. The Rudston monolith and adjacent Norman church.*

(possibly built at different times). The old village church stands directly on the ditch of the middle segment (Plate 47), while the northernmost section aligns to the ancient and important Bury St Edmunds Abbey, less than three miles (4.8 km) away. These 'coincidences' suggest the cursuses were just the marked elements

*Plate 47. Airview looking south along the crop marks of a Neolithic cursus at Fornham All Saints, Suffolk. The section nearest the camera aligns to Bury St Edmunds, and the church at Fornham can be seen sitting on the western ditch of the next segment of the cursus (courtesy Cambridge University Collection of Air Photographs)*

of larger Neolithic linear schemes within certain districts, the pattern being in some cases 'locked into' the landscape by ancient churches evolving on sites of former significance, just as Watkins suggested.

Other kinds of linear features from prehistory are also scattered about the British landscape. Stone rows, particularly prevalent on Dartmoor, run in single or multiple lines linking cairns and standing stones. Only one archaeological excavation of a stone row has been undertaken, and nothing was found. Also on Dartmoor, and various other localised regions of the British Isles, are *reave* systems. These are the remnants of some kind of poorly understood Bronze Age boundary system. On Dartmoor, some of the reaves are very direct and run for kilometres. Archaeologist Andrew Fleming of Sheffield University has shown that on

*Plate 48. A double stone row on Dartmoor*

*Plate 49. A Bronze Age boundary, over 3500 years old, cuts straight across Walkhampton Common, Dartmoor. Prehistoric Britons could survey straight lines across country.*

Dartmoor at least, Bronze Age peoples were capable of surveying lines on a large-scale basis, over rough country including ridges and deep ravines.[20] He calls such lines 'terrain oblivious'.[21] There is little practical difference in such findings and Watkins' basic discovery.

Even more curious features show up on aerial photographs: geometrically regular lines of unexplained prehistoric pit marks, curious parallel ditch patterns, and so on. There are certainly secret lines in the British landscape.

Apart from evidence in Watkins' home country, we now know that peoples the world over *did* build leys. And there is now nowhere better to study them than in the Americas.

The best-known New World straight lines are those at Nasca, Peru. On the pampa above Nasca, ruler-straight lines score the desert pavement. Hundreds of them, of varying width and some parallel, converge or diverge at mounds ('ray centres'), and boulders for all the world like Watkins' mark stones are to be found along some of them. These lines run for over 6 miles (10 km) and cut straight across hills as if they were not there. How they were created is easy – the removal of the dark, oxidised desert surface revealed a lighter subsoil and there was no rain or other disturbance to affect the lines once made. But no one knows why.

These desert markings seem to have been forgotten by everyone for many centuries. They were first noticed on the ground by Alfred Kroeber and Mejia Xesspe in 1926, both thinking them to be remnants of irrigation channels. But later, Xesspe came to consider them as similar to the Inca *ceques* or sacred paths (below). When Paul Kosok of Long Island University visited them in 1941, he immediately saw that they were not irrigation works. He happened to witness the sun setting beyond the end of one of the lines shortly after the June solstice and this led him to see the lines as 'the largest astronomy book in the world'. He became convinced they served a calendrical function. This conviction was passed on to Maria Reiche, a German mathematician who has studied and guarded the lines since 1941.[22,23]

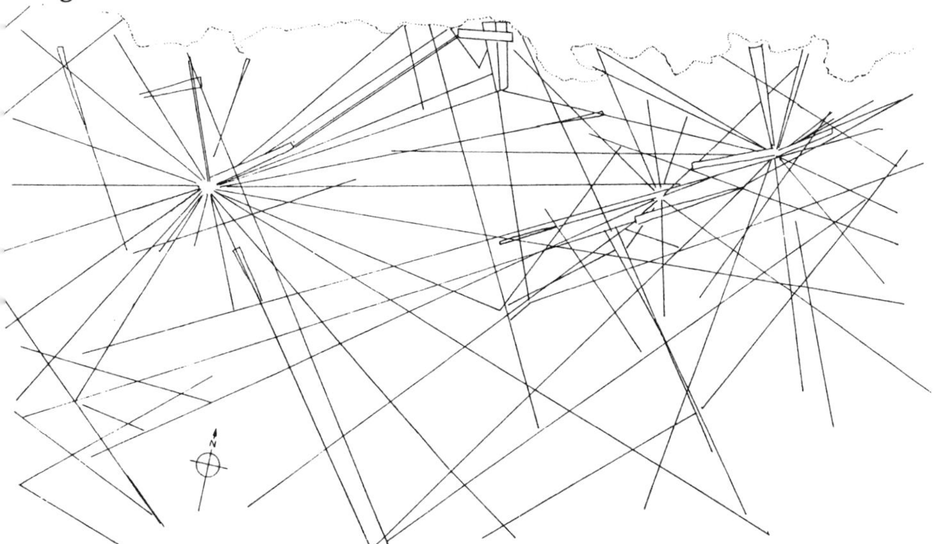

*Figure 77. Plan showing a 3.5 mile (5.6 km) wide section of the Nazca lines on the pampa adjacent to the southern edge of the Ingenio valley (after Maria Reiche)*

The date of the markings is not known with any certainty. A wooden peg found in the midst of a stone heap was dated by radiocarbon to the sixth century AD, but dating has mainly been by inference from fragments of pottery found amongst the markings. These ceramic pieces are from various periods of the Nascan Culture, which developed out of the earlier Paracus culture around the second century BC and lasted until the seventh or eighth centuries when it began to be influenced by the highland Huari empire. In the early 1980s, Canadian researcher Persis Clarkson conducted hundreds of miles of foot surveys of many of the markings. She has found that earlier periods of pottery seem associated with the animal and other figures, while later periods appear associated with the lines, and then mainly with the ray centres, pottery of all kinds being scarce on the lines themselves. This has led archaeologist Evan Hadingham to suggest that the animal figures came first, during the centuries around the beginning of the Christian era in the Old World, followed much later by all or most of the lines. Clarkson's investigations have also revealed hitherto unremarked stone rings and semi-circles, and maybe the remnants of shrines on the lines.[24]

Astronomy has been a main candidate for an explanation of the lines. Maria Reiche feels the lines mark certain solar and lunar positions, and perhaps particular star groups too.

The problem is, there are so many lines pointing in so many directions that astronomical events could be indicated purely by chance. This is compounded by the fact that no one knows what specific time-periods are involved. In an attempt to quantify these variables to some extent, Gerald Hawkins (of *Stonehenge Decoded* fame) carried out ground, aerial and computer surveys of 93 lines (186 directions) in 1968. He came to the conclusion that astronomy could not be the answer.[25] Hawkins did discover, however, that the lines had been 'laid out straighter than could be measured with modern air-survey techniques.' This required exceptional surveying skills by the ancients. Maria Reiche noticed that an Indian who assisted her on certain occasions had 'telescopic vision', easily capable of seeing a stake at two-thirds of a mile and sensing accuracy of alignment. He was a *rayador* or 'furrow tracer' hired by cotton plantations to set out parallel rows for planting. Perhaps this special ability is a hereditary survival from the old days of desert geomancy.

In research programmes spanning 1980–4, A.F. Aveni and Gary Urton compiled data on 500 lines and 62 ray centres – many more than discovered by Maria Reiche. They found that 100 of the lines can be traced to the centres and that the centres are interconnected. This seems to have been the organising principle behind the layout of the lines. Like Hawkins, they feel that no 'overall astronomical solution' seems likely to be forthcoming.

The lines themselves give few clues. They do not always point to significant skyline features such as peaks or clefts. They can start and stop at places with no apparent significance. Archaeologist Josue Lancho has made an interesting observation that may point to a fresh answer for part of the lines' function. Studying the Cantelloc area on the southern edge of the Nasca Valley, he has noted that some lines point to the locations of ancient underground aqueducts. These lines are in the same area as a series of triangular shapes which point to the base of Cerro Blanco, a mountain associated with water in local lore.

Perhaps the lines had ceremonial purposes. The Indian processions and dances can often be single-file activities, and many of the lines do contain ancient footpaths, worn deep. But such tracks meander within the exactitude of the straight line containing them, and the need for the straightness is still not explained.

Further south, in the altiplano of western Bolivia, less well-known but even more remarkable old straight tracks cut through plains, ridges and valleys without deviation. These tracks range for up to 20 miles (32 km) in length. Dotted along them are Indian shrines, most of which have been Christianised, and at some points churches were erected on the lines by the original Spanish missionaries. These features are in every respect leys as Watkins defined them. They seem to have first been brought to Western attention by the anthropologist Alfred Métraux in the early 1930s. He found small earthen shrines running in straight rows out from a village on the altiplano. These rows extended several miles into the surrounding landscape. The term *Mal'ku* was so widely applied that Métraux felt its best definition was 'spirit of place' – *genius loci.* These shrines were linked by pathways cut through the tola bushes which 'led in absolutely straight lines, regardless of the irregularities and slope of the ground.'[26]

Hilltops were sacred to many Andean peoples. The Christianised hilltop shrine is now known as a *calvario,* its Pagan term being *silu.* The Andean Indian word for the old straight tracks means 'a row of things', whether sacred, such as shrines, or secular such as a line of people or animals. The lines are thus alignments of sites (the ley concept), with the straight track forming the secondary component.

In Mesoamerica, the Mayans also had straight roads, known as *sacbeob*, skilfully engineered through the jungles of their domain. Thomas Gann was amongst the first to recognise these roads in the 1920s. He saw 'a great elevated road, or causeway . . . [It] ran, as far as we followed it, straight as an arrow, and almost flat as a rule.'[27] More recent research has revealed straight stone paths on the island of Cozumel, off the eastern coast of Yucatan. Most of these connected areas within settlements, but some connected different settlements. The best preserved of these inter-site straight lines is between San Gervasio and the northeast coast. It was mapped for over three miles (5 km) before its course was lost in a small settlement. It had small shrines positioned along its length.

Over 100 miles of other pre-Hispanic straight roads have been found around La Quemada in Mexico.

In North America, too, the ancient Amerindians built old straight tracks. In the California Sierras tracks belonging to the now extinguished Miwok Indians run straight for tens of miles, from one mountain peak to another. They are 'airline straight in their directness,'[28] and most are thought to date from before AD 900. In New Mexico, great systems of straight roads radiate around Chaco Canyon, the ceremonial centre of the lost Anasazi

*Plate 50. This picture of one of the 30-metres-wide straight Chacoan roads was taken in 1916 (courtesy F.A. Wadleigh)*

*Figure 78. Principle Anasazi roads and sites around Chaco Canyon (after Chaco Roads Project)*

peoples. The Anasazi had neither horses nor wheeled vehicles, yet built these wonderfully engineered straight roads, 30 feet (9 m) wide, with tributary roads just half that width. Recent work by NASA using airborne infra-red photography is showing that some of the major Chacoan roads had parallel sections running for miles (personal communication).

The Chacoan roads were first noticed in 1901, but effectively forgotten by academics until the last few decades. It is only since the 1980s that any serious study of them has been made. The roads are difficult to perceive at ground level, being a thousand years old. Only vegetation changes during springtime and very low sunlight reveal the depressions or 'swales' where the roads ran through the high mesa. The main aid is aerial photography (the famed flier Charles Lindburgh was one of the first to take air photos of the features in the 1920s). What archaeologists call 'The Great North Road' runs for tens of miles to (or from) the northern perimeter of Chaco Canyon. The NASA infra-red work shows that this has another running closely parallel to it, and there is another pair running parallel to these two at a slight distance. A single road of this order would be difficult to explain in the Anasazi culture, but parallels like this are mystifying. At Chaco, the Great North Road first meets the ruins of a 'Great House', Pueblo Alto. A ruined gate in a wall allows the road access to the rimrock area of the canyon. Archaeologists feel that Pueblo Alto, like other Great Houses, was a ceremonial centre. The Great Houses seem to have had a special relationship with the roads, which suggests that the straight tracks were themselves ceremonial, sacred.

The course of a road over the bare rimrock between the high mesa and the lip of the canyon is marked by small edging stones. At the top of the walls, steps cut out of the living rock descend to the canyon floor. These rock stairways can be up to 25 feet (7.5 m) broad and very steep. They could only have been used for symbolic or ceremonial purposes, again suggesting a similar function for the roads. (Elsewhere in the canyon are narrow steps with handholds, seemingly for normal, everyday use.)

There is a system of roads within Chaco Canyon itself, linking the Great Houses there, which, with their great kivas, were obviously ceremonial centres.

Evidence that the northern Indians also made straight roads is preserved at Marietta, Ohio, where a modern road called Sacra Via runs along the course of a straight ritual road, 2000 years old, that ran from the Muskingham River to an earthworks enclosure, also still respected by the town's street grid.

*Plate 51. An example of the mysterious stone stairways at Chaco Canyon*

It is clear that the *straight line* was a geomantic feature common to Amerindians at some point, and now found spread throughout the Americas in various guises.

The straight landscape line is found elsewhere in the world: in Indonesia there is an alignment of Buddhist temples, involving the famous Borobudur, which is marked by an annual ceremonial procession. In Ireland, the fairy paths from one earthworked hill (rath or 'fairy fort') to another were thought to be straight. There are alignments of mosques in Cairo, and mosques can be found on straight ritual roads belonging to ancient Egypt, such as the one between the temples at Karnak and Luxor. And so on. Watkins had perceived the remnants of a very deep pattern. But what was it all about? That is where we run into the mystery: archaeologists do

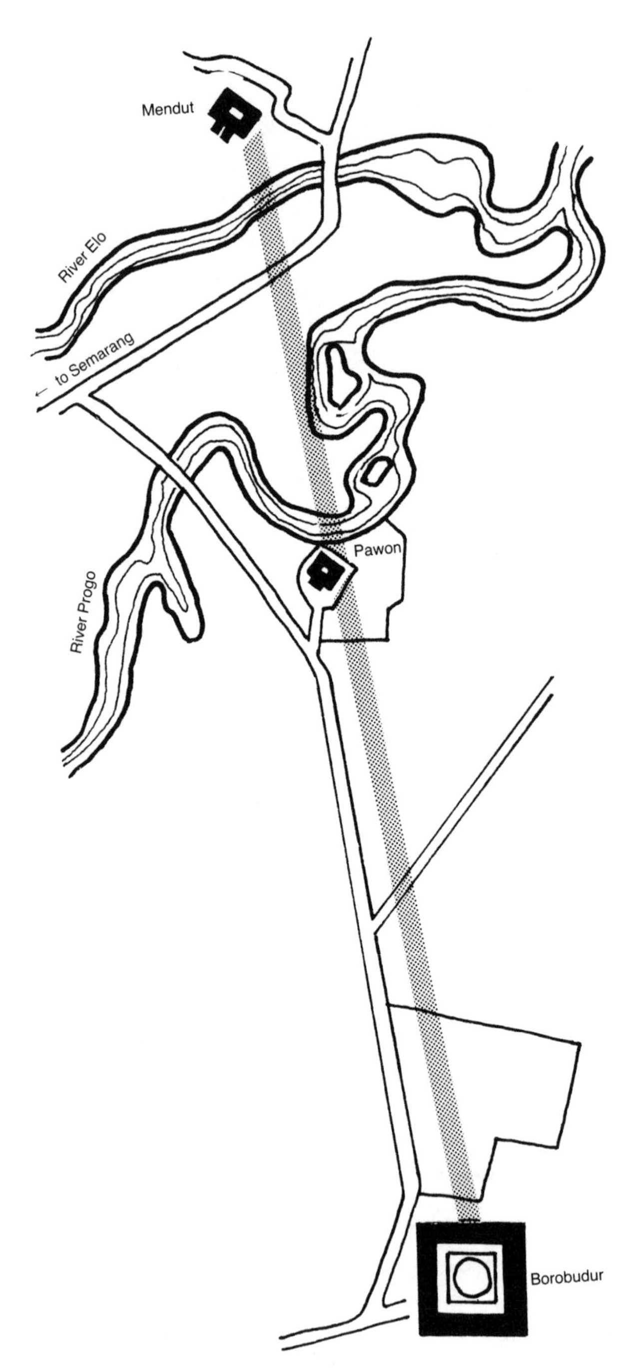


*Figure 79. Alignment of temples on Java, Indonesia*

*Plate 52. The Sacra Via at Marietta, Ohio, marking the course of a straight Indian ceremonial way about 2000 years old*

*Plate 53. The white building is a mosque, placed on the much earlier straight ceremonial way formerly linking the temples at Luxor and Karnak, Egypt*

not understand the function of linear features of antiquity. They seem to belong to some worldview lost to us. But there are a few clues that modern alignment researchers have uncovered, and these clues suggest that the use of straight landscape lines might reveal a deep-seated sense, an archetype, within human consciousness that was expressed in terms of a spirit landscape.

The main clue is provided by an Indo-European root word *reg* or *rect*, which meant 'movement along a straight line'. This has come to be included in a number of European words that relate, variously, to spatial concepts, such as rectangle, region or erect, to analogous straightness in the senses of social order or morality, like regular, regime, or correct, and to kingship – regal, for example. The Latin word for king, *rex*, comes directly from this ancient root word. Some words like 'right', which also derives from this origin, can have both spatial and moral meanings; another example would be 'direction', which can mean physical orientation or a command. In French, the word for king, *roi*, is found lodged also in *droit*, meaning right. We have the Old French *roial* from which we get English words like royal and realm. A straightedge in French is *règle*, and *en règle* means 'in order'. In German, *reich* means empire. Related to *rex* is *regulus*, a prince, and its feminine *regula* meant a straight piece of wood. Thus it is that we have the English word 'ruler' which means both a straightedge and a king or leader. Hence we have a monarch 'ruling the land'.

There seems to have been, therefore, some form of activity involving motion in straight lines about five thousand years ago in Europe, when *reg* was in use. It may have been the prototype of the modern ceremonial procession. But why should physical straightness have become associated with kingship? Well, we know that in many early cultures the king and the land were considered as one. If drought or pestilence struck the country, the king was held responsible. Moreover, the king was considered a god in some societies, while in others he was considered a human being but having a hotline to God. In other words, he was the repository for spiritual or supernatural power. This harks back to the tribal kind of social grouping where there was a shaman. J.G. Frazer, author of the epic mythological study *The Golden Bough* (1922), remarked that 'in many parts of the world the king is the lineal successor of the old magician or medicine man.'

The association between kingship and straight linearity also occurs outside the scope of the Indo-European zone. In old China, the emperor would sit on the Golden Throne in the Forbidden City at Beijing in order to deal with matters of state. The throne was on the straight, marbled meridian that forms the cosmological axis of the Forbidden City, and was at the focus of alignments of gateways. Only the emperor could use the straight landscape line, because, as we have noted, the Feng shui geomants saw to it that the populace neither lived nor were buried near straight lines. Likewise in Ireland, it was considered to be asking for trouble to build a home on a fairy path.

In Peru, the divine 'Son of the Sun', the Inca, ruled his empire from the Coricancha, the Temple of the Sun in Cuzco. Radiating out from the temple were 41 lines that the conquering Spanish referred to as *ceques.* These were marked by alignments of Inca holy places, the *huacas* that we noted in Chapter 4 represented the days of the year. They were traceable only by the lining up of ancient sites, like British leys, and it was not until 1985 that infrared photography by researcher Tony Morrison revealed that they were once also dead straight tracks radiating out over the Andes to all parts of the Inca empire: they show up as dark lines of vegetation in the photographs (personal communication). Archaeoastronomers Tom Zuidema and Anthony Aveni have studied the ceques and found only a quarter of the lines to have been for astronomical usage (towers, destroyed by the Spanish, had been placed on the horizon as foresights for solar observation), the rest were for ceremonial, religious and political purposes.

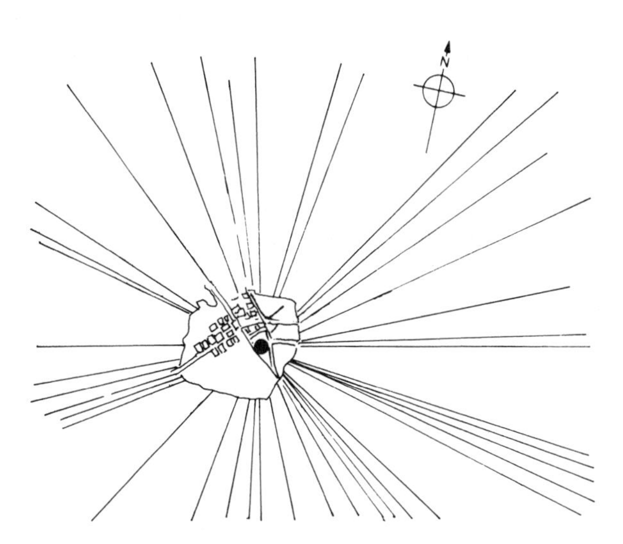


*Figure 80. The arrangement of* ceques *radiating from the Corichancha in Cuzco (after Evan Hadingham; based on the research of Tom Zuidema)*

So there seems to have been some ancient connection between straightness, kingship and spirit. The lines radiating from the seat of power (perhaps unconsciously perpetuated in places like Versailles, palace of another 'sun king') must have been seen as channels for the ruler's spiritual power. And that is probably the best way for us to understand the straight landscape lines of antiquity – as spirit lines. This is perhaps why we find the cursuses so often connected with long barrows and other sacred sites.

We can only make guesses today as to why spirit and straightness should have been so widely associated. Perhaps in the way that today we use light as a metaphor for spirit, ancient people seeing beams of sunlight streaming through clouds thought that the spirits and gods of the land must also move with such straight purity. Then again, we must always remember that it was typical of early peoples to make use of rituals and local botanical sources to produce visions of the Otherworld. Hallucinogens promoted shamanic ecstasy – out-of-body experience. Perhaps the landscape lines marked paths for the spirit of the living shaman.

Geomancy, then, served the human body, mind and psyche. It made a whole out of the cosmos, the Earth and the human soul. The ultimate act of systems thinking, pragmatic and spiritual at the same time. It is this harmony, this relationship with the environment, that we have lost today, and that is why the study of ancient geomantic systems is so crucial to our times. We need to rediscover principles that could be used in a revival of geomantic sensibility for the twenty-first century. HRH the Prince of Wales has effectively put his finger on this, in his wide-ranging criticism of modern architecture. He feels we have lost the basics of creating buildings that relate to the human scale and needs. It is a view that has struck a chord with many people, though numerous professional architects bristle at such views, seeing it as a call for pastiche treatments of bygone styles of architecture. There is a danger of that, but the principles the Prince calls for are sound and much deeper than some nostalgic whim.

The first of these he identifies is *place*. 'We must respect the land,' he wrote in *A Vision of Britain*.[29] 'New buildings can be intrusive or they can be designed and sited so that they fit in.' This is in effect a plea for geomantic sensibility. In *hierarchy*, the Prince calls for buildings that use their forms and spaces to emphasise those parts that are public and important. Architectural elements should be employed that 'uplift our spirits' when we enter. Different buildings for different purposes 'all have their scale and special sites.' Regarding *scale*, 'Man is the measure of all things,' Prince Charles reminded his readers. There is a difference, he remarked, between a public building like a cathedral which reflects our aspirations, and 'gargantuan out-of-scale developments that look like Gulliver in Lilliput.' Next, *harmony*. Here the Prince considered mainly the relationship of buildings in towns. Better, he suggested, to 'respect our indigenous roots' than to use 'transient international architectural fashions.' Contemporary buildings 'are designed from abstract principles . . . and are thrust . . . into the carefully scaled and painstakingly adjusted cities of the past.' A traditional image of paradise is the walled garden, so it is not surprising that the Prince selected *enclosure* as another principle. Whether it be the enclosure of a building, a town square or a garden, one should feel secure and focused. Here he echoes the ancient concept of the *temenos*, which is the boundary of sacred space. It is strange how in even a small circle of low stones, one can feel secure and centred. To stand within the Moel-ty-Uchaf circle high on a mountainside near Llandrillo, for example, is to feel protected and in absolute harmony with the wild Welsh mountain landscape all around.

Amongst the other principles he enumerated, Prince Charles included *materials*: 'Let where it is be what it's made of.' The modern standardisation of material has brought 'a bland uniformity'. Buildings need to look as if they belong to their region. An example he could have used are the sandstone Pueblos of the Anasazi, for instance, which not only blend with their environment, but have been found to be remarkably effective in passive heating: the local material in the local climate retains or shields from heat in a perfect cycle for human habitation.[30] Prince Charles notes that the manufacture of many new building materials damages the environment.

The only serious omission in the Prince's book was the word 'geomancy', though he did acknowledge sacred geometry and made the point that only in recent times have architects stopped drawing from 'the sacred in nature'.

There is no doubt that unless we can consciously recollect the principles of geomancy, we will not survive long into the next millennium. Geomancy must become an essential element in the new, and long overdue, Green thinking.

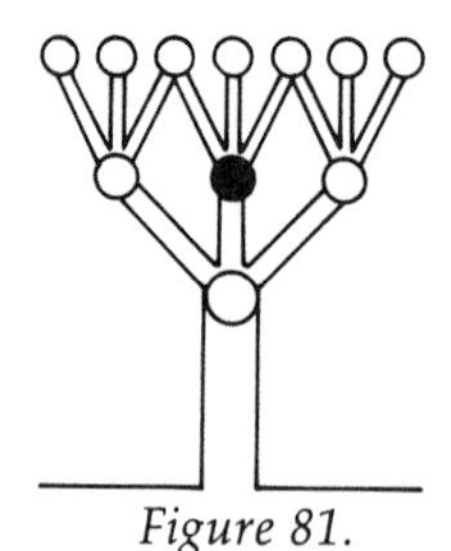

Figure 81.

CHAPTER 9

# CORRESPONDENCE AND SYMBOLISM

## Demonstration

The two circles Keith Critchlow used to produce the groundplan geometry evident at Castlerigg (Chapter 5) were derived, respectively, from solar and lunar axes relating to astronomical declinations observable at the site. One circle was effectively a solar circle, the other lunar. In *Time Stands Still,* Critchlow notes the symbolism of the overlapping solar and lunar circles in Tibetan Buddhism, as described by Lama Anagarika Govinda. According to this system, the solar circle represents universal or archetypal consciousness, the inner world of mind, and the lunar circle symbolises empirical

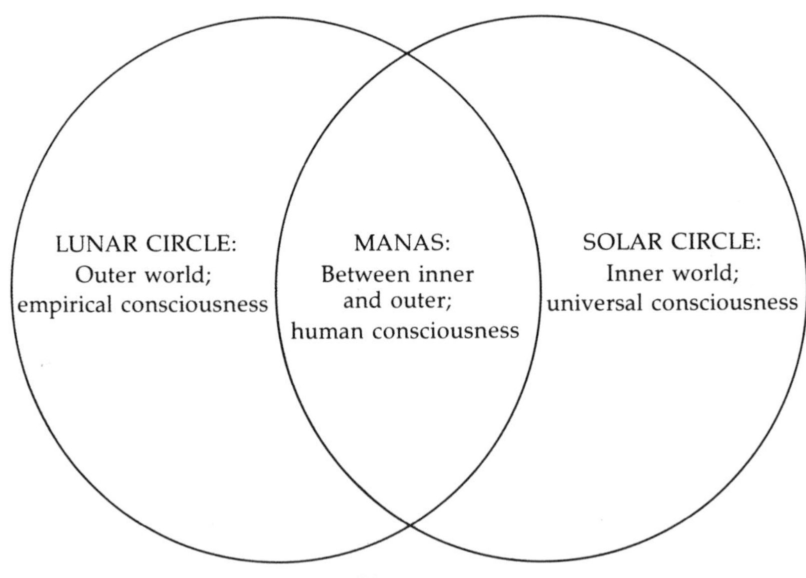


Figure 82.

consciousness, the outer world of appearance. Where the circles overlap, the vesica, is *manas.* Critchlow found that manas 'has been etymologically linked via the archaic Indo-European language with the word man – the conscious animal,' and in the symbolic diagram it represents, 'the balancing consciousness that "either binds us to the world of the senses or which liberates us from it,"' quoting Govinda in *Foundations of Tibetan Mysticism.*

Manas: we stand as if on a seashore strand, behind us the great hinterland of consciousness, and before us the rolling tides of the manifest world, the Tao's 'Ten Thousand Things'. Each of us attempts to balance our inner world of thoughts, intimations, insights and emotions with the activities and pressures of the 'outside' world. Our human consciousness is at the overlap. We can look one way or the other, or integrate the two great circles of being.

## Discussion

If geometry and number represent the ultimate systems language, then correspondence and its close companion symbolism represent the oldest and most profound form of systems thinking.

Thinking by correspondence means recognising a pattern that can manifest at many scales in many modes. Take, for instance, the branches of a tree – we can see the same pattern in forked lightning or a river delta viewed from above. In correspondence, the pattern, the archetypal inherent framework, remains the same, but the ratios change. Nature expresses the principle of correspondence in growth. Let us look again at the golden rectangle in Figure 40 (Chapter 5). From this figure we can draw one of the logarithmic or growth spirals to be found in nature (Figure 83). An arc is drawn at

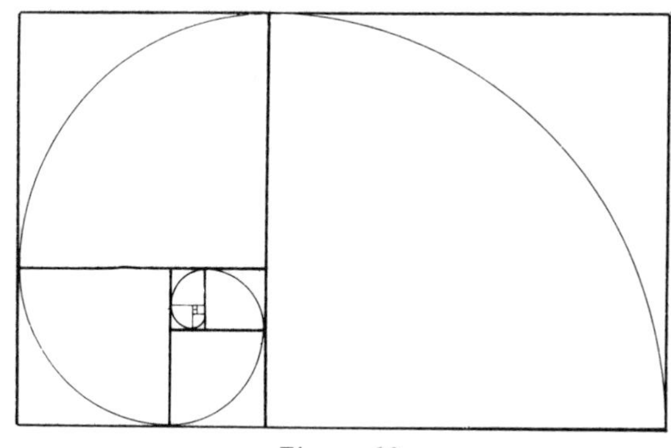

*Figure 83.*

each scale of the proportionally related set of rectangles. Connected up, the arcs form the spiral. The arc's curve at each level remains the same, only the ratios change. The very image of correspondence.

Correspondence allows the thinker to soar through various manifestations of creation, whether material forms, behaviour patterns, energy interactions, or ideas, following the same thread. Something that is true is true at all levels. Principles operative at the level of manifest, outer nature, can be found to apply within the human psyche as well. If a frame is placed around any one manifestation of a pattern being studied by means of correspondence, then beginning and end, cause and effect, can come into play, but the fluid nature of correspondence itself is not affected by these 'freeze frame' conditions. The use of correspondence allows the grand patterns of being and creation to be perceived, the workings of the universe to be grasped, and specific items of knowledge to be acquired, yet is as different to analytical thought as is possible to imagine – indeed, it *encompasses* analytical thought.

The very nature of correspondence makes it difficult to discuss in linear, verbal form. So let us employ example instead, and follow just one (multi) track of correspondence a short distance. Our themes will be the sun and moon, which are not just celestial bodies but symbols which shine as strongly in our psyche as in our sky, and the Earth itself.

In Chapter 5 we saw how to derive the profile of the Great Pyramid from the *vesica piscis*. Having that profile, or triangle, we can use it to produce a further geometric figure which can tell us something about our material environment. If we take a square as representing the plan of the pyramid, and use the half-way line across it as the base for the profile triangle, the Pyramid elevation, the apex gives a radius for a circle drawn from the centre of the square (Figure 84). We have squared the circle, the perimeters of both square and circle being equal. If we draw a circle within the square, and another centred on the outer circle as shown in Figure 85, we get two circles which accurately represent the relative proportions of the disks of Earth and moon. There is *much* more information that can be obtained from this geometrical figure, but there is no need to enter into that here.

Now, this piece of simple geometry has its own inner logic. It could be drawn anywhere – on a spaceship floating through some far starfield, or on a planet circling another sun. But it so happens that it yields actual, physical information about *our* planet and *our*

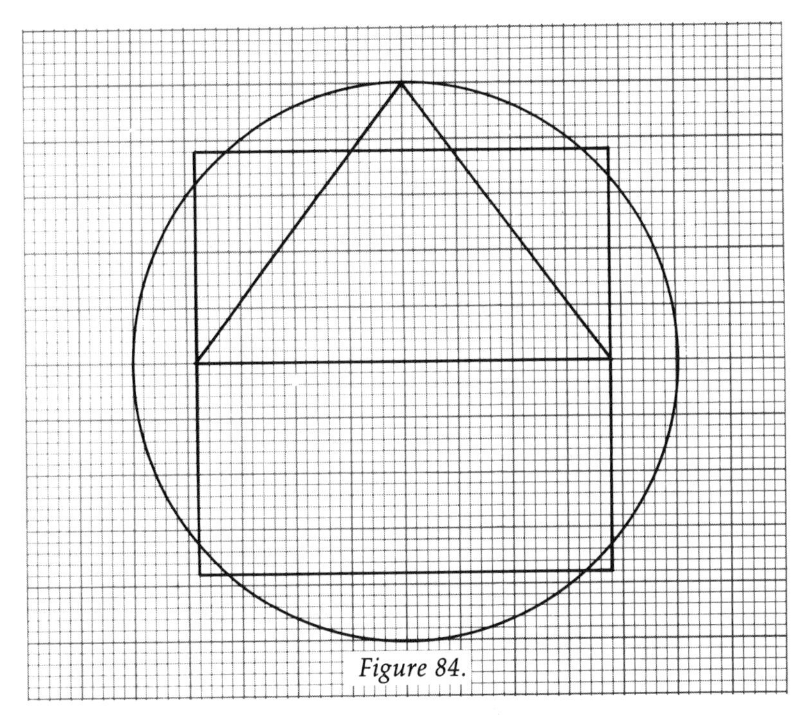

*Figure 84.*

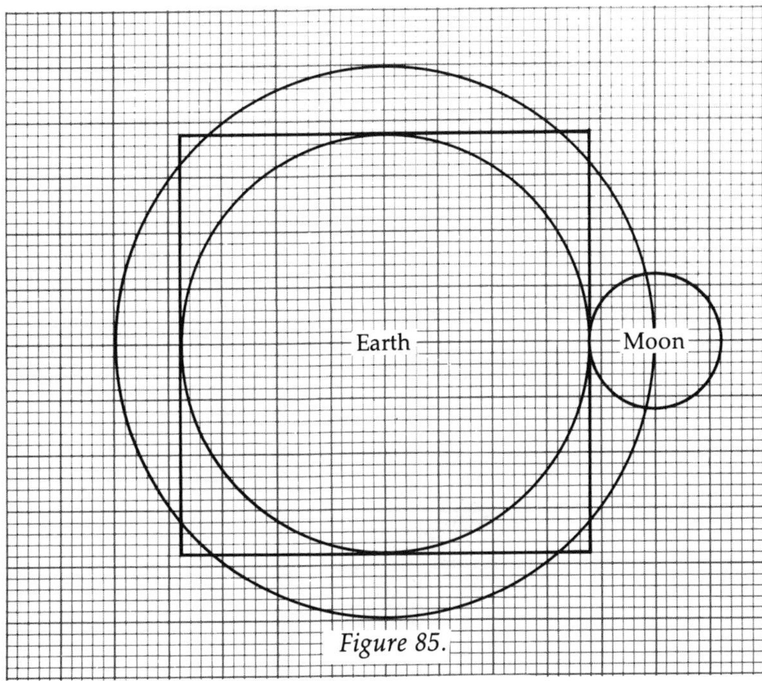


*Figure 85.*

moon. How can this be? The matter can no more be handled by the logical mind than can the curious 'coincidence' that is demonstrated every time we experience a solar eclipse. Earth is the only place we know of where there is sentient life. What a remarkable chance it is, then, that this rare and favoured planet also provides the base for observing the spectacle of its moon pass in front of its local star, the sun, one disc so exactly matching the other that a total eclipse is possible. The moon is about a quarter of a million miles away and has a diameter of approximately 2160 miles; the sun is roughly 400 times larger, but is also about 400 times further away, so the two disks are virtually the same size when viewed from Earth. Without the happenstance of intelligent life, ourselves, there would be no consciousness to witness this literally astronomical coincidence.

Modern thought dismisses such things as curiosities, and so misses worlds of wisdom unawares.

In most traditions around the world – there are one or two exceptions – the sun symbolises the masculine principle, and the moon, the Queen of the Night, the feminine. In the Chinese system, the male and female principles of creation were known as yang and yin. In the Cabala, they are called Binah and Chokmah. These two creative principles emerge from the godhead, the monad; they are differentiation coming forth out of the Divine Ground. They are active in mind and matter.

In no philosophical system were they more central than in alchemy, which was a synthesis of earlier arcane thought.

Medieval and Renaissance alchemy had its origins in ancient Egypt, its name deriving from the Arabic words *Al Kimiya*, meaning the magical craft of the Black Country, a reference to the dark soil of the Nile delta. Traditionally, alchemy was initially associated with a supposed ancient personage known as Hermes Trismegistos (almost certainly a version of the Egyptian god Thoth, the Greek's Mercury) who possessed 'the three parts of the philosophy of the whole world'. He is the reputed author of the

*Figure 86. The Yin Yang symbol*

Emerald or Smaragdine Table, said to have been discovered in a cave near Hebron, which laid out 13 statements in Phoenician script on the principles of alchemy, including that famous motto of correspondence, 'What is below is like that which is above . . .' The first historically secure alchemical texts, however, came from Arabian scholars during the first millennium of the current era. These eventually found their way to medieval Europe, and there was a great revival of the 'Hermetic Art'.

The aims of alchemy were to transmute base metals to gold, to discover the nature of the Philosopher's Stone with which the transmutation could be effected, and to find the Elixir of Life. These goals could be taken at the literal, exoteric level – the metallurgic attempt to produce gold, and to find or produce objective substances for the Stone and Elixir. But, by correspondence, these features and processes were also applied to inner, psychological or spiritual changes within the alchemist. The true alchemical process was essentially sacramental – an outward sign of inward grace. It was an obscure and trying business, and the alchemical texts abound with complex symbolism and brain-teasing commentaries. Most appear as gibberish, a term, appropriately, derived from the name of one of the early Arabian alchemists, Geber.

The essence of the alchemical Great Work was the union of sulphur and mercury to produce the Philosopher's Stone. But the correspondence was *philosophical* sulphur and mercury. The union was imaged as a marriage, and the sulphur and mercury, themselves symbols as the king and queen, sun and moon, gold and silver, red lion and white eagle. The geometrical correspondence of the alchemical marriage was given by the seventeenth-century alchemist Michael Maier in *Atalanta fugiens* (1618): 'Make

*Figure 87. A detail from a 1618 alchemical engraving by Johann Daniel Mylius showing a plethora of sun/moon (masculine feminine principles) symbolism and correspondences*

from the male and female a circle, then a square, afterwards a triangle, from which make a circle, and thou shalt have the Philosopher's Stone.' The circle squared.

The master pattern behind alchemy was that metals, the human psyche, or anything else, could be reduced down to the *prima materia,* an underlying matrix from which all life and form came forth. The alchemists' motto was *Solve et coagula,* to dissolve to basic matter and recombine into new substance. The *prima materia* was referred to by the great sixteenth-century alchemist, Paracelsus, as 'the Spirit of Truth . . . of a mysterious nature, wondrous strength, boundless power . . . this Spirit [does] move all bodies . . . It is sought by many and found by few. It is beheld from afar and found near; for it exists in every thing, in every place and at all times.' The eleventh-century Arabic alchemist, Avicenna, called it the 'Soul of the World', echoing the earlier Platonic thesis of a World Soul. The Emerald Tablet stated that 'the Earth is its nurse'. In depicting this (Figure 88), Michael Maier added, 'The Earth is the true heart.'

Gothic architecture developed in this milieu, and it is perhaps not surprising that the Gothic cathedrals, the 'books of stone', should contain references to alchemical philosophy. The master builders were certainly involved in the arcane traditions, and Chartres, particularly, may have been a deliberate attempt to record the mystery tradition which had so recently been invigorated by contact with the Middle East. So we find the west towers at Chartres (which, remember, were built first) displaying the sun-moon, masculine-feminine, principles. Facing the west front, the

*Figure 88. 'The Earth is its nurse.' Detail from an alchemical engraving by Michael Maier, 1618*

*Plate 54. The west front of Chartres Cathedral, showing the different heights of the 'solar' and 'lunar' towers*

left-hand tower rises 365 feet and the right-hand tower is 28 feet shorter. The left-hand tower therefore represents the number of days in the solar year, the 28-foot shortfall of the right-hand tower representing the number of days in a lunar month, 13 of these months take the solar year's tally of days to the nearest whole number ('month' in fact derives from 'moon')[1]. The solar and lunar symbolism of the towers is further reinforced in that each tower has the appropriate sun or moon symbol on its weather vane. The measures, proportions, patterns, siting and astronomy of Chartres provide a whole library of arcane knowledge. As Nigel Pennick has said in a slightly different context, 'Complex concepts could be transmitted from one initiate to another . . . without the ignorant even realizing that any communication had taken place.'[2]

*Figure 89. (William Blake)*

We can follow the sun-moon, yin yang, thread of correspondence to many places. In an illustration to his epic, visionary poem *Jerusalem,* William Blake, a mystic and esoteric scholar, conveys a whole set of correspondences while seemingly conducting an illustrative function (Figure 89). The central figure places dividers on the ground. We are being told about geometry, earth measure. Further, it is earth measure as the vehicle for sacred space and ancient wisdom, for in the background is a hybrid of Stonehenge and Avebury. On the left, a male figure holds the sun; on the right, a female figure is linked with a crescent moon and stars (another association of the archetypal female – see Figure 87). The dividers are the balance point, and the reconstituted Avebury avenues which reach out to the archetypal male and female, the sun and moon, centre on the circle symbolised by Stonehenge. The ancient site brings it all together.

There is another possible layer of correspondence. In Blake's illustration, as in the towers at Chartres, the masculine sun is on the left, the feminine moon on the right. This has echoes in human brain function in that the left hemisphere of the brain tends to be associated with 'masculine' consciousness – stage by stage cognition, analysis, logic – while the right brain tends to be associated with 'feminine' elements of mind, such as intuition, *gestalt,* new pathways of thought, creativity. These left-right hemispherical activities of the brain cannot be so simply divided, as some writers have maintained, but the trend is there. We may further see the masculine element as that of structure, with the feminine principle symbolising energy.

No one could deny that 'solar' and 'lunar' principles can be observed in human consciousness. There are people who are too influenced by the male principle, who 'have no time' for the arts, or spiritual matters. Anything that cannot be analysed and dissected is not 'real'. They have what De Ropp called 'horizontal mental cleavage'. On the other hand, we all know people overly susceptible to the feminine principle; they are 'vibing' away all the time, floating on Cloud Nine, their feet never touching the ground. Being so excessively ungrounded, they cannot discriminate between genuine mystery and concocted fantasy. These characteristics can dominate people of either gender, though the human sexes do generally mirror the powers and limitations of each principle. A balance, an alchemical marriage, is required: energy without structure, like water without a vessel, just dissipates. But structure without energy, becomes solid, musclebound, lifeless.

As with the individual, so with society. At present, Western culture errs too much on the side of the archetypal male, and this is expressed in its social structure, academic and scientific institutions, outlook and behaviour. A prime example of an extreme form of solar principle society was Nazi Germany: militaristic behaviour, racial domination, monolithic architecture. The Nazi symbol was, of course, the swastika, a solar symbol. Correspondence works at all levels. It is not some academic exercise: symbols and the archetypal patterns of correspondence relate to real forces underlying creation.

The solar number was used secretly in sacred structures in all sorts of surprising ways. Take Glastonbury Abbey, where Bligh Bond discovered that the groundplan was based on a grid of squares measuring 74 feet each. The abbey plan was contained in a rectangle of 9 × 4 rectangles, which John Michell has pointed out[3,4] gives a rectangle 666 feet long. The number 666 is the sum of 1–36, and there are 36 squares in the rectangle. These two numbers, 666 and 36, clearly refer to the sun, for they are the key numbers in the magic square of the sun. Magic squares are devices in which numbers are so arranged in a square grid that their sum, whether added in rows, columns or diagonals, comes to the same figure. Geometric glyphs or sigils can be produced from them too. Magic squares have always been associated with esoteric traditions in a great many ancient cultures, and examples have been found in twelfth-century Chinese literature which were copied from still older sources. W.S. Andrews opined that the 'study of magic squares probably goes back to prehistoric times.'[5] The magic square of the sun is a 6 × 6 grid (thus has 36 inner squares) and each column, row and diagonal adds up to 111, the sum of the six rows or columns thus being 666 – the solar number.

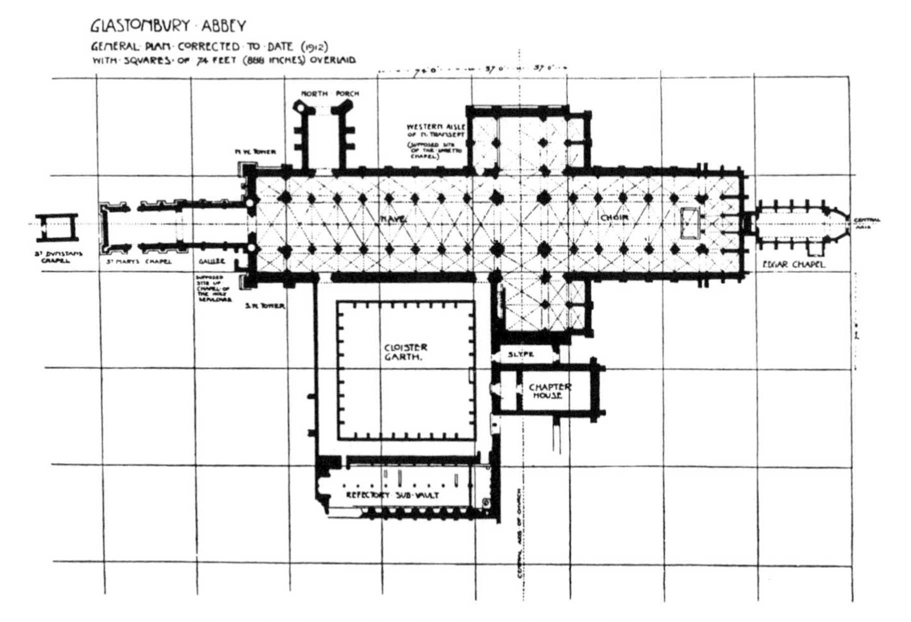


*Figure 90. Bligh Bond's plan of Glastonbury Abbey*

Magic squares are now seen purely as curiosities by the modern mind, but as W. S. Andrews pointed out:

> That magic squares have had in centuries past a deeper meaning for the minds of men than that of simple mathematical curios we may infer from the celebrated picture by Albert Dürer entitled 'Melancolia', engraved in 1514. The symbolism of this engraving has interested to marked degree almost every observer . . . these . . . details reveal an attitude of mind and a connection of thought, which the great artist never expressed in words, but left for every beholder to interpret for himself.[6]

'Connection of thought' is a good phrase to define correspondence. The magic square shown in *Melancolia* (Figure 92) is that of Jupiter. Michell observed that magic squares were 'highly regarded as numerical illustrations of cosmic laws'.[7] It may be difficult for the modern mind to believe that interplays of number or other notation can possibly reveal cosmic laws, but the precarious posture of this attitude is exposed by many curious facts of nature. A recent (late 1980s) case in point is that of David Hindley, a Cambridge musician who has been studying birdsong. He has found that the structure of birds' warbling relates precisely to principles of human musical composition. The time scale of birds

| 6 | 32 | 3 | 34 | 35 | 1 |
|---|---|---|---|---|---|
| 7 | 11 | 27 | 28 | 8 | 30 |
| 19 | 14 | 16 | 15 | 23 | 24 |
| 18 | 20 | 22 | 21 | 17 | 13 |
| 25 | 29 | 10 | 9 | 26 | 12 |
| 36 | 5 | 33 | 4 | 2 | 31 |

*Figure 91. The magic square of the sun*

is faster than that of human beings, so their perception is equivalent to slow motion from our viewpoint (Chapter 1), hence their songs are highly compressed sequences of notes. With the skylark, Hindley had to slow down recordings of its song by a factor of 16 in order to be able to record its notes. A 48-second burst of skylark song ran to nearly 13-minutes' worth of sheet music. Hindley discovered that the principles governing the skylark's song were the same as those underlying the music of Beethoven. Other birds evoked the structural qualities of other composers. Clearly, the

*Figure 92. Albert Dürer's 'Melencolia'*

instinctive singing of birds and the creative patterns of the musical mind adhere to some deep, natural patterns. In a single day, a few birds can compose the equivalent of hundreds of symphonies of human composition.[8] Again, in another area of correspondence, there is Bode's Law. Bode was an eighteenth-century astronomer who discovered that a certain numerical relationship revealed the radii of the orbits of the visible planets. He started with the sequence 0,3,6,12,24,28 and so on, and added 4 to each number: 4,7,10,28,52, 100 . . . Taking the radius of the Earth's orbit round the sun as 10, Mercury fell into place at 4, Venus at 7, Mars at 16, Jupiter at 52, and Saturn at 100.

While on the subject of magic squares, it is worth recalling the clutch of correspondences surrounding Lichfield Cathedral and Mars, uncovered by John Michell in the 1960s[9]. The cathedral is a Gothic building, marking the omphalos of England, according to Bede. It is dedicated to St Chad, whose feast day is March 2, the same as that of the god Mars – from which March takes its name. Red is the colour of Mars, and Lichfield Cathedral was built from red stone. Mars is the god of war, hence *mar*tial, and the name Lichfield was, according to a medieval document in the church archives, 'formerly called *Liches* from War'. When the cathedral was surrounded during the Civil War, with Royalists defending and the Parliamentary forces besieging, the commander of the Parliamentary forces had a cannon trained on the building. He prayed aloud for some omen to indicate whether or not he should go through with the sacrilegious act of firing on the cathedral. At that moment a defender, deaf from birth, fired a lead musket ball made from the cathedral's roof which killed the Parliamentary commander. The date was March 2. To cap it all, Michell found that the magic square of Mars yields a sigil which governed the elevational geometry of the cathedral!

This introduces us to another tool that was, and is, used in the service of correspondence. The site of Lichfield Cathedral was supposedly the spot where 888 Christian martyrs met their death, and Michell points out that by gematria this refers to the name of Jesus. Gematria is the esoteric system used by many mystery traditions such as the Cabala, in which the letters of the Greek or Hebrew alphabets are assigned numbers. In this way, key names in sacred texts can be transcribed into numbers, and into geometry. Michell has entertainingly demonstrated that parables in the New Testament can be read as number and geometry.[10] So it is that the major sacred texts can pass on hidden knowledge to the initiate.

We have seen that the solar number is 666. In gematria the lunar number is 1080. This also happens to be about the actual radius of the lunar disk in miles. The number 1746, the sum of 666 and 1080, represents the fusion of sun and moon. By gematria 1746 gives the phrase 'the Universal Spirit', the *prima materia* of the alchemist. Interestingly, in Greek the phrases 'the Holy Spirit' and 'the Earth Spirit' are anagrams of one another, and yield the lunar number 1080, so the fusion number 1746 also symbolises the harmony of heaven and Earth, the essence of geomancy. The magical union of the mystic sun and the Earth Spirit yields the Universal Spirit. (It also means that in symbolical terms, Jesus and the Holy Spirit represent the male-female principles emerging out of the Divine Ground of God the Father. Further, the Holy Spirit seems to represent a Christianisation of the earlier Earth Religion, but keeping the same magical power as expressed in the gematria.)

Although an unfamiliar usage of number for the modern mind, these arcane systems yield profound knowledge, and are probably the only way in which lost ancient wisdom, which never was common knowledge, is still recorded. We should not assume it is all some abstract confection, as is so much of the modern statistical and economic usage of number. Like sacred geometry, it is not invented but deduced from nature itself. These numbers, the geometry too, refer to real forces operative in nature. Anyone who feels that, on the small scale, number, geometry, ritual and sound cannot conjure up real forces, sometimes made visibly manifest, are deluding themselves. That is why authentic ritual magicians employ those tools. On the large scale, that of the actual planet, these numbers sigils and geometrical figures record mysteries of unutterable depth, but which also have practical correspondences. We will dare to glimpse at the Earth Spirit, the Soul of the World, in the final part of this book.

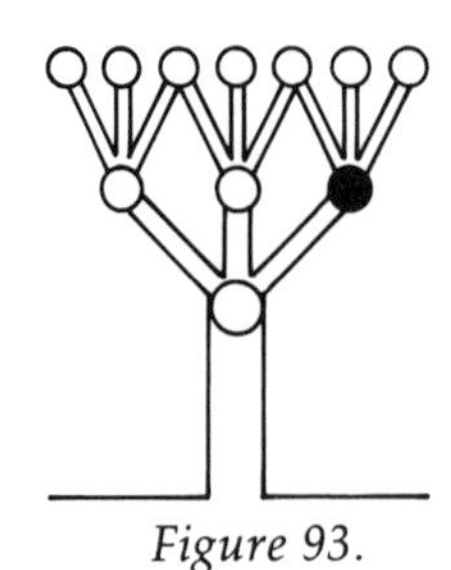

Figure 93.

# CHAPTER 10

# USE OF SITES

## Demonstration

The principle use of Castlerigg today is as a site to visit. It is visually dramatic, in good condition and accessible from Keswick, so is on the tourist route. This is not to be denigrated. Making pilgrimages to ancient sites is quoted in surveys as a major motive amongst tourists. It is a way modern people can connect back with their earlier relationship with the land. Just being at a sacred site can impart some indefinable quality of well-being to the visitor. The second use to which Castlerigg, along with many other sites, is put is as a learning tool; a subject of study, as this book testifies. This is a principle function of ancient sacred sites; they are repositories of perennial knowledge.

We cannot know the precise nature of the activities carried out at the site by Castlerigg's builders, but from the evidence that can be garnered, we can be sure that the megalith builders, who were geomants and astronomers, would have built their sacred places for ceremony and ritual, and for contacting non-ordinary realities – the spirit-world. The original users of Castlerigg would have been practising some version or other of shamanism.

One pre-dawn morning, a Dragon Project team inadvertently interrupted a modern ritual at the site, as I have done elsewhere. This was an example of the neo-paganism that has sprung up in modern times: people are again returning to the ancient places.

## Discussion

The underlying environmental awareness of primary peoples seems to have been animistic: everything was seen as alive, as sharing the breath of some unifying force or power. By definition, there is no room for anything 'inanimate' in such a worldview. Animism was the longest-lived and deepest element of ancient

*Plate 55.*

wisdom. Its final traces were lost to Western consciousness in a cultural sense only a few centuries ago. (In our superior modern way we may sneer at such a 'primitive' attitude as animism, but, then, we are in the final stages of killing our environment, are we not?)

Totemism arose out of animism. There were many versions of it, but in broad terms totemism was the indentification by a tribe or clan with a specific living creature – usually a mammal or bird. The totem animal of a person or group either would not be eaten, or only certain parts devoured, with the killing governed by certain rules. It was a power creature, carrying authority from the spirit world. In more structured religious systems, there are the concepts of the sacred beast and sacrificial animals.

Shamanism emerged, in turn, from the animistic-totemistic worldview. 'Shaman' comes from *saman,* the word the Tungus peoples of Siberia had for the person in the tribe who could journey to the spirit worlds for instruction on healing tribal members, finding lost souls, or determining circumstances affecting the tribe. This was the *ecstatic journey:* the tasks were carried out in an altered state of consciousness. A shaman was not a spirit medium, a passive role, but an active interloper of the spirit world. Nor was he or she just a medicine man or witchdoctor: a healer need not necessarily be a shaman. The shaman may have been an introverted child, quiet, seeking the solitude of lonely places. In some tribes, the shaman was androgenous, a 'she-male', dressed in clothing of the opposite sex.

Shamanism was the first known means of exploring altered states, and underpins all later religions. It was not a production just of the peoples of the arctic circle – the Eskimos of arctic North America, Siberia, and arctic Europe, particularly Lapland – but was also found throughout the Americas and in parts of Asia, including China and Japan (the Ainu), and in Australasia. Some of this may be due to diffusion, but it is mainly because shamanism was what Mircea Eliade called 'a primary phenomenon'. He could see

> . . . no reason whatever for regarding it as the result of a particular historical moment, that is, as produced by a certain form of civilisation. Rather, we would consider it fundamental in the human condition, and hence known to the whole of archaic humanity; what changed and was modified with the different forms of culture and religion was the interpretation and evaluation of the ecstatic experience.[1]

In an altered state, the shaman would leave the world of normal experience, the Middle World, and either go down into the Lower World or ascend into the Upper World, depending on the reasons for his journey. The shamanistic role was *the experiential aspect of the geomantic omphalos* (Chapter 8). As well as the Four Directions, there was up and down as well – the Six Directions of the spiritual landscape. The omphalos was where space, time *and consciousness* met: the Cosmic Axis. Hence its presence in some form, obvious or implied, in all temples and sacred places of antiquity. We have already noted that in the Etruscan tradition the omphalos stone would be removed to allow the influx of spirits into the human world on certain days. The shaman, on the other hand, left *here,* to journey to the other worlds. He left and returned; died and was reborn: as Eliade put it, the shaman is the one 'who *knows* and *remembers,* that is, who understands the mysteries of life and death.' He pointed out that:

> . . . the initiatory ecstasy very closely follows certain exemplary themes: the novice encounters several divine figures . . . before being led by his animal guides to the 'centre of the world', on the summit of the Cosmic Mountain, where are the World Tree and the Universal Lord . . .[2]

The holy mountain as the centre of the Four Directions, as the navel of the world, is universal, the best-known example being Mount Meru; the tradition of the World Tree is well expressed by the Norse Yggdrassil. Further, Eliade observed that:

> . . . the symbolism of the 'Centre of the World' . . . is implicitly present in all ascents to heaven. Jacob dreams of a ladder whose top reaches heaven, 'with the angels of God ascending and descending on it'. The stone on which Jacob goes to sleep is a *bethel* (that is, a sacred stone) and is situated 'at the centre of the world', for it is there that there was connection among all the cosmic religions. In Islamic tradition Mohammed sees a ladder rising from the temple in Jerusalem (pre-eminently the 'Centre') to heaven, with angels to right and left; on this ladder the souls of the righteous mounted to God.[3]

The symbol of the ladder was associated with alchemical initiation, and is found repeatedly in the accounts of Islamic and Christian mystics; it also occurs in shamanic traditions of Africa, Oceania and North America. In Tibet, it was a rope, and the image of 'a chain of arrows' occurred in the Americas and Melanesia. Other images included ascent by means of smoke, sunbeams, or climbing a tree, mountain or vine. Symbolic entrance to the Lower World was usually by entering a (visionary) hole in the ground, or going to the bottom of a river or the sea. Modern psychologists have found that the passage to the Other World of the Near Death Experience is frequently, even usually, imaged as a tunnel of some kind. Clearly, these symbols of passage are archetypal, which explains their recurrence worldwide and throughout time.

Perhaps we may begin to think of the ceremonial stairs on the walls of Chaco Canyon as part of the universal imagery of the passage between the worlds, linking as they do to the mysterious straight roads which traverse the spiritual landscape in the first instance, and only happen to be visible in the physical one.

The shaman made his journey up or down the Cosmic Axis, in whatever form visualised, by altering his consciousness. A number of techniques were employed (and still are in the vestigial shamanic traditions still extant). The prime one was that of drumming. The shaman's drum is mythically constructed from a branch of the World Tree. The meaning of the symbolism is clear, Eliade suggested, representing:

> . . . communication between the sky and earth by means of . . . the Axis that passed through the 'Centre of the World'. *By the fact that the shell of his drum is derived from the actual wood of the Cosmic Tree, the shaman, through his drumming, is magically*

*Figure 94. A Siberian tungus shaman drumming and chanting (Nicolas Witsen, 1705)*

> *projected into the vicinity of the Tree;* he is projected to the 'Centre of the World', and thus can ascend to the sky.[4]

The drum is typically oval in shape, covered by animal skin such as elk, reindeer or horse hide, and is often decorated in a variety of symbols. The drum is seen as a vehicle to transport the shaman to the other worlds; it is his spiritual canoe or steed. American anthropologist Michael Harner has carried out a great deal of practical research on shamanic drumming. 'The steady, monotonous beat of the drum acts like a carrier wave,' he has found, 'first to help the shaman enter the shamanic state of consciousness, and then to sustain him on his journey.'[5] Harner has reported research showing that drumming can produce changes in the central nervous system, a single beat of the drum containing many sound frequencies that can affect various neural pathways. The low frequency of the sound also means that 'more energy can be transmitted to the brain . . . than a sound stimulus of higher frequency.' Researcher Wolfgang Jilek has discovered that drum beat frequencies between four and seven cycles per second predominate in the ceremonies of the Salish Indians of America's Northwest Coast. These can entrain theta brain rhythms which are associated with deep states of meditative consciousness, trance and dreams.

Supporting implements which provide higher frequency sounds can include rattles, click sticks and gongs. It is thought that some bones found at certain prehistoric sites might be drum sticks or one of these other implements.

Breathing and posture techniques are also employed by shamans to attain altered states, but the most important method after drumming is the use of hallucinogenic plants, particularly common in central and south America. In Mexico, peyote is an important sacred plant. It was known to the Aztecs, and its use has been maintained by the Huichol Indians, who consider that a universal life force, *kupuri,* is concentrated in the peyote cactus. Varieties of psilocybe mushrooms occur widely around the world, and they are particularly used by the Indians of Mexico and other Mesoamerican countries. These 'magic mushrooms' may well have been used in prehistoric Europe. Though no direct evidence of this exists, it is difficult to believe that the archaic peoples of Europe would be unaware of their mind-altering properties. Morning Glory *(ololiuhqui)* is another sacred plant known from ancient times. The major sacramental plant of South America is a vine called Banisteriopsis – also called *caapi, yaje* and *ayahuasca.* Another important psychotropic plant is *Datura,* or jimson weed, known to have been used by the Indians of the American Southwest, and by the Chinese too.[6] In Siberia, the key psychotropic was the *amanita muscaria* (fly agaric) mushroom. A first-century-AD clay sculpture depicting a shaman sitting beneath an *amanita muscaria* mushroom, which seems to be symbolising the World Axis, has been found in Nyarit, Mexico.[7] When ingested, these plants can, variously, cause visions, out-of-the-body (ecstasis) sensations, ESP, transcendence of time and space, and allow apparent inter-species communication.

Many herbs, plants, and mushrooms contain mind-altering alkaloids in varying concentrations. It is estimated that there are around 40 native hallucinogens that grow in the British Isles alone. Mugwort, mandrake root and scullcap, amongst those botanical items associated with European witchcraft, can be hallucinogenic and may have been used for mind-change (perhaps recalled in the folk image of the witch flying on a broomstick). Mugwort was also one of the herbs used by the California Chumash Indians for dreamwork.

Whatever the technique employed, the shaman can 'abolish time and re-establish the primordial condition of which the myths tell,' Eliade asserted. 'We are in the presence of a mystical experience that allows the shaman to transcend time and space . . . [the]

re-establishment of a "paradisal" existence lost in the depths of mythic time.'[8]

Here we have the key point; the other worlds are *other states of consciousness.* That is why behind the myriad gods, spirits and demons of various traditions, archetypal patterns can be deduced. The forms may vary, but the underlying configurations of the psyche are constant. At the omphalos, the centre of the world, the Cosmic Axis can take the shaman into the Dreamtime, into mythic consciousness. Some anthropologists have called this aeonic time *Urzeit* or 'pre-time', and Lévy-Bruhl has used the fascinating term 'pre-temporal time'. Anyone who undergoes a major mind-change experience encounters this much-extended sense of time, where the winds of eternity blow. It is not merely the Long Ago, but the Eternal Present. It can be accessed from mundane time. The navel of the world is the point of entry to the other worlds, and to where one returns – a sort of combined departure and arrival terminal. It is where mundane time and Great Time, eternity, meet.

The sites that were used in the animistic-totemic-shamanic traditions that we know about tended to be natural locations, identified as sacred. The hilltop and mountain peak were important, they were the abodes of gods and spirits, and, to the shaman, symbolic of the Cosmic Mountain. Other sites could be springs, trees, large boulders or isolated rock outcrops. They had special properties; they were 'eternal sites'.[9] When Australian aborigine young men were being initiated, by absorbing the appropriate lore of the tribe, and undergoing physical ordeals such as being rolled on a fire, having a tooth knocked out or quartz crystals implanted in their bodies, the ceremonies they performed were for practice only. They did not have power until they were performed at the known, sacred totem sites where the *altirangamatjina* (mythical beings of the Dreamtime) dwelt. At these places, the correct rituals, songs, costumes and imagery could elicit *kurunba,* the life essence, which would permeate the locale bringing fecundity upon the group soul of the totem creature concerned. Hence the totem sites were known as 'increase centres'.

A.P. Elkin described the basic concept behind the increase ritual:

> The pre-existent spirits live at the sacred sites, and the purpose of the rites is to send them out into, or make them available for, the various totemic species or even man himself . . . The performers actually throw dust or stones from the spirit-home, mentioning, as they do so the name of the species . . .[10]

*Plate 56. An Aboriginal elder releasing the mystic force* kurunba *from the Malatji rock at Ngama (courtesy Charles P. Mountford)*

Around midwinter an increase ceremony takes (or took) place at Ngama, an outcrop of rocks near Mount Eclipse in central Australia. A low, isolated rocky hill a few hundred yards west of Ngama is where Malatji, leader of the mystical Dog-People and his clan, made camp during the Dreamtime. A boulder on this hillock is 'a concentrated mass of the life essence or *kurunba* of wild dogs'.[11] In the increase ceremony, an aboriginal Elder, taking a piece of rock and chanting the appropriate songs, breaks off pieces of the boulder, causing *kurunba* to permeate the environment, fertilising the female dogs of the region. An aborigine told anthropologist Charles Mountford that the *kurunba* spread through the air 'like a mist'.

Mountford pointed out the need for learning the 'totemic geography' of the paths or routes connecting the sacred, totem sites, before the aborigine Elders, the repositories of the knowledge, died out.

Caves were major sites for shamanistic practice. The initiate shaman of the Arunta aboriginal tribe has to go to the mouth of a cave where he is 'noticed' by the Dreamtime beings.[12] The Smith Sound Eskimo shaman as part of his initiation has to walk in darkness towards a cliff face in which there are caves. If he is destined to become a shaman he will walk into a cave entrance, if not, he presumably gets a painful bump on the nose. 'Caves play an important part in the initiation of North American shamans,' Eliade has written. 'It is in caves that aspirants have their dreams and meet their helping spirits.'[13]

The use of caves for animistic and shamanistic practice goes back to the remotest times, as testified by the Palaeolithic (Old Stone Age) paintings in the caves of southern France and Spain. The late Joseph Campbell called these 'vast underground natural temples' and 'Stone Age cathedrals'.[14] The remarkable images on the cave walls in these places are tens of thousands of years old. One scene in the Lascaux cave shows a man prostrate before a bull which is wounded by a spear entering through the anus and coming out via its sexual organ (Figure 95). This has been interpreted by some as the depiction of a hunting accident, but Campbell rightly poured scorn on such a notion, stating that the man was 'certainly a shaman' in shamanistic trance. 'He wears a bird mask; his phallus, erect, is pointing at the pierced bull; a throwing stick lies on the ground at his feet; and beside him stands a wand or staff, bearing on its tip the image of a bird.' Campbell goes on to knowledgeably associate the erect penis with the Australian 'lethal phallic rite of magic known as the "pointing bone"' which is

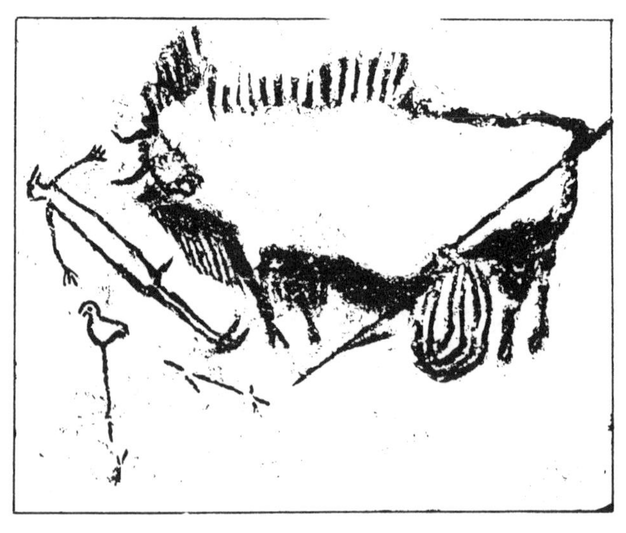

*Figure 95.*

*Figure 96. 'The Trois Frères sorcerer (after Ariège/Breuil and Begouen)*

directed at the person or creature the shaman wishes to injure or bind. Thus the Lascaux imagery in Campbell's view is representative of a hunting spell. German ethnologist Andreas Lommel has suggested that, on the basis of surviving Siberian legends, the scene depicts a battle between shamans.[15]

The Trois Frères cave in the Pyrenees was so named because three brothers happened across it in 1914. The cave art here is in a great cavern reached only after considerable difficulty. The images are engraved on the wall rather than painted. All depict animals except one, the 'Sorcerer of Trois Frères', 'above them all, predominant . . . watching, peering at the visitor with penetrating eyes.'[16] The figure is of a bearded man dressed in an animal skin, on his head stag antlers, his eyes concentric circles enhancing their staring quality. It is the only painted image, and has been called 'an eerie, thrilling picture'. The proto-shaman looking down the ages at us. Perhaps his memory haunts the European folk mind in the ancient images of the foliated Green Man (Jack-in-the-Green, the Wild Man of the Woods), in the legend of Robin Hood, and in the Abbots Bromley Horn Dance in England in which the dancers shoulder ancient antlers and twist and turn, just avoiding locking the horns. This folk dance used to be carried out at midwinter (but now early September) and is accompanied by a retinue of traditional characters, including a Bowman (Robin Hood) and 'Maid Marian', a she-male, amongst others.

The use of caves for magical, shamanic use is not surprising. A cave provides a retreat from the normal world, deep within the womb of Mother Earth. It also provides an environment suitable for sensory deprivation, which is known to cause altered states. Campbell noted that the painted caves were 'far from the natural entrances of the grottos, deep within the dark, wandering, chill corridors and vast chambers . . . Their absolute, cosmic dark, their silence . . . their timeless remoteness from every concern and requirement of the normal, waking field of human consciousness . . .'[17] There can also be geophysical properties in caves that enhance altered states – ionisation (lightning strikes are prevalent at cave mouths) and possible gamma radiation from the rocks (see next chapter).

The Old Stone Age sites were probably the precursors of the New Stone Age chambered mounds like Newgrange, Maes Howe and Gavrinis, the underground Iron Age ritual chambers of north-

*Plate 57. Interior of Carn Euny fogou, Cornwall, typical of the enigmatic, Iron Age underground chambers or souterrains to be found in specific areas of Europe's western Celtic fringe*

*Plate 58. Inside the much-restored Kuaua Kiva, New Mexico. One of the ancient wall paintings depicts a medicine man holding jimson weed, a hallucinogenic plant (not shown in this view)*

west Europe called soutterrains (fogous in Cornwall), and the kivas of the Pueblo Indians. These sites were, in effect, artificial caves.

From North America we gain evidence that such places were used in conjunction with hallucinogenic plants. At the Kuaua kiva in New Mexico, a pre-Columbian wall painting depicts a man, probably the shaman, holding jimson weed. At Burro Flats near Los Angeles there is a panel of rock paintings, the shrine of a Chumash shaman, depicting winged figures with headdresses, animals, hand prints and abstract designs of crosses, dots, lines, circles. The midwinter sunrise sunbeam enters through a natural aperture and interacts with these images. A similar thing happens at other Chumash sites. The Chumash shamans, we noted in Chapter 4, took jimson weed, and may have produced the rock paintings while under its influence. The Tukano Indians of the Colombian Amazon take *yaje*, and state that the source of their art is the imagery they see under its influence. At certain stages in the hallucinogenic experience the neurophysiological circuitry of sight is stimulated, producing phosphenes which fill the visual field with dancing, highly coloured geometric forms, very much in keeping with the imagery in Chumash rock paintings, and some other examples of rock art around the world.

'For the *"alchuklash"*, or astronomer-shaman,' American astronomer E.C. Krupp has written, 'winter-solstice sunrise was not something watched with scientific dispassion. It was a religious experience, a revelation . . . In the play of winter-solstice sunlight upon symbolic rock art, the shaman . . . experienced a *hierophany* – a "showing of the sacred".'[18] We can guess that something similar happened inside Newgrange and the other Neolithic chambered mounds of Europe when the sunbeams penetrated their darkened interiors. Surely the sunbeams would be the shaman's means of ascending to the Upper World; the bridge to allow universal wisdom and knowledge to be brought back to the tribe from the heart of all things.

Eliade linked cave and labyrinth: 'The cave and the labyrinth continue to have a function of the first importance in the initiation rites of . . . archaic cultures . . . both, indeed, are concrete symbols of passage into another world.'[19] Campbell concurred: 'In archaic art, the labyrinth – home of the child-consuming Minotaur – was represented in the figure of a spiral. The spiral also appears spontaneously in certain stages of meditation, as well as to people going to sleep under ether. It is a prominent device, furthermore, at the silent entrances and within the dark passages of . . . New Grange.'[20] True labyrinth designs, laid out in boulders, carved on rocks or built out of turf, emerge from pre- and protohistory at many points around the world. The Cretan labyrinth of the minotaur is the most famous nowadays, but the labyrinth seems to have been of primary importance in Russia and northern Europe, the areas so associated with shamanism. Some 500 stone labyrinths are known in Scandinavia, for instance, and many in western Russia. Most are probably of medieval date, but it is possible that a group in the Solovecke Archipelago date to 4000 BC,

*Figure 97. Left, a stone labyrinth from Visby, Gotland, Sweden (courtesy John Kraft and* Caerdroia *magazine); right, the Chartres Cathedral labyrinth*

*Figure 98. Meander patterns on the back of an ivory bird figurine from the Ukraine, dating back about 20 000 years.*

and meander patterns, from which the labyrinth configuration can be developed,[21] have been found on mammoth ivory figurines of birds in Siberia dating back perhaps 20 000 years. Medieval turf labyrinths have survived in England and Germany, and these may be reworkings by the Church of earlier, pagan versions. These ecclesiastical labyrinths are found in pavement form in some Gothic cathedrals, notably Chartres, which encoded so much

*Plate 59. This is arguably the most accessible and used of the several new labyrinths to have been built in the USA to the ancient pattern. It is situated at the Omega Institute, New York, and was constructed by the author and his Earth Mysteries workshop group in 1987 (courtesy Howard McCoy)*

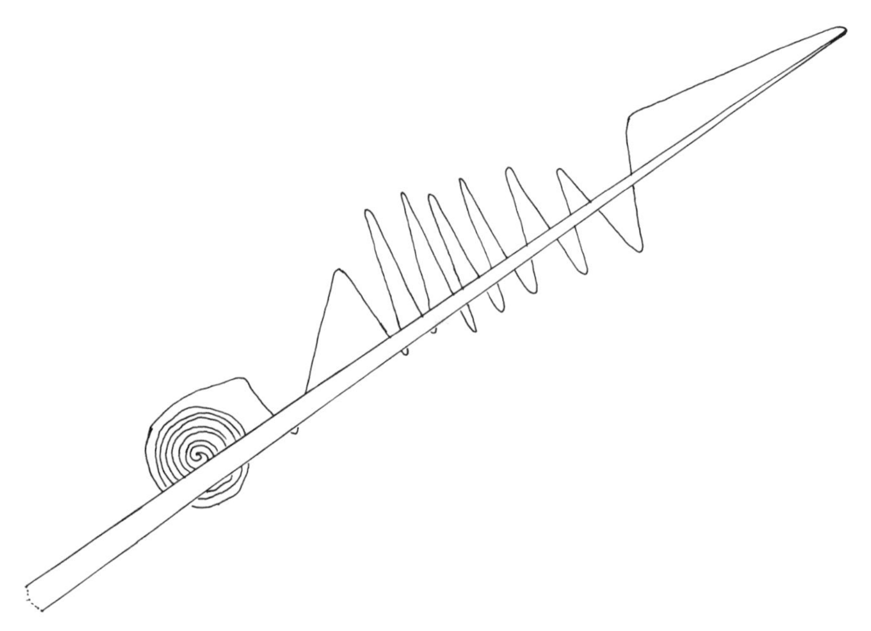

*Figure 99. The 'Needle and Thread' Nascan ground drawing (after Maria Reiche)*

arcane information. It is interesting to note that a common medieval name for the labyrinth was 'Road to Jerusalem', bringing us back once more to the theme of the omphalos. In eastern Germany, British researchers Jeff and Deb Saward of the Caerdroia Project found turf labyrinths with central trees – obviously symbolic of the World Tree.

Many spirals and one labyrinthine symbol appear on the pampa at Nasca, along with continuous-line ground drawings of animals and abstract design, in amongst the straight lines that traverse the desert. When archaeologist Evan Hadingham followed one of the curvilinear ground drawings he became disoriented, a common result of running around a labyrinth (which may cause neurophysiological effects in several ways). He felt these features were used for group, ceremonial dances, but that the straight lines were used for some other, more solitary purpose.[22] He noted the appearance on Nasca pottery of designs reminiscent of san pedro cactus, a powerful hallucinogenic which promotes out-of-the-body experiences. I suggest that it is not beyond the bounds of probability that the straight lines of Nasca were related to shamanic out-of-the-body flight. This could be a better explanation of why the desert figures are seen best from above than Von

Daniken's notions of alien spacecraft. The spirit landscape might not only be haunted by the spirits of the Dead and nature spirits or gods, *but also by the spirit-bodies of living human beings.*

Don Eduardo Calderon is a well-known living Peruvian shaman. He uses san pedro cactus for such ecstatic flight himself. He also feels that the maze-like designs on the pampa were used to initiate healers in hallucinogenic states.[23] American psychologist Alberto Villoldo has described experiences he and a group of companions had with Calderon on the Nasca lines at night under the influence of the hallucinogenic cactus. Calderon took them to the ground drawing known as 'the needle and thread'. At one point, a woman followed the linear path across the spiral, and many members of the group shared the collective vision of seeing her burst into flames; symbolic, Calderon said, of painful memories. Other collective hallucinations were experienced by other members of the group who crossed the 'energy spiral'.

We can see the use of altered states in another form at one of Greece's most important sanctuaries, Delphi, discussed previously. This 'navel of the world' on the slopes of Mount Parnassos was founded over a fissure in the rocks, from which issued mind-changing fumes. The prophetess, the Pythia, would mount a bronze tripod over the fumes. Her mumblings during trance were interpreted by another priestess in answer to questions. Delphi was the pre-eminent oracle site of its time.

Strong evidence has been presented suggesting that the 'wine' used in the Mysteries of Eleusis, also in Greece, was made from 'ergot-infested grain', very similar to LSD.[24]

Other sites – healing temples – were used in Graeco-Roman times for *dreaming*, the most common altered state of them all. The most famous site of this kind is probably the temple of Epidaurus, but there were some 300 such places in the Mediterranean area alone. The temples were usually, but not necessarily, dedicated to the healing god, Aesculapius: a dream temple at Lydney near Gloucester in England, for instance, was dedicated to the pagan British god, Nodens, and in Egypt the dreaming temple at Denderah was dedicated to Hathor. All the dream temples were located at major water sources. The patient would bathe in and drink the waters, then *incubate* a dream in special cells known as *abatons*. The ambience of the temple and the procedures the patient would be instructed in would be such as to encourage a dream of the healing god or some symbol relating to him. Patients would be aided in recalling and interpreting their dreams by temple assistants called *therapeutes*, from which we derive the modern English word therapist. Ideally, the dream would reveal instructions from the god how the illness was to be dealt with, or, in some traditions, the 'Temple Sleep' was considered healing in its own right.

Another version of sacred sleeping comes from Scotland, where a seer would be wrapped in animal hide or a blanket, with only the head free, and lie all night by a holy well or waterfall in order to experience visions.[25] (Sleeping by water emerging from the ground seems to have been the primary theme in sacred dreaming traditions.) This may be a practice that came down from the Druids, who considered wells and springs sacred. The Druids are the nearest we can get to knowing about the users of the gaunt, silent megalithic sites of northern and western Europe. The Druids belonged to Celtic society in the first millenium BC. As with the Etruscans, we know nothing about them directly, but only from the remains of sites, artefacts and the writings of Romans. The Druids kept a strictly oral tradition, committing nothing to writing. An initiate took 20 years to learn the knowledge of the priesthood. It used to be thought that they conducted their rituals only in natural places such as sacred wells (later Christianised), trees and groves, holy hills, and the precincts of burial mounds, but archaeological work has now revealed rectilinear earthworks that show the Druids also built shrines.

Some of these enclosures contain ritual pits or offering shafts that go deep into the ground, reminiscent of the Etruscan omphalos pits (Chapter 8). A ritual pit at Wilsford, Wiltshire, has been radiocarbon dated to the fourteenth century BC, which is within the Bronze Age period, before Druidic times. Celtic expert Anne Ross has commented that this 'gives rise to new thought on the origins of the Celtic priests, the Druids, who certainly used this kind of shrine in Celtic times.'[26] A remarkable shaft, 250 feet (76 m) deep, was found at Findon, West Sussex, crammed with broken pottery and stags antlers. This was located close to a Celtic temple, which in turn had been superseded by a Romano-British shrine: an evolved site. A deer skeleton was found in another shaft, and a figurine in yet another. Navan Fort is a hilltop site in Northern Ireland with extensive views, and the prehistoric structures that have stood there speak of political and religious function. By the first century BC a timber building 125 feet (38 m) in diameter was standing, comprised of five concentric circles of oak posts, the sacred wood of the Druids. It may have been roofed. A long corridor led from the entrance to the centre, where archaeologists found evidence of an enormous oaken pole that had stood around 36 feet (11 m) tall. This great World Tree 'was the focal point not only for the sanctuary itself, but for the entire countryside where it must have acted as a sacred marker.'[27] The pole had been fashioned from an oak tree which had been 200 years old when it was felled, and Ross suggests that it 'may have been one of the sacred trees, *'bile'*, of Ireland which are so well-attested down the ages.' Much of the landscape around Navan shows evidence of ritual activity.

The Druids drank a concoction made from mistletoe, and in modern Irish and Scottish Gaelic, mistletoe means 'all healing'. There were male and female Druids, and their tasks included presiding over legal disputes, prophesy, astronomy and the defining of boundaries. They had an eightfold division of the year – the equinoxes, solstices and the cross-quarter day festivals of Imbolc, Beltane, Lughnassadh, and Samhain. Druids carried wands made of ash, and used idols and images, mainly of wood. The Celts were not a megalithic culture but did sometimes use stones as boundary markers and considered standing stones to possess powers. In Gaul, which received Druidism from Britain, there is evidence to suggest that they believed in the *wouivre*[28] or *nwyvre*[29], a serpentine power residing in the earth and permeating all things. It is perhaps noteworthy that in the entrance passage to Neolithic Gavrinis, serpentine carvings can be seen apparently climbing up a stone out of the ground, and the same imagery occurs at a menhir on the Manio I mound at Kermario. Prehistorian Aubrey Burl admits that these markings may represent the earth.[30]

It is extremely likely that Druidism was at the tail-end of traditions reaching from Neolithic times. Although Ross states that there is not 'the slightest evidence that the pagan priests of the early Celtic peoples were ever associated' with megalithic sites, she allows that 'their direct predecessors may well have been.'[31]

Although effectively exterminated by the Romans, Druidism probably lasted into the early centuries of the current era in the western fringes of Scotland, parts of northern England and in Ireland. From the traces of Druidism, and possibly other vestigial Old Religion traditions, a form of paganism, essentially shamanism, survived into historical times. This paganism and Christianity interchanged a number of times in Britain during early centuries, and even when Christianity became officially established, it is certain that in particular areas there was an undertone of paganism, with wise women and cunning men being known and resorted to. At points throughout the medieval period kings were obliged to denounce pagan gatherings at wells, groves and standing stones. The holy wells may have become Christianised, but worship at them maintained a pagan nature. Even today there are wells where people leave votive rags tied to local trees (Chapter 6). Pre-Reformation churches, too, display pagan influences in grotesques and gargoyles. At Kilpeck church near Hereford, for instance, which escaped the attentions of the Cromwellian iconoclasts and Victorian 'improvers', the pagan sheela-na-gig fertility image is clearly visible on the exterior of the building, as it is on a few other old churches. The witchcraft persecutions throughout Europe which reached their height in the sixteenth and seventeenth centuries, and in which millions of women were killed, broke the main thread of living pagan tradition, leaving only vestigial remnants here and there.

As the old traditions died in Europe and the Americas, revivals have come along to take their place.

Druidism, of a kind, started to be revived, or reinvented, in the eighteenth century, when all megalithic monuments were thought to be 'Druidic'. At the turn of the nineteenth century, the movement took on more impetus with the influence of Welsh antiquarian Iolo Morgannwg (Edward Williams). He claimed to have found previously unknown bardic texts from which he was able to determine the layout of the stone circle he claimed was used to mark the traditional Druidic gorsedd or gathering. Gorsedd circles were erected in Wales where the new Druids held their annual assemblies, a practice which still goes on. Numerous sects of new Druids emerged, so the white-robed figures who gather (or used to until modern government interference) at Stonehenge at midsummer are not in a direct lineage from the actual Iron Age priesthood, though the general patterns of their ceremonies do contain some basic motifs possibly present in prehistoric ritual.

The Old Religion enjoyed a revival as 'witchcraft' and, later, 'wicca' in the twentieth century. In Britain, the magician Aleister Crowley called for 'a natural religion' early in the century, and Margaret Murray's *The Witch-Cult in Western Europe* (1921) gave the process a boost. In the 1930s and 1940s Gerald Gardner acted as a catalyst in the witchcraft revival, but the repeal of the Witchcraft Act in 1951 allowed the proper commencement of a neo-pagan movement. Gardner published his influential *Witchcraft Today* in 1954. Neo-paganism draws on what is known of prehistoric fertility religions, traditional European (Anglo-Saxon) pagan practice, and modern occult research and tradition (which was itself boosted by the use of psychedelics in the 1960s). The neo-pagan

*Figure 100. The Sheela-na-gig carving on Whittlesford Church, Cambridgeshire (author)*

movement has many schools and strands of opinion. Essentially, there is a belief in a goddess and a god, who have taken many forms in the various cultures of humanity, representing the yin/yang principles of creation, and are worshipped in nature. The Earth is seen as the Mother Goddess. Neo-pagans gather at holy wells, stone circles and other sites as well as secluded natural locations. It is by and large a simple, healthy religious activity, nurturing deep-seated instincts within the human psyche, and provides a valuable direct interface for the modern mind with nature. Ritually slaughtered dogs and cats have been found by some of my colleagues at stone circles, but this sort of activity speaks more of 'black magic' cults than wiccan and other pagan practitioners to whom such acts are abhorrent. Many thousands of people in the West must now be active in neo-pagan activities of one kind or another, with its own specialist literature. It is a noteworthy religious trend of the late twentieth century.

Concurrent with the pagan revival has been the intellectual appreciation, especially by women, of the prehistoric Goddess traditions, largely eclipsed or marginalised by a masculinised version of the past. Powerful scholars like Marija Gimbutas have looked for evidence of the religion of the Old European (pre-Indo-European) Great Goddess, and found it in prehistoric art, archaeological discoveries and mythology. She finds the Goddess-centred religion to have stretched from Asia Minor to the Atlantic coast of Europe, and to have existed for 'much longer than the Indo-European and the Christian . . . leaving an indelible imprint on the Western psyche.'[32]

Neo-paganism is practised in America, too, where it also has another form as shamanistic revival. Joan B. Townsend identifies the roots of this as the '"hippie" and related movements that began in the 1960s and developed into various genres in the 1970s.'[33] These synchronised with the rise in America of the Human Potential movement, which in turn brought hitherto obscure academic anthropological material on traditional shamanism to the attention of a wider public through workshops and publications. This was augmented by the work of younger anthropologists who had become experientially involved in shamanism by studying with native practitioners. Among these were Michael Harner (with South American Indian shamans) and Peter Furst and Barbara Myerhoff (with Huichol shamans). The books of Carlos Castaneda, whether true, fictional or 'factional' treatments of anthropology, made neo-shamanism immensely popular. While there is much superficiality and half-truths in modern shamanism, there are those who excuse these aspects as necessary evils encountered in the urgent requirement to get Western consciousness back into a healthier relationship with nature.

Encouraged by the new interest in native traditions, individuals of the decimated Amerindian peoples have come forth to offer tribal teaching, lore and insight. Some of this, too, takes on a superficial 'New Age' gloss, perhaps as a result of the audiences these spokespersons are usually invited to address, but authentic Amerindian elements that might otherwise have perished are being recorded within this milieu.

But the surviving Indian lore is limited and fragmented. The mysterious straight tracks of various extinct or decimated Amerindian tribes, the geometric earthworks of the vanished Adena and

Hopewell peoples, and, even further back in time, the megaliths on the coast of Labrador by the 'Lost Red Paint People',[34] seem beyond the recall of modern Amerindian tribal memory. This can be turned into an advantage. White Americans have often said to me that they do not know if they relate to the megalithic sites of Europe, where their gene pool belongs, or to the Amerindian sites of the land they were born in. In some ways, they feel estranged from both. It seems to me that red, white, and black Americans stand as equals before the most ancient and mysterious relics of the American landscape. It is to this far, archaic land that they need to turn for insight. It will so provide, just as the megalithic sites are doing to Europeans and Westerners in general. But this needs to become a conscious act soon, for the ancient landscape in America is under constant threat for various reasons. That is why it is particularly sad to attend geomantic gatherings in the USA, as I have, and find 'geomants' there who promote the most fantastical notions of 'energy lines' (past, present and future ones, all dowsable . . . interplanetary leylines . . .), rather than learning from the ancient face of the land which nurtures them. 'Geomants' like these are part of the problem rather than the solution.

Shamanism and its offspring, then, add the dimension of consciousness to the geomantic omphalos, thus defining the basic *raison d'etre,* the use, of all sacred places.

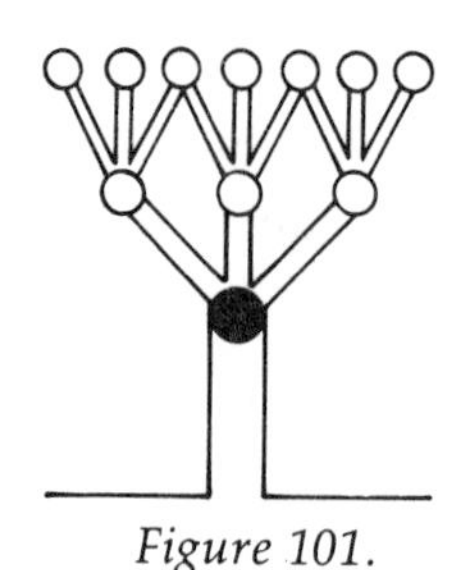

*Figure 101.*

# CHAPTER 11
# ENERGIES

## Demonstration

Writing in *English Mechanic and World of Science* (17 October 1919), a Mr T. Sington recounted an experience he and a colleague had one dark evening at the Castlerigg circle. Returning to their Keswick hotel from a hillwalking expedition, the men saw balls of white light floating hither and thither over the stone circle. As they stood by a field wall gazing in perplexity, one of the lights detached itself from the others and drifted towards them at about head height. Sington described it as 'globular, white, with a nucleus possibly six feet or so in diameter.' As it came up close to the field wall, the light 'slowed down, stopped, quivered, and slowly went out.' The other lights were still playing lazily above Castlerigg as Sington and friend beat a hasty path to their hotel. He wondered if the builders of the circle had themselves seen the lights in the area, caused 'by some local conditions at present unknown', and had erected the stones out of awe of what they interpreted as spirits or gods.

Regarding other energy aspects of the site, it has already been mentioned that apparent ultrasound was detected in modern monitoring work, and a resistivity meter behaved in a strange fashion when between the stones. More recent work (1988) has revealed that just one of the circle's 38 stones, that on the most westerly point of the ring, contains material sufficiently magnetic that it will noticeably affect compass needles.[1] It seems unlikely to be chance that this one stone with this property should occur at a cardinal point of the circle, especially as, as will be shown, similar stones have now been found at key points in other megalithic sites.

*Plate 60. Two men saw balls of light over Castlerigg in 1919. (Simulation)*

*Plate 61. Castlerigg's magnetic stone being checked with a compass.*

## Discussion

We can see that the 'second order', more integrated, approaches to sites – geomancy, arcane systems, and use – ultimately distil down to a question of energies of some kind. There is the *ch'i* of the Chinese geomants, the *prima materia* of the alchemists, the 'Earth spirit' or Holy spirit' of the occult codes, the *kupuri* and *kurunba* of indigenous peoples, and the *wouivre* of ancient Druids.

The question of energies breaks down into three areas: the idea of there being some 'universal force' underlying all material manifestation, unknown to modern science but acknowledged in ancient traditions the world over; known, recordable and measurable energies at sites; and, finally, light phenomena of the kind reported at Castlerigg, which is an energy manifestation that fits somewhere between the two previous categories – it can be seen and photographed, seems to relate to electromagnetism, but has characteristics that go beyond anything currently known in geophysics.

Let us first look at the idea of a universal force. If it exists, it is more properly considered as a force rather than an energy, because it cannot be measured. There are many other traditional names for it than those mentioned above. Martial arts adepts use *ki* in Japan, the Pacific islanders have their *mana*, and numerous Amerindian tribes had names for the force: to the Pubelo it was *po-wa-ha;* the Algonquins spoke of *manitou;* the Sioux had *wakonda* or *waken;* the Crows knew of *maxpe;* the Iroquois referred to *orenda*, and the Eskimos to *sila*. In northern Europe the force was called *önd*,[2] personified by Woden or Odin. The ancient Greeks recognised *pneuma* permeating all things, which the Romans called *numen*. In North Africa it is *baraka;* it is known as *lunyensu* or *bu-nssi* to the Bantu and *n/um* to the !Kung bushmen of South Africa (the exclamation mark denotes a click sound). In Ndedema Gorge, !Kung rock art depicts two shamans with the force streaming out of their heads, and a freshly killed antelope is seen yielding up *n/um*.

It seems that only our own culture has no concept, and thus no word, for a universal force. But the notion lingers. Scientists used to think there was an 'ether', then Einstein sought his 'unified field', and now a 'fifth force' beyond the four known fundamentals of gravity, electromagnetism, and the strong and weak nuclear energies, has become the quarry for physicists. It is thought to be a type of gravity. Earlier dalliance with the idea of a pervading force was often mixed in with a developing awareness of electricity and magnetism.

In the eighteenth century, Mesmer invoked 'animal magnetism' as the force that allowed him to hypnotise patients, and for many years it was supposed that magnetism was some kind of subtle fluid. Since at least Cardan in 1554, it had been suggested that anaesthesia could be induced by magnetism, and nervous diseases treated by magnetised rings and bracelets. This had been developed the following century by Paracelsus who applied magnets directly to the body for healing purposes, considering that people had something magnetic within them identifiable with the life force.

Static electricity and the powers of the lodestone were known at least as far back as ancient Greece, and there are claims that magnetism was used in Egyptian temples.[3] In the sixteenth century, the brilliant Elizabethan, William Gilbert, distinguished between magnetism and electricity, coining the term 'electric force'. He announced that the Earth was a magnet, attributing a 'soul' to the lodestone because it was the offspring 'of its animate mother, the Earth.'

The idea of a universal force is not studied for long without the subject of 'auras' being encountered. Countless psychics down the ages have been able to perceive a subtle, coloured field effect around people, and have been able to spot impending health problems by distortion in it. In the 1840s, the German scientist, Karl von Reichenbach, found that psychics (he coined the term 'sensitives' for them) could see crystals, magnets, plants and other objects in total darkness because of a mysterious emanation of subtle light from them. One of his best sensitives, Angelika Sturman, saw a blue, undulating luminosity that occasionally flared into brilliance emerging from the pointed end of a crystal, while a haze of dull red-yellow light glowed around the blunt end. He found that a colleague, Professor Endlicher, could identify a plant in total darkness even when the man had no idea what the object was that he was being asked to see. Reichenbach conducted many experiments, the most impressive using a powerful horseshoe magnet. He learned that his sensitives were able to distinguish a 'fine light' coming out from it in two streams:

> . . . which do attract each other, do not cease, do not affect each other as does the magnetic power of both poles, but which quietly stream upwards side by side, teeming with white luminous points and, together, forming a column of light about a man's height, which was described by each one who saw it as arrestingly beautiful.[4]

The human body was also a powerful producer of this light, which he called 'Odyle Force', or OD, named after Wodan, the 'all penetrating'. He found it had a polarity and that it could travel through conductors at about 40 inches per second, too fast for conducting heat and too slow for electricity or magnetism.

Early in the twentieth century, Dr E. Boirac of the Salpetrière Hospital in France was able to corroborate some of Reichenbach's findings, frequently using hypnotised sensitives. He was apparently sometimes able to use spectroscopes and other apparatus to support the sensitives' claims. Boirac also found the human body could naturally produce the force, and that some people could store it; it had a left- and right-hand polarity, and it was emitted most strongly through a person's fingertips, an effect which could be intensified by placing a wire coil around the subject's arm.

From the 1930s to the 1950s, physician and Freudian analyst Wilhelm Reich claimed discovery of a similar force he called 'orgone'. Reich concluded from his psychological work that mental tension could cause muscular tension, and sufferers would adopt rigid postures. He considered sexual repression and other problems played a great part in the creation of this muscular armouring, and treated such conditions with psycho-analysis and deep massage. Untreated, areas of constant muscular tension became focal points of disease. He came to the conclusion that some form of underlying force was being damned up in the armoured areas. He teased at the idea of this 'life force' for years and eventually made a breakthrough with his claimed discovery of what he called *bions.*

Reich was able to produce these bions from a range of substances. When he filtered water through soil, for example, and froze the resulting yellowish liquid, flakes would appear on thawing. Magnified 3000 times these flakes displayed pulsating phenomena which Reich likened to living cells. These bions seemed halfway between living and non-living matter. He found energy radiating from bions produced from sea-sand and concluded it was a force unknown to science. Opinion is now sharply divided on Reich: everyone accepts that he was a brilliant Freudian scholar, but many feel he slipped into lunacy when he started his pursuit of orgone energy.

Whatever the rights or wrongs of that argument, Reich went on to conduct many experiments and make challenging observations about his orgone energy. He claimed that by looking at the sky through a tube made of organic material orgone energy could be discerned spiralling in the air, a motion which the Austrian scientist considered as being the origin of growth patterns and celestial mechanics. Being the fundamental force of the universe, orgone was naturally everywhere, but Reich found that he could concentrate it in 'accumulators', boxes made from alternating layers of organic and inorganic material, usually wood and metal. By looking through a peephole in an accumulator, it was said to be possible to observe the dimly glowing orgone spiralling around in the darkness of the box. Reich worked at different locations in Europe, always having to move on due to various forms of intolerance, and finally settled in America. He ran into trouble there, however, because he claimed that people sick with cancer and other diseases could be healed by being placed in large orgone accumulators. When demanded by the courts to prove his claims, he refused to do so as a matter of pride, and was jailed for contempt. He died, incarcerated, in 1957.

(Geomancy students have long noticed the curious coincidence that many Neolithic mounds were constructed of alternating layers of organic and inorganic materials. Nowhere is this more dramatic than at Newgrange and Knowth. No archaeological explanation for this practice has been forthcoming.)

Over approximately the same period, Harold Saxon Burr of Yale was finding electrical fields around and electric potentials on the surfaces of living things. Burr went on to claim that these fields, which he called 'L-fields' (Life fields), were the organising force behind an organism's growth. This echoed the 'vitalist' school of biology, active in the nineteenth century and early decades of this one, which postulated that there was some non-material vital principle acting on living organisms to frame their morphology or form. Though vitalist concepts are not encouraged in modern biology, we do have the sophisticated field model of formative causation promoted by biologist Rupert Sheldrake.[5,6]

There is a considerable history of other experiments and theories involving electrical, magnetic, dowsing and occult means of detecting a fundamental, organising force underlying all manifest creation. This urge reveals the innate conviction possessed by the human mind that such a universal force exists. This urge also manifested in the attempts to image the force.

In 1842, an English researcher called Carsten made a condenser system to produce 'electric patterns' of coins on a mica plate, a precursor of Kirlian and other forms of electrophotography. Similarly around the turn of this century, Hippolite Baraduc, a French doctor, attempted to image what he called 'the lights of the human soul' by using a generator of high voltage static electricity. His picture of the hand of an 'over electrified' person registered on a photographic plate was the world's first electrophotograph of part of a human being. He also asked subjects in different emotional states to simply place their hands – without contact – over photographic plates. Images were formed in the emulsion. In this work Baraduc was following the lead of Professor Blondlot, who believed in 'certain ether radiations of a special order of frequency, near the electromagnetic in the ether scale' which were given off by nerve tissue, especially during concentrated thought or emotional disturbance. He called these radiations 'N-rays' and found they could affect photographic plates.

In the 1890s, the respected British scientist, W.J. Russell, also produced photographic images without recourse to electrical energy. Russell learned from the French scientist, H. Becquerel, that uranium could leave an effect on photographic emulsion, and he set up a test in which perforated zinc was interposed between a uranium sample and a photographic plate, expecting that the holes in the zinc sheet would be clearly delineated on the plate. Instead, he found that the greatest amount of activity occurred beneath the zinc itself. By extensive further experimentation, Russell found that metals could on their own account give off photographically recordable emanations of some kind, even at a distance of several inches. He discovered that certain types of wood were very active. Annual tree rings could leave impressions on photographic emulsion. Essential oils such as peppermint,

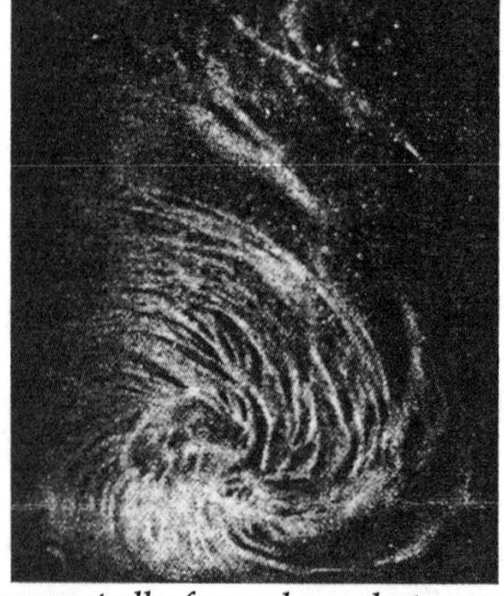

*Plate 62. An image purportedly formed on photographic emulsion without light or physical contact by one of Baraduc's subjects. The French researcher had people in various emotional states hold their hands near a photographic plate. In this case the vortex pattern was created by someone thinking 'sad and violent' thoughts*

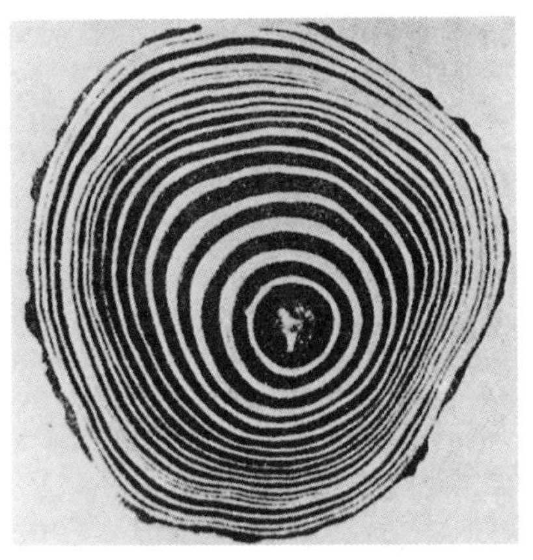

*Plate 63. W.J. Russell's photograph of tree-rings in Scots Fir. The wood apparently photographed itself by means of an unidentified emanation (courtesy W.J. Russell)*

eucalyptus, lavender, pine, winter green and others containing terpenes were also notably active. Substances such as gelatin, celluloid, parchment and ordinary paper allowed the Russell Effect to pass through them more or less unhindered, while materials such as mica, dry glass, arabic gum and paraffin blocked it. It is tempting to see the Russell Effect as related to the subtle emana-

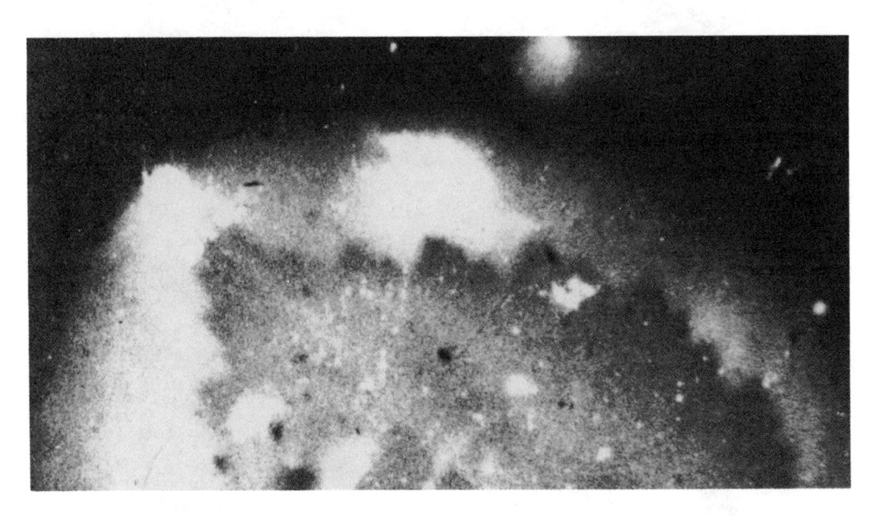

*Plate 64. A Russell-effect picture of a leaf. This leaf photographed itself after being left in contact with a piece of high contrast line film (Kodalith ortho) for a period of about five days. The image is considerably enlarged here. No light or artificial enhancement was used*

tions perceived by Reichenbach's sensitives, and, indeed, in 1938 Lord Rayleigh succeeded in obtaining faint images from magnets laid on very sensitive film emulsion.

Because exposures of many hours are required for Russell Effect images to form on film, which occurs even with a barrier such as cling-film or aluminium foil, electrophotography has taken precedence in 'energy photography' over recent decades. 'Kirlian photography' was accidentally discovered in 1939 when Russian electrician Semyon Kirlian found his hand could leave an image on film shortly after he had received an electrical shock. This led to much research and development in electrophotography in the USSR. One of the leading Russian researchers, Victor Inyushin, was convinced that living things have an 'energy body' consisting of what he called 'bioplasma'.

This work was announced to the West in Sheila Ostrander's and Lynn Schroeder's *Psychic Discoveries Behind the Iron Curtain* in

*Plate 65. A typical Kirlian photograph of a leaf*

1970.[7] This news intrigued Californian psychologist Thelma Moss who visited Russian researchers and began her own experimentation on her return to America.

A Kirlian 'camera' uses no lenses. The photographic image is recorded on film by placing an object in a high tension, high frequency electric field. In practice, this means placing an object – leaf, human hand, or whatever – on a sheet of film lying on an insulated plate electrode. A coil produces high voltage but as there is effectively no current, objects that are imaged come to no harm. Typical Kirlian pictures show streamers and blobs of light emerging from the tips of leaves or fingers, which are often surrounded by a corona of light. Initially, everyone enthusiastically thought this was the elusive aura captured on film at last, but there is a more sober view today.

So many variables – humidity, pressure, composition of air, and so on – can affect the outcome of a Kirlian picture that it became clear the early work was not sufficiently rigorous. It was shown that the corona effect was created in film emulsion by the electrical field permeating the object being imaged – a 'cold emission of electrons'. Nevertheless, it remains true that Kirlian photography can be of some value if it is carried out with sufficient control of variables, of which Arthur Ellison, a professor of engineering, has identified about 30.

It needs to be understood what a Kirlian image is showing. While it is certainly an artefact of the electrical field, a Kirlian photograph is a *disclosing artefact*. To take a mundane analogy, special dye can reveal areas of plaque on teeth: what is seen is the dye, not the plaque, but it shows where the plaque is. In just the same manner, the actual image on a Kirlian photograph may be caused by the effect of the instrument's electrical discharge on an object, but it can disclose information about the object's natural field – perhaps the sort of thing Russell was recording.

A number of clinical researchers around the world now use Kirlian photography to diagnose cancer. Cancerous tissue yields powerful, disorganised coronal images while healthy tissue shows a more restrained and balanced coronal pattern. Some work has shown that fingertip electrophotographs of women with breast cancer differ to those of healthy subjects. The work goes on.

Arguably the leading Western exponent of electrophotography is Florin Dumitrescu, a Romanian now based in France. He feels that different methods of recording 'bio-electrical fields' are required because they are of varying frequencies. Bio-electric fields can be made visible, he has found, because surrounding ionised

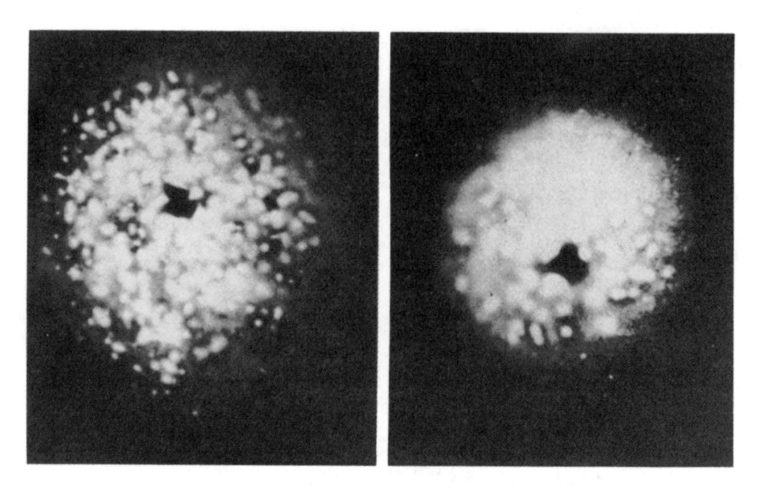

*Plate 66. Electronographic images of an acupuncture point (courtesy Ion Dumitrescu, Neville Spearman)*

gases can take on their pattern. Dumitrescu has pioneered various 'electronographic' techniques, conducted with consummate care and rigour, and can image energy effects on and around large portions of the human body. He produces still, movie and video images.[8] Plate 66 shows electronographic images of an acupuncture point taken with (left) a negative impulse and (right) a positive impulse.

Much of the Western search for a *ch'i*-like force over the last century or so is permeated with sheer hokum and mistaken identity of forces which were to become better understood. Nevertheless, some aspects remain unresolved. The account with the universal force has not yet been closed even in our culture.

While we can presently only guess at how a universal force relates to ancient sites, what about known energies? That was largely the question the Dragon Project (Chapter 7) was set up to investigate. Resources did not allow work to the level that was really required, but it was realised that whatever might be discovered would be more than had been known hitherto – it was virgin research territory. Mainstream science by and large had ignored the area as 'lunatic fringe', while the lunatic fringe itself would not condescend to consider the possible presence of known energies, everything having to be occult and 'spiritual'. The Dragon Project thus trod difficult ground between the extreme viewpoints. The full story is provided in my *Places of Power*[9] but a summary of some aspects can be given here.

*Plate 67. Dragon Project monitoring taking place at the Llangynidr Stone, Wales, probably the first monolith to be checked for electromagnetic anomalies*

The first physical, instrumental investigation I know of at a megalithic site was at the 14-foot (4-m) tall Llangynidr Stone near Crickhowell, Wales, in the mid-1970s. Two investigations by physicists did reveal magnetic anomalies on the surface of the stone, corresponding remarkably well with earlier findings by a dowser.[10] This work convinced us that magnetic monitoring should be part of the Dragon Project's brief. When resources allowed, we used magnetometers, instruments which can measure very small levels of magnetic change. These revealed that sporadic, low-level changes of magnetism could occur in standing stones. At Rollright in July 1983, we found one stone in the western sector of the circle that was fluctuating quite dramatically for a few hours in the millioersted range (the scale on the machine being used). It eventually settled down and gave a completely level reading like all the stones we monitored around it. This tallied with earlier findings[11] by independent researcher Charles Brooker, who had measured two other magnetically pulsing stones in the circle. The reasons for this effect are currently unknown. I must emphasise that in most cases *no* unusual readings were obtained.

In the late 1980s, a different kind of magnetic effect began to be noted at certain sites. In 1987, a local Welsh journalist told me of a curious happening at Carn Ingli, one of the peaks of Mynedd Preseli, a hill range in southwest Wales. A woman passing by the peak had been overcome by sudden physical discomfort that she felt had somehow been triggered by the hill. It was later discovered that Carn Ingli had anomalous magnetic areas on it where a compass needle would point due south! Carn Ingli means 'Hill of the Angels', so named because a sixth-century holy man, St Brynach, had experienced visions and 'spoken with angels' there. In the Iron Age, if not before, people had laced stone walls around the peak. I told an archaeologist about the phenomena on the hill, and when he visited it he and two companions saw a rainbow-like effect over the top of the peak – at night!

The magnetic anomalies on Carn Ingli are dramatic but not mysterious. They occur because iron content in the rock contains the 'imprint' of the Earth's magnetic field as it was hundreds of millions of years ago, when the magnetic poles were apparently reversed. A fossilised geomagnetic field, in effect. Not paranormal in any way , but possibly of great significance. Such dramatic compass responses could not be reproduced elsewhere along the Preseli ridge, and Carn Ingli had clearly been singled out by prehistoric peoples. It is a possibility that St Brynach's visions may have been helped by the geophysical environment on the peak. One can sit on rocks there with the lower part of the body in the archaic magnetic field, and head and shoulders in the present one. It was, after all, human response which had drawn attention to the magnetic anomalies in the first place.

Thus alerted, I started checking structured monuments for 'magnetic stones' using simple, liquid-filled compasses. My wife, Charla, discovered the stone at Castlerigg (above), and we went on to find magnetic stones at other circles. At Gors Fawr in Wales, for example, there are two outlying stones that Thom claimed indicated summer solstice sunrise. The stones in the circle did not affect a compass, but one of the two midsummer outliers,

*Plate 68. This outlier of the Gors Fawr circle, Wales, indicates midsummer sunrise and also affects magnetic compasses held near it. Note its curious seat-like shape*

the furthest from the circle, did. Also, its shape was such that one could sit on the stone and rest the head against the most magnetic part of the rock.

Sites with magnetic stones have been found in Scotland and Wales, but a wide survey has not yet (1990) been carried out. A parallel case, however, was discovered on Mount Tamalpais, outside San Francisco. Four 'power spots' have been identified on the mountain by an Amerindian Elder. I was shown one of these in 1986, and later noticed that a rock sample from the site was strongly magnetic. Subsequent compass work (1989) confirmed points of magnetic anomaly at the location. A power spot indeed.

*Plate 69. One of the 'power spots' on Mount Tamalpais, San Francisco. The location is an outcrop of magnetic serpentine, and a person sitting in the natural seat there can have the base of the spine in contact with magnetic rock*

Another fundamental, known energy the Dragon Project looked at in an ancient site context was natural radioactivity, mainly because of Keith Critchlow's anecdote (Chapter 7). Most people think of radiation in terms of nuclear weapons or power stations, but in fact we are subjected to low-level radiation all the time in the form of cosmic rays from outer space and gamma radiation from rocks and minerals in the ground. There is always a background count. In certain areas where there are particularly radioactive rocks, such as granite, the background readings are relatively higher. There had not been a great deal of official concern about natural radiation in the landscape until the scare about radon gas and the Chernobyl disaster. The Dragon Project was at work prior to either of these events. Radon gas issues from the ground as a result of uranium decay. Some areas are more prone to this than others, and it has been found that houses with insufficient ventilation situated on radon emission points can experience a build up of the gas which creates particles in the air that can be breathed in. Over *long* periods of such exposure, it is thought lung cancer can be provoked, hence the concern.

But what about ceremonial sites? We knew that uranium deposits had been found under Amerindian and Aborigine holy places, thus causing the 'land rights' controversies, and a French writer, Marc Dem,[12] had pointed out that the distribution of megaliths in France corresponded well with known uranium deposits, so we thought there may be a connection.

At the Welsh site of Moel ty Uchaf, source of Critchlow's anecdote, we almost always obtained higher readings on the northwest quadrant of the circle. I can only suggest that there is a radon source there that had been particularly activated at the time of the earth tremor and associated sound and light phenomena that was centred on the monument's mountain location in 1974. (Critchlow was there just days after these events.) At the huge ring of Long Meg, Cumbria, a project volunteer noted in 1983 that small zones on three stones emitted constant streams of radiation. I confirmed this a few years later: a geiger counter clicking away lazily would suddenly issue a staccato burst near one of these localised spots. American Project volunteers Cosimo and Ann Favaloro monitored a Scottish stone circle, Easter Aquorthies, and its environment continuously for 12 hours over a Major Standstill moonset period in 1987. On one occasion, there was a huge 'flare up' of readings within the circle while the background remained normal, and at the precise moment of moonset the values of site and environment readings switched over for a short time. Our most usual finding at stone circles was that they tended to occupy slightly *lower* areas of background readings than their environments. But no clear patterns emerged.

We found that a number of the holy wells we checked yielded higher-than-background radiation *at water surface* – considerably higher in some cases. Once removed in a container, the water was not anomalous. I presume the higher radiation must be caused by radon filtering into the water as it rises through the strata or from granite stonework around the well (water surfaces gave higher readings than surrounding stonework). In Bath, Britain's most famous Neolithic and, later, Roman springs, have been known to be mildly radioactive since early this century.[13] It is also said that the Chalice Well at Glastonbury is slightly radioactive. If such waters have enhanced radiation only while at the well, it may explain why those seeking healing nearly always had to come to the site, rather than water being taken to the patient, if radiation is a factor.

So concerned were we at finding some remarkable geophysical anomaly, the real, subtle energy secret of certain sites slipped by unnoticed for quite a while.

In the way some members of traditional peoples today have

*Plate 70. A cornish dolmen or 'Quoit'. This is Chûn Quoit and has an interior Geiger count significantly higher than background. Odd light radiation phenomena inside the Quoit have been reported*

superior knowledge of their botanical environment (they still teach Western pharmacologists), earlier societies, or, at least, their shamans, would also have been just as intimately aware of the geophysical aspects of their surroundings. The megalith builders were opportunistic, in that if they could create an effect in an easy manner, they would not choose a difficult one. So in areas with high background radiation we tend to find sites that are enclosed – either 'boxes' of stone as with dolmens, or underground chambers such as souterrains (fogous in Cornwall), and kivas. The Iron Age souterrain/fogou sites occur in Brittany, Cornwall, Aberdeenshire, Orkney and Ireland. The first three zones are all granite areas, and in Orkney uranium has been found in stream water.[14] I do not have geological information on the relevant Irish region. In America, the kivas are semi-subterranean features in the Southwest where there are uranium deposits. I have taken background readings in New Mexico which are identical to those in Cornwall. Kivas are known to be ritual chambers, but some archaeological opinions still claim that souterrains were storage places for Iron Age villages. The reasons why this borders on the ludicrous have been well summarised elsewhere.[15] There can be little doubt that the fogous of Cornwall are ritual chambers.

What we found at dolmens and fogous in Cornwall was entirely to be expected in enclosed granite chambers – they were environments of enhanced natural radiation, typically two or three times the local, already high, background. Now, an accidental discovery at the Rollright started me wondering if this geophysical factor might in itself be significant. The Rollright circle had yielded no radiation anomalies, except for occasional flares like the Easter Aquorthies incident. But our environmental monitoring revealed that the stretch of country road immediately alongside the site gave high natural readings. This was presumably because rocks in its foundations were radioactive (tests showed the road surface to be normal). It was ironic that we found a modern feature to be radioactive! However, something odd became apparent to me over the years of the project: the 200-hundred-yard stretch of radioactive road produced three outstanding paranormal events, experienced by three independent and reliable witnesses, one of them a scientist, and each incident reported to me independently. All three cases involved the fleeting appearance and disappearance of apparently solid objects or creatures. I published this matter only in 1990.[16]

Interestingly, I had obtained the same readings inside the King's chamber in the Great Pyramid as in the Cornish sites. The Pyramid is limestone but the chamber is clad in Aswan granite brought hundreds of kilometres from the south. This chamber was also probably used for initiation and ritual. On the coast of the Gulf of Bengal are house-sized blocks of granite, some of which have been hollowed out into temples. In eastern Germany, at Teudelsmauen, a seat has been carved out of granite in an area noted for its high natural radiation. Could enhanced zones of natural radiation cause transient mind-change? Had it been used as part of the old shamans' armoury of techniques?

We discovered that people had, indeed, experienced the transient altered states in fogous, and as we enquired further, we heard of other people elsewhere in the world who experienced exactly the same kind of mind effects while living over large granite deposits.

Other, surprising factors emerged about the Cornish sites: we began to collect accounts from reliable witnesses, including an archaeologist, that inside a dolmen and a fogou curious light phenomena had been observed. It was a soft light, usually white and sometimes accompanied by pin-prick sparkles, that *moved over* the interior surfaces of the granite in these dark, radon-charged places. The nature of this light has not yet been determined. I have no doubt that it would have been known to the megalithic master masons, and perhaps seen as a manifestation of spirit.

Apart from altered states, it appears that in suitable doses and exposures, natural levels of radiation may have healing properties. In the late nineteenth century, when Europeans were visiting spas (some of them mildly radioactive, remember), their American counterparts were visiting the radon caves of Colorado for the same purposes. In the 1950s, radon kits were sold containing canisters of radon from which the purchaser could have a quick sniff when feeling out of sorts! At the present time, people frequent the old gold and uranium mines in Montana for carefully timed periods inside the radon-permeated mine levels for curative purposes. People claim cures or help with diabetes, arthritis and other ailments.[17] Long-term exposure to radon is, we have noted, harmful; but perhaps limited, 'homoeopathic' exposures can be beneficial.

I believe that further research into the magnetic and radiation aspects of ancient monuments may lead us to some fascinating insights. We had overlooked the actual nature of the megalithic instruments themselves, yet it is obvious with hindsight that a prehistoric 'energy' technology would be as natural as the materials in the megalith builders' environment. So basic and elemental that it was easy for late twentieth-century eyes to overlook it.

The other long-term monitoring programme on the Dragon Project involved ultrasound (Chapter 7). In the late 1970s we obtained apparent ultrasound signals at Rollright and a few other sites, nearly always over a few hours around sunrise. There was a tantalising hint in the data that lunar phase was related to how soon the signals would start prior to actual sunrise,[18,19] but it proved impossible to follow this up. Signals were obtained most strongly over February–March, and least activity – usually none at all – over the summer months. The apparent signals occurred in vague patches in or around the monitored sites. But in 1987, with new tunable instrumentation, we did obtain what appears to have been our first identified source – a metre-deep band around the tallest stone in the Rollright circle. The readings were again obtained over sunrise. We are not sure if the sandstone pillar was truly emitting ultrasound, or whether it was possibly acting as a dielectric waveguide for cosmic or artificial electromagnetic waves that triggered the ultrasound receiver. The whole matter of ultrasound at ancient sites remains annoyingly unresolved.

Ultrasound presented itself in another guise, too. We had British Kirlian researcher Harry Oldfield on site on a number of

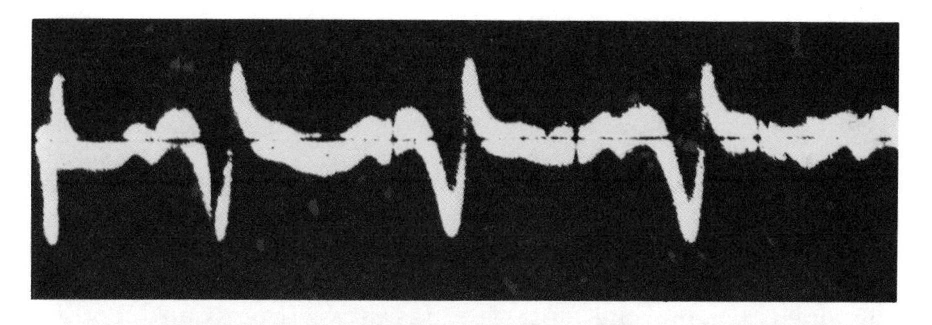

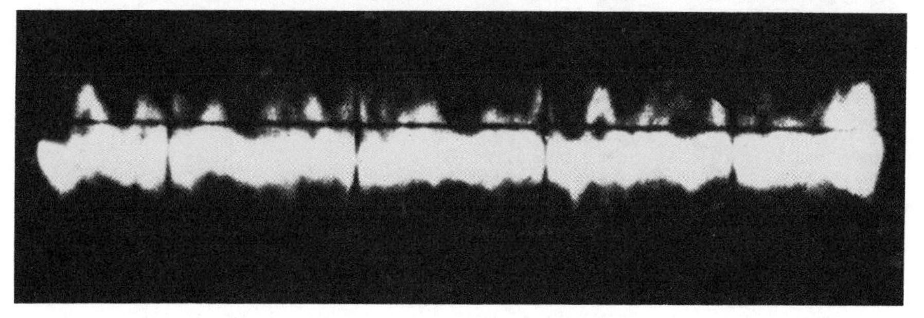

*Plate 71. Oscilloscope images of ultrasound emissions from a Rollright stone undergoing Tesla coil energisation. (top) shows a normal wave pattern from the coil's input; (bottom) shows disruption of the pattern during sunrise*

occasions with a view to conducting Kirlian photography at a stone. Oldfield had developed a system for medical use in which a person was energised by a Kirlian camera causing them to become a 'beacon' for radio and ultrasound emissions. By using an appropriate detector linked to an oscilloscope, Oldfield was able to observe variations of the signal around the person's body as a diagnostic method. At our request, he tried this on a standing stone, using an ultrasonic receiver. The stone was energised shortly before sunrise and the signal coming off it was a uniform wave resulting from the Kirlian camera's input (Plate 71, top), but as the sun rose the signal coming off the stone changed markedly (Plate 71, bottom). On another occasion, Oldfield was able to produce a partial corona around a stone using Kirlian methods. It appeared as a dancing blue light. The set-up was difficult and complex, though, so the experiment was never repeated.

Infra-red photography was tried from time to time. On two occasions, at dawn, I obtained 'glow' effects around the top of a megalith at Rollright on infra-red film, which experts were never able to satisfactorily explain. More dramatically, however, infra-red work by other photographers at Rollright and a megalithic site in Kent revealed what appeared to be a 'cloud' about 15 feet (4.5 m) above the ground. In neither case was a cloud visible to the photographers. Again, this is work that requires further investigation.

Amongst many other trials and experiments, monitoring of electronic voice phenomena (EVP – see Chapter 7) took place on several occasions around 1980. Many hours of taping took place but barely two-minutes' worth of apparent paranormal voices was obtained. For me, the most eerie result was from Cairn T, the Neolithic chamber at Loughcrew (Chapter 4). I left an unattended tape machine recording inside the radio-silent interior for ten minutes. On analysis, the background hiss of the fresh tape was interrupted only once, by a rapid 'voice'. Slowed down, this seemed to say 'Ghost is the listener'!

We learned that similar work to the Dragon Project had been going on in Brittany. The researcher was the Belgian Pierre Méreaux.[20] He, too, had picked up magnetic anomalies around the Carnac stone rows. He also had discovered gravity anomalies there which the rows marked out. (The pull of gravity varies over the Earth's surface due to different types of rocks and mineral deposits.)

In the 1960s John Michell suspected[21] that standing stones in Britain occurred near fault lines, those areas of the crust where seismic action has caused breaks or fissures, or where mineral bodies butt up against one another. It was not until geologist Paul McCartney's work on the Dragon Project, however, that this intuition was scientifically confirmed. McCartney found in a detailed study of sites in England and Wales that all stone circles were situated within a mile of a surface fault or an associated tectonic intrusion which tend to be faulted themselves or have faulting around their periphery (granite is intruded into the Earth's crust, for example). Henge monuments did not show such an exact correspondence. No study was done for other megalithic sites, though some standing stones are known to stand on faults. Méreaux, too, had noted that the Carnac stones, the most concentrated area of megaliths in the world, were hemmed in by faulting.

No wider-ranging survey of this aspect of monument siting, essentially a geological aspect of geomancy, has yet been made, but it is known that other important ceremonial sites around the world are associated with faulting. Delphi, Greece, was over a fault from which we have already noted fumes used to issue. The ceremonial *Althing* in Iceland was deliberately located on the Mid-

Atlantic Rift in the tenth century. The 2000-year-old Serpent Mound in Ohio, USA, is situated on a 'crypto-volcanic' area, unique in the USA, where there is a great concentration of faults. Many of the Anasazi pueblos are fault-related, especially in Arizona where they are near 'blow holes', natural orifices which inhale and exhale air in a daily cycle and which connect with extensive fault systems. Machu Picchu high in the Andes of Peru is also on a faulted site. There are many more.

If we are not dealing with some bizarre coincidence, what could the ancients have been seeking at fault zones? The first, obvious answer is that these parts of the Earth's crust have been subjected to considerable tectonic forces; they are natural 'energy zones'. Faults tend to have high mineralisation around them affecting local electric and magnetic fields, and to be points of weakness where stress and strain in the crust can manifest, again causing energy effects within and above the ground. If there was a physics, as well as a botany, of shamanism, then fault zones might have been sought for certain activities.

Strange lightforms also have a high incidence in faulted geology. I give a very full account of these phenomena, with research data and photographs, in *Earth Lights Revelation*[22] for those who want the full range of solid evidence; here I will simply give an outline.

The explanation that ET spacecraft are to blame for mysterious lights in the sky is recent and belongs to our technological age. Previously, the lights were omens or dragons. To Australian aborigines their *min min* lights are ancestor spirits or the work of sorcerers. West African tribespeople call the lights *aku*, devil. The Danes and Germans of old Europe called them 'treasure lights', believing them to mark buried riches, an idea carried over into the New World with the *Mae de Ouro* (Mother of Gold) lights of Brazil and *la loz el dinero* ('the money lights') of Peru. In the British Isles the lights either foretold death or, especially in the Celtic countries, were fairies. The Penobscot Indians of Maine thought the lights were shamans flying in fireball form, and called them *medeoli'nuwak* or *eskuda'hit*, 'fire creatures'. Hawaiian islanders thought of their *akualele* lights as spirits. The Malaysians called the lights *pennangal* and said they were the spectral heads of women who had died in childbirth. These lights haunted the hill of Changkat Asah, and in 1895 Sir George Maxwell, a British government official, witnessed the lights there for a whole night. They were, indeed, head-sized, and there were dozens of them, flying with and against the wind, skimming the ground and soaring

*Plate 72. Four states in the appearance of an earth light from the ground. A composite depiction derived from eyewitness reports from various times and places*

high into the sky.

Earth lights may be related to ball lightning and earthquake lights, both of which are unexplained, but they have their own character. Research is revealing that they appear in highly localised regions – they are terrain-related. In some places locals have seen them for generations. These zones have so far been found to contain one or more specific characteristics of faulting, seismic history, mineral deposits or bodies of water (which can cause microquakes). Professor Michael Persinger, of Laurentian University, Ontario, proposes a 'Tectonic Strain Theory' in which pressures in the Earth's crust set up powerful electromagnetic fields causing the lights to appear.[23] Whether this correctly identifies how they form or not, they do appear to be related to geological factors and seem as if they are somehow born of Earth. There are in fact eyewitness reports, some going back nearly a century, of columns of light emerging from the ground and lightballs forming within them or at their upper ends. These globes of light then flash off over the surrounding countryside. Sometimes they are seen trailing the umbilical column of light, and this is often interpreted as a 'searchlight'. In some cases the column fades away, or does not produce lightballs. On occasion a sphere of light is seen hovering above the ground – perhaps it is attached to the earth by a strand of energy not emitting photons and thus invisible. These types of light usually just spring into visibility. Occasionally, amorphous

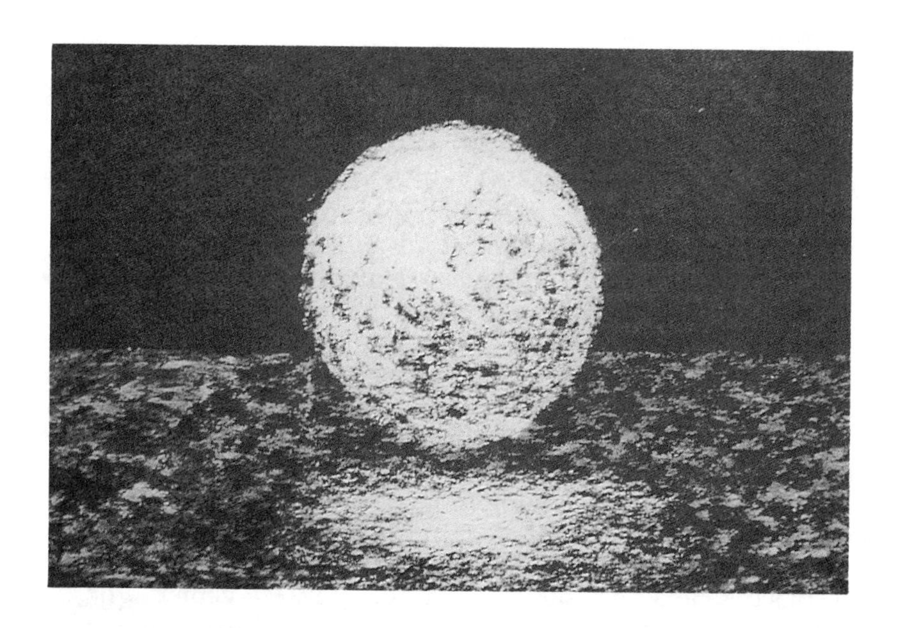

*Plate 73. Some other forms taken by earth lights: (left) a columnar discharge from the ground (top) sphere of light hovering above ground (typical size is that of a 'basketball', but smaller and larger are occasionally reported) (bottom) a 'blob' type lightform sitting on the ground. Many lights seen up close are reported as having teeming inner activity while the overall form remains stable*

'blobs' of light are seen sitting on the ground – sometimes moving around like an amoeba.

People who see these lights close to unanimously report a teeming, wriggling light effect within the coherent outline of the lightform. The lights range in size from inches to, only rarely, yards/metres. 'Basketball size' is the norm, and a common description. Amber is a frequent colour, though red and white also predominate. Most colours have been reported, however. The lightforms can split and coalesce, and can change shape: they are not always globular. Recent photographic and radar evidence suggests that earth lights pulse 'on' and 'off' rapidly, giving the illusion of being constant. They can display effects of mass and weightlessness, as though they hover on the very edge of material manifestation.

Many earth lights zones are now known in England, and only a few examples can be given. Areas in the Pennines, it has already been mentioned (Chapter 6), have histories of light phenomena, and place names and folklore reinforce this. Policemen who do night patrols on the moors around Skipton and Grassington, have seen lights, and excellent photographs have been taken. Project Pennine is uncovering remarkable earth lights material in the region.[24] Further south, Mere Down, Wiltshire, was a focus for light phenomena last century. A countryman saw a light flash across the moor, then it turned and came right up to him. 'We looked at one another a bit,' the fellow recalled, 'and I said, "What! Have 'ee a-lost your way?" and off he went again. It was a beautiful light as big as a plate.'[25] Mere is only nine miles from faulted Warminster where there was a huge UFO outbreak in the 1960s. Around Helpston, Cambridgeshire, an outbreak of lights was described by the 'peasant poet', John Clare, in 1830. Although many people reported them, and he had himself seen them at a distance, Clare found himself 'robbed . . . of the little philosophic reasoning which I had about them' when a light intercepted him as he was walking one night between Helpston and Ashton. The brilliant light crackled, and Clare admitted that it 'frit' him.[26] In the 1920s the church and holy well at Burton Dassett, south of Warwick, were at the centre of a great deal of light phenomena, which were well observed and reported by locals and visiting journalists. The church stands on the Burton Dassett Fault.

In Scotland there are at least eight identified earth lights zones, all associated with faulting and seismic activity. One is Loch Leven, where lights were seen for years. Earlier this century, locals and visitors used to come to the water's edge in the evenings to watch the lights gambol along the loch. In early 1905, between Barmouth and Harlech in Wales, lightforms of all shapes and sizes were seen by many people. Lights emerged from the ground and clung to rooftops. It coincided with the Welsh Methodist Revival, and people literally had the fear of God put into them. The phenomena were well recorded and my own research has precisely located the lights in relation to faulting and seismic activity over the period. Indeed, the incidence of reported lights dramatically increased with proximity to faulting. The region was additionally the epicentre of a quake registering 5.5 on the Richter Scale in 1984 – the largest recorded in the British Isles this century. In 1987, there was an outbreak of light phenomena in the Elan Valley in central Wales. Greenpeace members in this remote area thought that a British Aerospace unit in nearby Hafren Forest might be responsible, but enquiries by BBC reporter Philip Rickman and myself revealed that local farmers and shepherds had seen the lights in the region all their lives. In Northern Ireland, Loughs Erne and Beg have produced reports of light phenomena for over a century.

Eighteenth-century mining texts[27,28] reveal that copper and tin miners used to prospect for good mineral veins by watching for the emission of lights from the ground. A ball of light as big as a human head was a very good sign. British earth-lights researchers have noted a high percentage of light phenomena reported near old tin and lead mines. These are, of course, likely to be radon emission points.

Earth lights in America are known as 'ghost' or 'spook' lights, and over a hundred locations are known. It is claimed that virtually all of them occur near faulting.[29] Marfa, Texas, is one of the best-known zones and lights have been reported there for over a century. There are over 70 local folk tales accounting for them. The Apaches thought they were spirits. In the 1970s, two geologists chased a couple of 'basketball-sized' lights in a jeep, but could not catch them. Although there is an official viewing point on Highway 90 between Marfa and Alpine, the main focus of the lights is actually the mineralised Chinati Mountains a good distance to the south. In 1989, Japanese scientists claimed to video a set of lights cavorting over the desert.

Other US locations of earth lights are, or have been, Maco Station and Brown Mountain in North Carolina; Ada, Oklahoma; the Uintah Basin, Utah; several in the Ozarks, and the 'Hooker light' on the Ramapo Fault near Washington Township, New Jersey, amongst many others. On the Yakima Indian reservation in

*Plate 74. Llanfair Chapel, near Harlech, Wales. In 1905, lights were seen to emerge from the field in the foreground, which is now known to be on the Mochras Fault*

*Plate 75. Looking across Mitchell Flat, Marfa, Texas, scene of earth light appearances for at least a century. The noticeboard marks the 'official' viewing point and tells the story of the lights. The peaks on the horizon are the Chinati Mountains, a key focus of light phenomena*

*Plate 76. The Yakima Indian reservation, scene of light phenomena in the 1970s. On the left of the picture is Toppenish Ridge, a main location for the mystery lights. Snowcapped Mount Adams, one of the Cascade peaks, can be seen in the distance.*

Washington State, lights were seen by trained observers and photographed during the 1970s. The Yakima reservation is adjacent to the Cascade Mountains, where Kenneth Arnold saw the 'flying disks' in 1947 which started the 'flying saucer' craze. The Cascades are on a tectonic plate margin and are seismically active, as the eruption of Mount St Helens in 1980 indicated.

In Norway, the valley of Hessdalen was very active with lights over a period of a few years in the 1980s. Hundreds of photographs were taken, many eyewitness reports recorded, and instrumental study made in the field by Project Hessdalen. Distinct faulting, seismic and mineralisation connections were found.

Earth lights zones exist all around the world, but no thoroughgoing study has yet been attempted.

The phenomena seem to prefer specific types of geological terrain and display electromagnetic characteristics, such as frequenting charge collectors like TV masts, isolated buildings on faults, high tension cables and mountain peaks. But they also clearly possess more mysterious properties. The very fact of coherent lightforms is in itself currently inexplicable, not to mention the bizarre observation by many witnesses that the lights can seemingly exhibit a rudimentary intelligence (see next chapter). Their study is sure to take us beyond known science, as US Government geologist John Derr has predicted.[30]

On the basis of clinical knowledge, Persinger has proposed that energy fields surrounding the lights might affect brain function in close encounter witnesses, causing waking hallucinations, amnesia, and in some instances actual bodily harm such as burns (the lightballs can certainly scorch vegetation). There are traditional warnings. The Californian Wintu tribe gave the lights the ominous name of 'spirit eaters', and around Darjeeling, India, the lights are thought to be the lanterns of 'little men' (*chota admis*), and to get too close is to court illness or death. However, some people do get close to earth lights, and ball lightning for that matter, without harm; the frequency of the energies emitted by a specific light could be a key factor.

Accounts of lights at sites are only just beginning to be compiled. Apart from the case at the Castlerigg stone circle, stone circles on moorlands in Yorkshire, Derbyshire, Wales and the Isle of Arran have had lights reported around them. Lights have been seen within and around the great henge circle at Avebury, and in the summer of 1989 orange lightballs were seen to descend into a field where mystery crop circles appeared. Some researchers now think there may be a connection between these lights and the curious swirled and geometrically precise markings in British cornfields which have appeared in their hundreds over the last decade or so.

Occasionally, tongues of flame are seen over Carnac's stones, and orange or blue flame-like lights are seen hovering around the Great Pyramid. American psychologist Alberto Villoldo and companions saw 'an eerie light like a person, with a large, rounded head' at Machu Picchu.[31] Lights have been seen cavorting over the Nasca lines.[32] Lights were regularly seen to play around a temple near Darjeeling.

Holy hills and mountains are typical earth lights locations. Northern California's Mount Shasta, part of the Cascades range, was sacred to the Indians and there have been many accounts of strange lights and fleeting apparitions on its slopes. Sorte Mountain, Venezuela, is still used by native shamans. Towards sunset, they look for lights near the peak which give evidence that the 'spirits' and 'energies' of the place are suitable for ritual or healing.[33] In Lancashire, England, Pendle Hill was the gathering place of the seventeenth-century Pendle Witches, where George Fox, founder of the Quaker movement, was drawn to have his spiritual

*Plate 77. Mount Shasta, northern California*

vision, and where many lights and brief apparitions have been reported for centuries. Latterly, these have been dubbed 'UFOs'. A temple was built by the Buddhists on the southern pinnacle of the Chinese holy mountain, Wu Tai, to allow observation of orange lights that float around the peak. Glastonbury Tor is a famous holy hill where lightforms have been regularly reported.

As Sington suggested, the appearance of lights may have caused a place to have been seen as sacred by the ancients, and so they built a site there. In addition, the mind-changing properties of the lights, if Persinger is right, might have attracted the shamans. German ethnopsychologist Holger Kalweit has noted that there are many accounts in the anthropological literature of shamans getting their powers after a close contact with a lightball.[34] This is remarkably reminiscent of the modern accounts of witnesses who develop psychic or healing abilities after a 'close encounter' with a UFO.

While earth lights have electromagnetic properties, or, at least, are closely related to the electromagnetic spectrum, they clearly are an exotic energy form, probably known to ancient peoples who knew their landscape much better than we moderns.

In summary then, we can say little about any possible universal, *ch'i*-like force at sites. We can only look to the anthropological literature and the comments of traditional peoples, and, possibly, develop reliable means of primary detection. (If it improves its methodology, and removes the fantasy element, energy dowsing may have something to offer here.) The geophysical effects at some sites may have been used for both healing and mind-change, and this aspect requires much closer attention. It may also be that electromagnetism is an interface between the physical and non-physical realms, as astrophysicist Michael Shallis has hinted.[35] If so, the understanding of the nature and use of energies such as magnetism and radiation at sacred sites might by analogy tell us something further about *ch'i*, especially if linked with our bodies and minds at those places. Finally, the earth lights aspects of the landscape may enable us to learn some deep truths not only about our planet, but about our psychic and spiritual relationship with it.

The energy aspects of sites are really a deeper dimension of geomancy. It is to that deep geomany we must now turn, having explored the great tree of knowledge that grows from ancient sacred sites. It is time to make a few guesses at how deep and how far its roots may reach.

*PART THREE*

# ROOTS

CHAPTER 12

# THE LIVING EARTH

The extended description of ancient sacred sites displayed in the preceding chapters has taken us through a whole gamut of awareness and knowledge in various forms and modes. The sites are showing us the paths of knowledge down which we need to go to establish better relations between our physical environment and our inner selves. It is old – or, more accurately, perennial – information. The monuments are there to remind us. This knowledge needs to be integrated into a whole, 'glass bead game' approach.

The sites are also telling us that they can be used. They are instruments. The Irish nature mystic, poet, artist and agriculturist, George William Russell ('AE') likened them to senses. 'The body of the Earth,' he told Dr Monk Gibbon, has 'special regions through which the traffic of perception seemed most clearly to take place.'[1] Russell found that there were certain geographical locations where his perception of spiritual, visionary layers of the landscape could occur more easily than others. 'I have always found it comparatively easy to see visions while at ancient monuments like Newgrange and Dowth,' he informed W. Evans Wentz, 'because I think such places are naturally charged with psychical forces, and were for that reason made use of long ago as sacred places.'[2] In his visionary state, he saw what he called 'supernature', the 'dreamtime' Earth. He saw it as an actual, environmental reality.

Russell had an early experience in which 'Earth revealed itself to me as a living being, and rock and clay were made transparent so that I saw lovelier and lordlier beings than I had known before, and was made partner in memory of mighty things, happenings in ages long sunken behind me.'[3] In other words, he participated in what the ancients called the 'Soul of the World', or what we might refer to as the 'Earth Field'. We have already mentioned that the Earth was considered as a living being by virtually all earlier peoples[4,5]. Some people think that the view of the planet adopted by Western culture since about the seventeenth century, in which Earth is seen as a lifeless lump of matter available for our endless exploitation, is the crucial error that has led to our present environmental crisis. It is literally a question of worldview.

Russell's 'supernature' was, of course, a matter of a changed state of consciousness. He saw the world with his 'doors of perception cleansed', to use Blake's phrase. Those people and tribes who ingest hallucinogenic plants likewise often perceive the transcendent, 'Dreamtime' Earth. It is always present, interfused with the mundane facade of the land seen in 'normal' Western consciousness. The tree of knowledge produced by ancient sites is rooted in the concept of the living Earth, and that in turn is rooted in the nature of consciousness.

The idea of the living Earth has come back into Western thinking through four fairly recent developments. One has been the works of Professor James Lovelock[6,7] and Lynn Margulis, which detail the scientific observation that the Earth behaves as if it is a living organism. The great systems of the planet, temperature, chemical balance of the atmosphere and so on, self-regulate themselves; the interactions between living things – the biosphere – and aspects of their physical environment are deeply intertwined. Another prompt to reviewing our worldview has been at a less cerebral level – the deep-seated shock we experienced when we saw the images of Earth from space. Whether we articulated it or not, we felt for our planet as we might for an endangered creature. As I have said elsewhere, it was as if life recognised life.[8] Thirdly, we have become increasingly aware, primarily through our space-age telecommunications media, our electronic cortex, that we have an ecological crisis on our hands, and that delicate being we saw sailing through space may be rendered uninhabitable for us if we carry on with our cultural attitudes. Finally, there has been the growth of anthropological and general perception of the attitudes of traditional peoples, past and present, in which the Earth was considered as a living being, expressed in prehistory in images of the Mother Earth Goddess. This 'goddess awareness' has accompanied and augmented a feeling, especially expressed by women, that the feminine element in our culture needs to be given greater prominence.

This emerging, 'new' sense of the planet as alive is still very disparate, and, in many people, it is almost subliminal. But it is nevertheless an increasing sensibility.

By becoming aware again of the Earth as living, we put ourselves on a path that must ultimately cross a watershed. At some stage we are going to have to ask: 'If the Earth is alive, is it also conscious? Is it *sentient*?' This in turn brings us back to the ultimate dilemma – what is consciousness?

To modern science, it is a result, an epiphenomenon, of the complex interactions between brain cells. It exists only so long as the fabulous neuronal networks shimmer with energy transactions. For many years there were actual, surgical attempts to locate areas of consciousness such as memory. They naturally failed. Consciousness is a spectral presence called mind, occupying the physical organism of the brain: Koestler's 'ghost in the machine'. But is consciousness created by the brain, or is it rather that the brain processes some kind of *medium?* By analogy, we could ask whether the picture on a TV screen is created by the TV set, the signal being broadcast, or the activities in a distant studio. In the analogy and the actual question alike, the various interpretations are all possible, depending on how narrow a view of the matter is taken.

Consciousness as an epiphenomenon of brain activity is the ultimate systems view. In such a model, consciousness is the extra increment that is produced by the endless series of 'descriptions' going on within the cortex. At one level, this view has to be correct. Complex neuronal activity is unquestionably the means that allows consciousness to manifest. But the means of allowing its manifestion may not be the actual source of consciousness. In the same way that while it is undoubtedly the circuitry of the TV set that produces the image on the screen, the programme itself is produced elsewhere and broadcast from another source.

My personal view is that consciousness is better thought of as a medium, a field; that consciousness itself does not have a skull-centred source. It is processed rather than produced by the brain, and it is that processing which gives us our unique human dimension of consciousness. Consciousness could be a potential field, non-physical in itself, that manifests at different levels depending on the complexity and nature of the structure interacting with it. In such a view, consciousness is not restricted to the human brain, but can occur in all matter. It may seem bizarre to think of a rock as possessing consciousness, but even a rock is not solid and inert. All matter dissolves into energy fields, which dissolve into the more fundamental and mysterious quantum fields.

There have to be related consciousness fields, or a consciousness field, otherwise how could consciousness occur? It did not arrive in a package from some cosmic Santa Claus, it arose from the Earth, and the self-reflective awareness that we humans have been both blessed and cursed with came with that evolution. Teilhard de Chardin felt that the Earth passed on a 'quantum of consciousness' to its evolving biosphere. This is undoubtedly true, but we must not fall into the trap of thinking that then we alone possess consciousness, and that the Earth gave it all away.

Arguments about the possible field nature of consciousness, of it being a fundamental medium perhaps the *ch'i* of the Chinese geomants and all the other names the universal force has been given, need not be simply an abstract debate. It can be experienced directly, taking the matter out of the sphere of conjecture for the participants concerned. We have seen above that George William Russell, through his natural body chemistry, was able to change the level or frequency of his consciousness, allowing him to see deeper into the nature of the world; actually to participate in the Earth's field of consciousness (which he called variously 'Earth spirit', the 'memory of the Earth' or 'memory of nature'). But throughout human time shamans and tribal seers have done likewise. We have discussed the ways this was done, and noted that one of the key methods for certain groups was the use of hallucinogenic plants. One of the states engendered by this means is ecstasy – out-of-body experience (OOBE), classic shamanic flight. The shamans use OOBEs to travel to other parts of the world to obtain information, as well as to travel to the Otherworlds of spirit. The many thousands of Westerners who have experienced involuntary OOBEs similarly experience not merely other states but also a peripatetic view of their environment, be it bedroom, backyard or further afield. Can a person's consciousness exist apart from the brain? Can it float around as a point of awareness, sentient, observing, but non-material? The most recent work suggests that in a state known as lucid dreaming the human mind can produce incredibly detailed replicas of places known to it, or invent new ones, and apparently move around disembodied within these pseudo-locations. (A lucid dream is one in which the dreamer becomes fully conscious that he or she is dreaming without waking up.) In laboratory work it is now possible for lucid dreamers to communicate from within the dreamstate to researchers by making signals with their eyeballs.[9]

In certain cases, however, those undergoing OOBE's do seem able to obtain information as if they were able to travel mentally in the real, physical world. Anthropologists have remarked on such instances while working with tribal peoples using psychotropic plants, particularly *ayahuasca* (Banisteriopsis). Indians have seen things in distant cities they could not possibly have known about, and in some cases have been able to tell anthropologists of distant events which were only confirmed days later by field radio.[10] Perhaps we have a situation where consciousness can be used as a medium for obtaining information by extra-sensory means, but is presented to the individual in a pictorial form involving flight out of the body.

However this may be, the psychedelic experience also offers other ways to transcend the normally experienced limitations of time and space. Stanislav Grof, we noted in Chapter 2, is one of the world's most experienced researchers into altered states of consciousness. He is a medical doctor, a psychiatrist and psychotherapist, and has been involved in LSD research for 30 years, making thousands of studies in Czechoslovakia and the USA. He is one of the leading researchers in the remarkable developments in the understanding of consciousness that has gone on over the last few decades, especially in America. From his vast experience, Grof comments that the greatest challenge to our accepted, Western worldview, based on Newtonian and Cartesian logic, comes from *transpersonal* experiences had under hallucinogenics, whether in a traditional context or in research work.

'During normal conditions, we clearly and concretely experience with all of our sensory organs only the present moment and immediate conditions,' Grof has written. 'During transpersonal experiences, one or more of the . . . restrictions of our everyday perception of the world is apparently suspended.'[11] He identifies three general categories of transpersonal experiences: those in which the individual appears to regress into the historical past, even far back along the evolutionary tree of creation (the phylogenetic tree); those in which personal consciousness slips into some object or organism in the subject's environment, so it is possible to experience being a plant, animal, or 'in extreme cases . . . all life, the entire planet', and, thirdly, to enter a world 'outside of the conceptions of Western science and culture', a world of archetypes – gods, demons and primordial forces.

It is the normal, mainstream reaction to treat such experiences as 'dream-like and obviously insane products of the brain,' Grof admitted, but warned 'the situation is not so simple'. This is because people in psychedelic sessions can bring back startlingly accurate information quite outside their range of education or knowledge, some of it profoundly obscure, specialist knowledge. Details of medieval clothing and habits, mating patterns of certain creatures, 'an abundance of medically correct insights into the anatomical, physiological and biochemical' processes, and so on. Moreover, there is nothing at all dreamlike in the vivid sense of reality of the experiences.

If an individual's awareness really can move into its physical surroundings, slipping into other beings and objects, then a field model of consciousness has to be seriously entertained. Grof remarks that, 'In the case of the lower animals, plants, and inorganic matter . . . we may be surprised that we encounter consciousness or perception in something which we normally hold to be unconscious.' It is 'the possibility of experiencing and of consciously identifying with various aspects of the world without the aid of sensory perception' which is so challenging. Such experiences:

> . . . have led many subjects – including those with college educations – to suggest independently that consciousness is not a product of the central nervous system and thus cannot be restricted to humans and the higher vertebrates. They suddenly viewed consciousness as an attribute of existence which can neither be reduced to nor derived from anything else.[12]

Grof has been forced into accepting that 'from the perspective of our new knowledge . . . consciousness appears to be the primary property of existence and is threaded into the structure of the phenomenal world.'[13]

George William Russell, it has been noted, posited a 'memory of the Earth' that allowed him to see past events. Such a planetary field of consciousness is well described by Prem Das when he was with the Mexican Huichol Indians during their peyote ceremonies. He had ingested the hallucinogenic cactus, and was pondering the nature of his Western society, which he saw as having become so 'isolated and estranged from the harmony and beauty of our wonderful planet.' He began to weep. Suddenly, he experienced

> . . . a great time-lapse vision. I saw a human being rise from the earth, stand for a moment, and then dissolve back into it. It was only a brief moment, and in that moment our whole lives passed. Then I saw a huge city rise out of the desert floor beneath me, exist for a second, and then vanish back into the vastness of the desert. The plants, rocks, and the earth under me were saying, 'Yes, this is how it really is, your life, the city you live in.' *It was as if in my peyotized state I was able to perceive and communicate with a resonance or vibration that surrounded me.* Those inner barriers which defined 'me' as a separate identity from 'that' –

my environment – had dissolved . . . The painful problem that had confronted me disappeared entirely, to be replaced with a vision of people and their technology as temporary forms through which Mother Earth was expressing herself.[14] (My italics.)

The Earth-level structure of consciousness – the Earth Field, the Soul of the World, the *anima mundi*, call it what we will – is planet-sized. It is not a 'person', nor operative at the levels of consciousness we recognise, because it is structured differently. But that does not mean the Earth is not at its level a sentient entity.

If this is so – and I am putting forward nothing other than personal views and suggestions here – then can human and planetary structures of consciousness interact? Can we speak to the Earth, as it were, and allow it to communicate directly to us? Can we take Chardin's idea of planetisation to its ultimate extreme?

Let us assume the answer to these questions is 'Yes.' (Let's live dangerously!) The next question is 'How?' This brings us back to the sites. Their fundamental lesson is that *they cannot be used in what we view as 'normal' consciousness.* They were designed to be used in altered states, whether by initiatory ordeal, drumming, dance and rhythm, dreaming, or by means of mind-changing plants, infusions or fumes. They were so built or located that they often had geophysical and geographical attributes to aid in this process. They were the selected places at which human consciousness was set temporarily free. Let us briefly look at these various factors.

First, the geophysical aspect. We have noted in earlier chapters that stone with magnetic or radioactive properties seems to have been incorporated into some monuments. 'Magnetic' stones so far found at sites are selectively placed – at cardinal points in circles, on astronomical sightlines, or exist as the dominant megalith in a monument. How could they have been used to augment altered states? Certain parts of the brain are sensitive to magnetic fields – particularly the temporal lobe region which houses the organs that process memory, dreams and feeling. There is an archaic tradition of sleeping on stones of power to achieve visions. The classic case is of course Jacob (Chapter 10) who slept with his head on a *bethel,* or sacred stone. The Japanese emperors also had a special dreaming stone (kamudoko). We can perhaps envisage the megalithic shaman, in an altered state of consciousness, lying or sleeping in head contact with the stone of power at a site. This might have helped to engender special visions, acting as a sort of 'waveguide' to consciousness, in the way that St Brynach (Chapter 11) used the magnetically anomalous peak of Carn Ingli to 'speak with the angels'.

It is my guess that the magnetic stones found strategically placed at sites are the ones that were used for dreaming and visions. This can be tested now that we have begun to identify the relevant stones at sites. It is work still waiting to be done, but the technique can still be used.

But what of the radioactive stones? It has already been remarked that the enclosed interiors of granite monuments like dolmens and underground chambers (or the King's Chamber in the Great Pyramid) are relatively high radiation zones, and that such places have been associated with involuntary, short-lived experiences of mind-change. A bemushroomed shaman sitting in the sensory-depriving interior of these places, subject to the apparently mind-affecting radiation, would be ejected into very profound, and perhaps specialised, altered states.

Individual stones emitting radiation may also have had a role. Examples of these were reported, it may be recalled, at the Long Meg stone circle in Cumbria (Chapter 11). We may have a hint of their usage in the procedures Alberto Villoldo and his colleagues were put through by shaman Don Eduardo Calderon at Machu Picchu. One of these involved Inti Huatana, the 'hitching post of the sun'. This is a granite megalith comprised of an upright, the 'post', on a platform of complex geometry. Every midwinter, the Incas held a ceremony at this feature, in the highest temple at Machu Picchu, in which they 'tied the sun' to stop it swinging even farther north in its daily progression. The shamanic legends, Calderon told Villoldo, 'say that when one touches one's forehead to the stone, the Inti Huatana opens one's vision into the spirit world.'[15] When members of Villoldo's group pressed their heads to the stone they 'felt a sensation of warmth on their foreheads . . . Others reported seeing a light go on inside their heads like a bursting sun.' Calderon dismissed these accounts, however, predicting that:

> . . . the real effect of the ceremony would not be felt for weeks as each of us learned the shaman's way to 'see' with his or her inner vision . . .[16]

Calderon then took Villoldo's group to another location within the granite site, the Pachamama stone. This is over 20 feet (6 m) long and 10 feet (3 m) high. Calderon said it represented Mother Earth. Under instruction, Villoldo and colleagues pressed their backs against the stone and prayed to the Great Mother. Again, in the Great Temple at Machu Picchu, Calderon had his charges lay on a stone bed to experience a 'spirit flight initiation'. On an earlier occasion with Calderon, Villoldo had experienced a remarkable happening:

> The first time I lay on the stone of the spirit flight and felt the shaman place his hand on my forehead, I felt a great peace and relaxation. Yet nothing unusual occurred. I did not soar like an eagle . . . After what appeared to be ten minutes, don Eduardo said, 'Okay, come up.' I sat up from the stone and walked away to join my companions . . . To my surprise, everyone was looking intently at the stone bed. I turned around and saw my physical body – and a smiling don Eduardo signalling for me to come back and lie again on the stone so as to reconnect with my physical self.[17]

Unfortunately, we do not have a Calderon to show us the workings of the European megalithic sites, but it is my guess that the particularly active granite stones at certain sites were used for similar purposes to those at Machu Picchu.

Then there is the matter of water. Dowsers have for decades noted the association of sites with underground water, and water sources were also a key feature in temples where 'temple sleep' took place (Chapter 10). Dragon Project findings show that some holy wells have relatively high radiation, but there seems to be something else about water that is significant and mysterious. Holy wells have always been places for prophesy and vision, and all sacred waters seem to have had similar associations. We noted in Chapter 10 that there was a Scottish tradition of sacred sleep alongside springs and waterfalls. Supposed visions of the Blessed Virgin Mary, too, have been associated with water. At Lourdes, for instance, a spring erupted where the visionary Virgin appeared to Bernadette Soubirous. Again, at La Salette, a light containing the image of a woman appeared next to a stream, and at Willesden, a tenth-century visionary Virgin caused a spring to flow. There are numerous other examples. In Celtic tradition, sacred waters were the entrance to Tir-na-nog, the Land of Eternal Youth.

Water, while ubiquitous and thought of as simple, is in fact a mysterious substance. It has unique physical and chemical properties, it is deeply involved with living organisms, it occupies about the same percentage of the Earth's surface as it does the bodies of mammals, and recent work has shown that it can 'memorise' electrical frequencies.[18] Decades ago, Italian scientist Giorgio Piccardi demonstrated that water was sensitive to cosmic influences, such as sunspots and cosmic ray showers, and German engineer Theodore Schwenk considered water to be 'a receptive "sense organ" . . . the impressionable medium *par excellence*,' open to the universe. Scientist Jacques Benveniste and colleagues published a paper in *Nature*,[19] which purported to show that water could somehow 'remember' the molecules of an antibody even when the substance was so diluted it could not be chemically present. This caused a huge uproar in scientific circles.

Magnetism, radiation, water . . . these are just some of the factors found incorporated into ancient sacred sites. It may be that altered states entered into at such places allow human consciousness to 'tune into' the 'frequency' of the Earth Field more effectively or accurately than elsewhere. Magnetic and radioactive fields, and the presence and nature of pure groundwater, may act as kinds of interfaces between human and planetary structures of consciousness. Only time and experimentation will tell.

If there is an Earth Field, it may in some way be influenced by the presence of mineral deposits and great bodies of water, creating different manifest qualities in various places. In the way that gravity (and thus the passage of time which is associated with the strength of gravity) varies minutely over the globe due to different densities of the Earth's crust, so too might a terrestrial field of consciousness. In such a geography of consciousness, ancient sites would be placed like markers of the mind.

Geology is certainly a factor in site geomancy.

Some kinds of monuments occur in geologically faulted country, and it has been shown that these zones not only tend to have high mineralisation, to respond to seismic stress, and harbour gravity anomalies – all factors which can affect the local energy fields – but also display a high incidence of 'earth light' phenomena (Chapters 6 and 11). When we discussed these earlier, a number of recurring characteristics were noted. One very controversial property, however, was barely mentioned: the lights have regularly been reported in cases worldwide to behave as if they are *intelligent*. This intelligence usually takes a rudimentary, often playful, quality. The geologists at the Texan Marfa earth-lights zone (Chapter 11), chased two lights across the prairie without success. The balls of light seemed to play a game with them, stopping, allowing the men's jeep almost to catch up with them, then flash off at an angle behind a bush. The lights 'had intelligence, definitely,' Elwood Wright, one of the geologists, stated quite flatly.

When biologist Frank Salisbury investigated an outbreak of light phenomena in the Unitah Basin, Utah, in the 1970s, he noted that 'many witnesses reported the feeling that the UFOs seemed to react to their actions or even their thoughts. Reaction to *thoughts* would be difficult to prove . . . Nevertheless, there are many cases when some action taken by the observer . . . resulted in the rapid departure of the UFO. This seems to be a clearly discernible pattern.'[20] Dr Harley Rutledge, who led a field team to study light phenomena around Piedmont, Missouri, also in the 1970s, noted 32 cases in which the lights and the observers seemed to share 'a relationship, a cognisance'.[21] Project Hessadalen, the team who monitored light phenomena in the Norwegian valley, also found that a certain percentage of the lights they observed seemed to 'play' with them. I only fully realised what a major element this characteristic of apparent intelligence was in earth lights sightings when I came to compile the index for *Earth Lights Revelation* – I ended up with three index lines packed with page references! (It is also noteworthy that the same index has *five* lines referring to the association between light phenomena and bodies of water: the appearance of the lights and the presence of water seems intimately connected. Perhaps another aspect of water's mysterious qualities. It may be no coincidence that the Chinese Feng shui geomants claimed that water could act as a carrier of *ch'i*.)

It is my firm opinion, based on research and direct experience of the phenomena, that the lights are an energy expression of the Earth Field. Their appearance relies on complex geophysics – they are born from Mother Earth's body – but their nature is exotic and only barely framed within the material universe, just as is the case with the mind in the brain. Of all the possible interfaces between human and planetary consciousness, I suggest that earth lights are the most direct. Nature always provides a means.

All the above observations are simply personal conclusions drawn from a wide range of evidence. Can they be tested? I think so. Work on earth-light phenomena by small groups of researchers in Europe and North American continues. The more this happens, the closer we will come to understanding them. It is work, however, conducted outside of mainstream science and mainstream ufology, both parties having prescribed views that prevent them dealing with the matter adequately. Earth-lights research basically depends on the endeavour of a handful of dedicated individuals working independently within scientific, ufological and Earth Mysteries fields.

In addition, the Dragon Project Trust is set to commence work on a research programme during 1990 in which dream incubation techniques will be used at British sites specially selected as prime examples of those possessing magnetic or radiation properties, or which are situated directly on faulting and attract light phenomena. This research effort, called Operation Interface, will run for at least three years. Dream imagery from a 'dream team' will be catalogued and stored on computer, ultimately being cross-referenced to see if site-specific images and themes occur. If so, we will have made a start on uncovering the lineaments of the geography of consciousness. A concurrent programme, but independent of the Dragon Project, staffed by people working in an individual capacity, is also to be run in which natural psychotropic plants will be employed to investigate altered states at these sacred places of prehistory.

The analogy of prehistory with the human subconscious will become literal in both programmes.

It is also hoped that direct interfacing with earth lights might be achieved.

The work will not be some vague, isolated 'turning on' or 'nodding off' at sites which individuals have done for years, but rigorous hard work, recorded, cross-referenced and contextualised. But it is almost by definition research outside the frame of Western mainstream acceptance, outside the Indo-European cognitive framework we have discussed earlier. Nevertheless, it can, and will, be undertaken regardless.

It is an ambitious programme, equivalent in consciousness-studies terms to NASA's Apollo Program, though with virtually no financial resources! Fortunately, there are not a lot of expensive high-tech requirements for this inner space planetary probe, but the Trust will be looking for support from individuals and groups worldwide to help maintain the research effort. Those who care will come forward.[22]

It will be years before an outcome, if any, can be assessed, but the work must begin now, for there is a profound need for a new psychophysical philosophy; one in which fresh connections are made, in which psyche and environment can be brought together in a new synthesis. (This is becoming more widely accepted in the realm of human health, in mind-brain-body symbiotics, but needs to be extended to mind, brain, body and planetary environment. The Chinese did this, of course, with their acupuncture system of *ch'i* control for the body, and the Feng shui system for the landscape.) This synthesis was expressed traditionally in the geomantic omphalos, the archetype of the Navel of the World, and its dimension of consciousness as provided by the shaman's journey to and along the Cosmic Axis (Chapters 8 and 10). Our

# REFERENCES

An excellent source for readers seeking further information and contantact with those working in the areas covered by *Earth Memory*, is *The Ley Hunter* magazine, PO Box 92, Penzance, Cornwall TR18 2XL.


**CHAPTER 1: Sites as Systems of Knowing**

1. Marilyn Ferguson, *The Aquarian Conspiracy*, (1980), Granada ed. 1982.
2. Ludwig von Bertalanffy, *General Systems Theory*, Braziller, 1968.
3. Gregory Bateson, *Mind and Nature*, (1979), Bantam ed. 1980.
4. Ervin Laszlo, *The Systems View of the World*, Braziller, 1972.
5. Bertalanffy, op. cit.
6. Bateson, op. cit.
7. Rupert Sheldrake, *A New Science of Life*, Blond & Briggs, 1981.
8. Rupert Sheldrake, *The Presence of the Past*, Collins, 1988.
9. Ibid.
10. Bertalanffy, op. cit.
11. Teilhard de Chardin, *Human Energy*, (1962), Collins ed. 1969.
12. Peter Russell, *The Awakening Earth*, RKP, 1982.
13. Teilhard de Chardin, *The Future of Man*, Fontana, 1959.
14. Laszlo, op. cit.
15. Quoted in *The Fate of the Forest* by Susanna Hecht and Alexander Cockburn, Verso, 1989.
16. Henry Munn, 'The Mushrooms of Language', in Michael Harner's *Shamanism and Hallucinogens*, OUP, 1973.
17. Bateson, op. cit.
18. Ibid.
19. Fritjof Capra, *The Turning Point* (1982), Flamingo ed. 1983.

**CHAPTER 2: Archaeology**

1. Charles Mountford, *Winbaraku and the Myth of the Jarapiri*, Rigby, 1968.
2. Extracted from *Argonauts of the Western Pacific*, quoted in *Primitive Mythology*, by Lucien Lévy-Bruhl, (1935), Univ. of Queensland Press ed. 1983.

3. Lévy-Bruhl, ibid.
4. Holger Kalweit, *Dreamtime and Inner Space,* (1984), Shambhala ed. 1988.
5. Stanislav Grof, 'Beyond the Brain', in *Gateway to Inner Space,* Christian Rätsch (Ed.), Prism, 1989.
6. Glyn Daniel, *A Short History of Archaeology,* Thames & Hudson, 1981.
7. David Miles in *The Atlas of Archaeology* (Ed. K. Branigan), Macdonald, 1982.
8. E.G. Squier and E.H. Davis, *Ancient Monuments of the Mississippi Valley,* Smithsonian Institution, 1848.
9. Susan L. Woodward & Jerry N. McDonald, *Indian Mounds of the Middle Ohio Valley,* McDonald & Woodward Publishing Co., 1986.
10. Nigel Pennick & Paul Devereux, *Lines on the Landscape,* Hale, 1989.
11. Daniel, op. cit.
12. Ibid.
13. Quoted by David Miles, op. cit.
14. Daniel, op. cit.
15. Warwick Bray and David Tromp, *A Dictionary of Archaeology,* Allen Lane, 1970.
16. Riane Eisler, *The Chalice and the Blade,* Harper & Row, 1987
17. Miles, op. cit.

**CHAPTER 3: Being and Seeing**

1. John Glover, 'Alignment for Issue 94', *The Ley Hunter* 94, 1982.
2. John Glover, 'Paths of Shadow and Light', *The Ley Hunter* 87, 1979.
3. David Fraser, 'Land and Society in Neolithic Orkney', BAR 117 Part 2, 1983.
4. Chris Kincaid (Ed.), *Chaco Roads Project Phase I,* US Bureau of Land Management, 1983.
5. Glover, 1982, op. cit.
6. Helen Woodley, 'Prehistoric Sites in their Landscape Context', *The Ley Hunter* 108, 1989.
7. *Field Monuments in the National Park,* Brecon Beacons National Park Committee, 1983.
8. But an account has been given in *The Ley Hunter* magazine: Paul Devereux, 'Silbury's Secrets', issue 110, 1989.
9. Aubrey Burl, *Prehistoric Avebury,* Yale Univ. Press, 1979.
10. Caroline Malone, *Avebury,* Batsford, 1989.
11. Ibid.
12. Michael Dames, *The Silbury Treasure,* Thames & Hudson, 1976.
13. Michael Dames, *The Avebury Cycle,* Thames & Hudson, 1977.
14. *Riddles of the Stones,* BBC, Radio 4, Nov–Dec, 1989.
15. As I write, preliminary calculations by R.D.Y. Perrett suggest that the 'Lammas/Beltane window' viewable from Silbury would also accommodate the rising moon at Minor Lunar Standstill.

16. G.T. Meaden, *The Circles Effect and its Mysteries,* Artetech Publishing, 1989.
17. Pat Delgado and Colin Andrews, *Circular Evidence,* Bloomsbury, 1989.
18. Jenny Randles and Paul Fuller, *Controversy of the Circles,* BUFORA, 1989.
19. Ralph Noyes, 'Cropfield Circles Books Reviewed', *The Ley Hunter* 109, 1989.

**CHAPTER 4: Ancient Astronomy**

1. John Goulstone, *The Summer Solstice Games,* private (ISBN 0 9510556 07), 1985.
2. Ibid.
3. John Michell, *A Little History of Astro-Archaeology,* Thames & Hudson, 1977; revised ed. 1989.
4. Martin Brennan, *The Boyne Valley Vision,* Dolmen Press, 1980.
5. Christopher Chippindale, *Stonehenge Complete,* Thames & Hudson, 1983.
6. Aubrey Burl, *The Stonehenge People,* (1987) Barrie & Jenkins ed., 1989.
7. A. Thom, *Megalithic Sites in Britain,* OUP, 1967.
8. Euan MacKie, *Science and Society in Prehistoric Britain,* Elek, 1977.
9. Burl, op. cit.
10. Michell, op. cit.
11. Chippindale, op. cit.
12. Burl, op. cit.
13. Douglas Heggie, *Megalithic Science,* Thames & Hudson, 1981.
14. Ray A. Williamson, *Living the Sky,* Univ. of Oklahoma Press, 1987.
15. Described in Evan Hadingham's *Lines to the Mountain Gods,* Random House, 1987.
16. Quoted by Anthony F. Aveni, 'Tropical Astronomy', *Science,* 10 July 1981.
17. John Eddy, in *In Search of Ancient Astronomies,* (Ed. E.C. Krupp) Doubleday, 1978.
18. Aveni, op. cit.
19. Ibid.
20. E.C. Krupp, *Echoes of the Ancient Skies,* Harper & Row, 1983.
21. E.C. Krupp, 'Uxmal: Architecture, Alignment and Astronomy', *The Ley Hunter* 80, 1978.
22. John Glover, 'Paths of Shadow and Light', *The Ley Hunter* 87, 1979.
23. G. Vaucouleurs, quoted in *Stonehenge Decoded,* by Gerald Hawkins and John B. White, Souvenir Press, 1965.
24. Aubrey Burl, *The Stone Circles of the British Isles,* Yale Univ. Press, 1976.
25. Aubrey Burl, in *Antiquity* 54, 1980.
26. Aubrey Burl, in *The Ley Hunter* 102, 1987.
27. Aubrey Burl, *Megalithic Brittany,* Thames & Hudson, 1985.

28. Brennan, 1980, op. cit.
29. Martin Brennan, *The Stars and the Stones,* Thames & Hudson, 1983.
30. Ibid.
31. In interview with Janet Saad-Cook, *Archaeoastronomy* VIII, 1985.
32. Tom Ray, in *The New York Times,* 31 January, 1989.
33. Heggie, op. cit.

**CHAPTER 5: Sacred Geometry**

1. A. Thom, *Megalithic Sites in Britain,* OUP, 1967.
2. Keith Critchlow, *Time Stands Still,* Gordon Fraser, 1979.
3. John Michell, *The New View Over Atlantis,* Thames & Hudson, 1983.
4. Michael Lawlor, *Sacred Geometry,* Thames & Hudson, 1982.
5. Nigel Pennick, *Sacred Geometry,* Turnstone Press, 1980.
6. Lawlor, op. cit.
7. Pennick, op. cit.
8. John Michell, *The Dimensions of Paradise,* Thames & Hudson, 1988.
9. Pennick, op. cit.
10. Michell, 1988, op. cit.
11. John Anthony West, *The Traveller's Key to Ancient Egypt,* Knopf, 1985.
12. Jean Lassus, *The Early Christian and Byzantine World,* Paul Hamlyn, 1967.
13. Ibid.
14. Keith Critchlow 'Introductory Notes on a New Theory of Proportion in Architecture', in *Glastonbury – A Study in Patterns,* RILKO, 1969.
15. Louis Charpentier, *The Mysteries of Chartres Cathedral,* (1966), RILKO ed., 1972
16. F. Bligh Bond, *The Gate of Remembrance,* (1918), Thorsons ed. 1978.
17. Frances A. Yates, *The Occult Philosophy in the Elizabethan Age,* (1979), Ark ed. 1983.
18. Pennick, op. cit.
19. Michell, 1983, op. cit.
20. The books of John Michell referenced here, for example, or comprehensive works like *The Great Pyramid Decoded,* by Peter Lemesurier, Compton Russell, 1971.
21. John Michell, *Ancient Metrology,* Pentacle, 1981.
22. John Michell, 'The Dimensions of Stonehenge and the Whole World', in *The Ley Hunter* 90, 1981.

**CHAPTER 6: Folklore**

1. Jeremy Harte, *Cuckoo Pounds and Singing Barrows,* Dorset Nat. Hist. & Arch. Soc., 1986.
2. Chris Castle, 'Megaliths in the Senegambia', *The Ley Hunter* 85, 1979.
3. Leslie Grinsell, *The Folklore of Prehistoric Sites in Britain,* David & Charles, 1976.

4. Dermot Mac Manus, *The Middle Kingdom*, Colin Smythe, 1973.
5. Harte, op. cit.
6. Paul Screeton, *The Lambton Worm and Other Northumbrian Dragon Legends*, Zodiac House, 1978.
7. J.C. Cooper, *An Illustrated Encyclopaedia of Traditional Symbols*, Thames & Hudson, 1978.
8. Laurence Main, 'Down to Earth' column, *The Ley Hunter* 104, 1987.
9. *The Mabinogion* (Jones, T. & G. trans.), Everyman Edn., 1949.
10. Jeremy Harte, *Cuckoo Pounds & Singing Barrows*, Dorset Nat. Hist. & Arch. Soc., 1986.
11. Paul Devereux, *Earth Lights Revelation*, Blandford Press, 1989.
12. Leslie V. Grinsell, *Folklore of Prehistoric Sites in Britain*, David & Charles, 1976.

**CHAPTER 7: Sensing and Monitoring at Sites**

1. *The Ley Hunter* magazine, P O Box 92, Penzance, Cornwall TR18 2XL. UK.
2. Janet Saad-Cook, 'Touching the Sky', *Archaeoastronomy* VIII, 1985.
3. John Beardsley, *Earthworks and Beyond*, Abbeville Press, 1989.
4. Work by some of these artists is reproduced in *Megalithomania*, by John Michell, Thames & Hudson, 1982.
5. F. Bligh Bond, *The Gate of Remembrance*, (1918), Thorsons ed. 1978.
6. Chris Walker, 'Psychic Archaeology in Ireland', *The Ley Hunter* 90, 1981.
7. Quoted in *Quicksilver Heritage*, by Paul Screeton, Thorsons, 1974.
8. Jeffrey Goodman, *Psychic Archaeology*, (1977), Wildwood House ed. 1978.
9. David D. Zink, *The Ancient Stones Speak*, Paddington Press, 1979.
10. Several archaeologists have told me of digs where dowsing has proved useful. It is also mentioned as a technique in *Understanding Archaeological Excavation*, by Philip Barber, Batsford, 1986. *Dowsing and Archaeology*, Tom Graves (Ed.), Turnstone Press, 1980, gives a historical look at the association between dowsing and archaeology.
11. Sir William Barrett and Theodore Besterman, *The Divining Rod*, (1926), University Books edition, 1968.
12. Christopher Bird, *Divining* (*The Divining Hand* in the US), (1979), Macdonalds & Janes edition, 1980.
13. Barrett and Besterman, op. cit.
14. Guy Underwood, *The Pattern of the Past*, (1969), Abacus ed, 1972.
15. Tom Graves, *Dowsing*, Turnstone Press, 1976 (re-issued as *The Diviner's Handbook*, Aquarian Press, 1986.)
16. Dion Fortune, *The Goat-Food God*, (1936), Star ed. 1976.
17. Tom Graves, *Needles of Stone*, Turnstone Press, 1978; (re-issued as *Needles of Stone Revisited*, Gothic Image, 1988.)
18. Paul Devereux and John Steele, David Kubrin *Earthmind*, Harper & Row, 1989.

19. C. Maxwell Cade and Nona Coxhead, *The Awakened Mind,* Element, 1979.
20. Ralph Whitlock, *Water Divining,* David & Charles, 1982.
21. J. Cecil Maby and T. Bedford Franklin, *The Physics of the Divining Rod.* Bell, 1939.
22. S.W. Tromp, *Psychical Physics,* Elsevier, 1949.
23. John Downer, *Supersense,* BBC Books, 1988.
24. Devereux, Steele, Kubrin, 1989, op. cit.
25. Francis Hitching, *Earth Magic,* Cassell, 1976.
26. Peter Bander, *Voices from the Tapes,* Drake, 1973.
27. Paul Devereux, *Places of Power,* Blandford Press, 1990.
28. The Dragon Project Trust, c/o Empress, Box 92, Penzance, Cornwall TR18 2XL, U.K. The Trust always needs funds or facilities. Donations by British tax-payers are tax deductible.

**CHAPTER 8: Geomancy**

1. Nigel Pennick, *Earth Harmony,* Century, 1987.
2. Ibid.
3. From Hershon's *Talmudic Miscellany,* quoted in *The Canon,* by William Stirling, (1897), Garnstone ed. 1974.
4. Vincent Scully, *The Earth, The Temple and the Gods,* Yale Univ. Press, 1962.
5. Quoted in Stirling, 1897/1974, op. cit.
6. Ray A. Williamson, *Living the Sky,* Univ. of Oklahoma Press, 1987.
7. Lucien Lévy-Bruhl, *Primitive Mythology,* (1935), Univ. of Queensland Press ed,. 1983.
8. Quoted in Lévy-Bruhl, op. cit.
9. Charles Mountford, *Winbaraku and the Myth of the Jarapiri,* Rigby, 1968.
10. E.J. Eitel, *The Rudiments of Natural Science in China,* (1873), Cockagyne ed. 1973 (published as *Feng Shui*).
11. Leonard Cottrell, *The Penguin Book of Lost Worlds,* (1962), Penguin ed. 1966.
12. Raymond Bloch, *The Etruscans,* (1956), Thames & Hudson ed., 1958.
13. Allen Watkins, *Alfred Watkins of Hereford,* Garnstone Press, 1972.
14. Alfred Watkins, *The Old Straight Track,* (1925) Garnstone Press ed. 1970.
15. John Michell, *The Old Stones of Land's End,* Garnstone Press, 1974.
16. Paul Devereux and Ian Thompson, *The Ley Hunter's Companion,* Thames & Hudson, 1979; (re-issued in digest form as *The Ley Guide,* Empress, 1987).
17. Nigel Pennick and Paul Devereux, *Lines on the Landscape,* Hale, 1989.
18. John Michell, *The New View Over Atlantis,* Thames & Hudson, 1983.
19. Pennick and Devereux, 1989, op. cit.
20. Andrew Fleming, *The Dartmoor Reaves,* Batsford, 1988.

21. Andrew Fleming, 'Coaxial Field Systems: Some Questions of Time and Space', *Antiquity* 61, 1987.
22. Tony Morrison, *Pathways to the Gods*, Michael Russell, 1978.
23. Tony Morrison, *The Mystery of the Nasca Lines*, Nonesuch Expeditions, 1987.
24. Evan Hadingham, *Lines to the Mountain Gods*, Random House, 1987.
25. Gerald Hawkins, *Beyond Stonehenge*, Hutchinson, 1973.
26. Quoted in Hadingham, op. cit.
27. Quoted in *Chaco Roads Project Phase I*, Chris Kincaid (Ed.), U.S. Bureau of Land Management, 1983.
28. J.A. Barrett and E.W. Gifford, 1933, quoted in ibid.
29. HRH The Prince of Wales, *A Vision of Britain*, Doubleday, 1989.
30. Ray A. Williams, *Living the Sky*, Univ. of Oklahoma Press, 1987.

**CHAPTER 9: Correspondence and Symbolism**

1. Keith Critchlow, Jean Carroll and Llewylyn Vaughen Lee, *Chartres Maze – A Model of the Universe?*, RILKO, 1975.
2. Nigel Pennick, *Sacred Geometry*, Turnstone Press, 1980.
3. John Michell, in *A Study in Patterns*, RILKO, 1969.
4. John Michell, *The View Over Atlantis*, (1969) Abacus ed. 1973.
5. W.S. Andrews, *Magic Squares and Cubes*, (1917), Dover ed. 1960.
6. Ibid.
7. Michell, 1969/1973, op. cit.
8. QED, 'A Man Who Writes Birdsong', BBC TV, 14 March, 1990.
9. Michell, 1969/1973 op. cit.
10. John Michell, *The Dimensions of Paradise*, Thames & Hudson, 1988.

**CHAPTER 10: Use of Sites**

1. Mircea Eliade, *Shamanism – Archaic Techniques of Ecstasy*, (1951), Princetown Univ. Press, Bollingen ed. 1964.
2. Ibid.
3. Ibid.
4. Ibid.
5. Michael Harner, *The Way of the Shaman*, (1980), Bantam ed. 1982.
6. E.C. Krupp, *Echoes of the Ancient Skies*, Harper & Row, 1983.
7. Joan Halifax, *Shamanism*, Crossroad, 1982.
8. Eliade, op. cit.
9. Carl Strehlow, quoted in *Primitive Mythology* by Lucien Lévy-Bruhl, (1935), Univ. of Queensland Press ed., 1983.
10. Quoted in ibid
11. Charles Mountford, *Winbaraku and the Myth of the Jarapiri*, Rigby 1968.
12. Nevill Drury, *The Elements of Shamanism*, Element, 1989.
13. Eliade, op. cit.
14. Joseph Campbell, *Primitive Mythology*, (1959), Penguin ed. 1976.
15. Andreas Lommel, *Prehistoric and Primitive Man*, Paul Hamlyn, 1966.

16. Campbell, op. cit.
17. Ibid.
18. Krupp, op. cit.
19. Eliade, op. cit.
20. Campbell, op. cit.
21. Jeff and Deb Saward, *The Caerdroia Field Guide,* Caerdroia Project, 1987.
22. Evan Hadingham, *Lines to the Mountain Gods,* Random House, 1987.
23. Alberto Villoldo and Stanley Krippner, *Healing States,* Simon & Schuster, 1987.
24. Rich Yenson, 'From Mysteries to Paradigms', in *Gateway to Inner Space,* Christian Rätsch (Ed.), Prism, 1989.
25. Nigel Pennick, *Practical Magic in the Northern Tradition,* Aquarian Press, 1989.
26. Anne Ross, *The Pagan Celts,* (1970), Batsford ed. 1986.
27. Ibid.
28. Louis Charpentier, *The Mysteries of Chartres Cathedral,* (1966), Thorsons/RILKO ed. 1972.
29. Pierre Méreaux, *Carnac – une Porte vers l'Inconnu,* Laffont, 1981.
30. Aubrey Burl, *Megalithic Brittany,* Thames & Hudson, 1985.
31. Ross, op. cit.
32. Marija Gimbutas, *The Language of the Goddess,* Thames & Hudson, 1989.
33. In *Shaman's Path,* Gary Doore (Ed), Shambhala, 1988
34. Nova, WGBH, *Secrets of the Lost Red Paint People,* Ted Timreck, 1987.

**CHAPTER 11: Energies**

1. Paul Devereux, *Places of Power,* Blandford Press, 1990.
2. According to the research of Nigel Pennick – see his *Practical Magic in the Northern Tradition.*
3. Joseph Ennemoser, *History of Magic,* Bohn, 1854.
4. Karl von Reichenbach, *The Mysterious Odic Force,* (1852), Aquarian Press ed. 1977.
5. Rupert Sheldrake, *A New Science of Life,* Blond & Briggs, 1981.
6. Rupert Sheldrake, *The Presence of the Past,* Collins, 1988.
7. Sheila Oestrander and Lynn Schroeder, *Psychic Discoveries Behind the Iron Curtain,* (1970), Bantam ed. 1971.
8. Ion Dumitrescu and Julian N. Kenyon, *Electrographic Imaging in Medicine and Biology,* Neville Spearman, 1983.
9. Devereux, 1990, op. cit.
10. Francis Hitching, *Earth Magic,* Cassell, 1976.
11. Charles Brooker, 'Magnetism and the Standing Stones', *New Scientist,* 13 January 1983.
12. Marc Dem, *Megaliths et Routes Secretes del'Uranium,* Michel, 1977.

13. Quoted in *Bath – Some Encounters with Science,* by W.J. Williams and D.M. Stoddart, Kingsmead Press, 1978.
14. U. McL. Mitchie and D.C. Cooper, *Uranium in the Old Red Sandstone of Orkney,* HMSO, 1979.
15. Ian Cooke, *Journey to the Stones,* Men-an-Tol Studio, 1987.
16. Devereux, 1990, op. cit.
17. CNN, 'Radon Mines', *Newsnight,* 22 November 1987.
18. Don Robins, 'The Dragon Project and the Talking Stones', *New Scientist,* 21 October 1982.
19. Don Robins, *Circles of Silence,* Souvenir Press, 1985.
20. Pierre Méreaux, *Carnac – une Porte vers l'Inconnu,* Laffont, 1981.
21. John Michell, *The View Over Atlantis,* (1969), Abacus ed. 1973.
22. Paul Devereux, *Earth Lights Revelation,* Blandford Press, 1989.
23. Michael A. Persinger, *Space-Time Transients . . .,* Nelson-Hall, 1977. (Persinger has also produced many research papers in *Perceptual and Motor Skills* and the *Journal* of the American Society of Psychic Research.)
24. Project Pennine, summarised in *Earth Lights Revelation,* can be contacted through *UFO Brigantia,* 84 Elland Road, Brighouse, W. Yorks., HD6 2QR, UK.
25. *Notes and Queries,* 4 April 1891.
26. John Clare, *The Journals, Essays and the Journey from Essex,* 1830.
27. William Pryce, *Mineralogia Cornubiensis,* 1778.
28. Geoff Bird, 'Mining Lights', *The Ley Hunter* 102, 1987.
29. 'Earth Emits Ghostly Light', *Science Digest,* July 1982.
30. John S. Derr, 'Luminous Phenomena and their Relationship to Rock Fracture', *Nature,* 29 May 1986.
31. Alberto Villoldo and Stanley Krippner, *Healing States,* Simon & Schuster, 1987.
32. Tony Morrison, *The Mystery of the Nasca Lines,* Nonesuch Expeditions, 1987.
33. Jim Swan, 'Sacred Places in Nature' in *Shaman's Path,* Gary Doore (Ed.), Shambhala, 1988.
34. Holger Kalweit, *Dreamtime and Inner Space,* (1984), Shambhala ed. 1988.
35. Michael Shallis, *The Electric Shock Book,* Souvenir Press, 1988.

**CHAPTER 12: The Living Earth**

1. Raynor C. Johnson, *The Light and the Gate,* Hodder and Stoughton, 1964.
2. W.Y. Evans Wentz, *The Fairy Faith in Celtic Countries,* (1911), Colin Smythe ed. 1977.
3. G.W. Russell, *Song and its Fountains,* (1932), in the Russell mystical compendium *The Descent of the Gods,* Raghavan and Nandini Iyer (Eds.), Colin Smythe, 1988.
4. Paul Devereux and John Steele, David Kubrin, *Earthmind,* Harper & Row, 1989.

5. David Kubrin, 'The War Against the Earth', *The Ley Hunter* 100, 1986.
6. J.E. Lovelock, *Gaia: A New Look at Life on Earth,* OUP, 1979.
7. J.E. Lovelock, *The Ages of Gaia,* OUP, 1988.
8. Devereux, Steele, Kubrin, 1989, op. cit.
9. Stephen LaBerge, *Lucid Dreaming,* (1985), Ballantine ed. 1986.
10. Holger Kalweit, *Dreamtime and Inner Space,* (1984), Shambhala, 1988.
11. Stanislav Grof, 'Beyond the Brain', in *Gateway to Inner Space,* Christian Rätsch (Ed.), Prism, 1989.
12. Ibid.
13. Ibid.
14. Prem Das, 'Initiation by a Huichol Shaman', *The Laughing Man,* Vol. 2, No. 4.
15. Alberto Villoldo and Stanley Krippner, *Healing States,* Simon & Schuster, 1987.
16. Ibid.
17. Ibid.
18. C.W. Smith 'Water – Friend or Foe?', *Laboratory Practice,* October 1985.
19. J. Benveniste et al., 'Human basophil degranulation triggered by very dilute antiserum against IgE', *Nature,* 30 June, 1988.
20. Frank B. Salisbury, *The Utah UFO Display,* Devin-Adair, 1974.
21. Harley D. Rutledge, *Project Identification,* Prentice-Hall, 1981.
22. Reference 28 in Chapter 7 gives the address of the Dragon Project Trust. A modest level of funding is constantly sought to further the work of the project. It operates outside of both normal academic and 'New Age' channels and relies on the generosity of individuals who feel its work is important enough to support. There is some, but less, need for facilities, field volunteers and informed consultants in various areas.

# INDEX